THE
COMPASS
OF
CHARACTER

Creating Complex Motivation for Compelling Characters in Fiction, Film, and TV

The Four Directional Forces That Guide Your Characters

DAVID CORBETT

WRITER'S DIGEST BOOKS

Dedication

For Mette, my Bride
a chuisle mo chroí

And in loving memory:
Dr. Arnold Ross, born Arnold Ephraim Chaimovich,
who taught me what it means to teach.

www.penguinrandomhouse.com

1 3 5 7 9 10 8 6 4 2

ISBN-13: 978-1-4403-0086-8

Edited by Amy Jones
Designed by Jason D. Williams and Danielle Lowery

Acknowledgments

The writer who claims to have done it all himself is lying above and beyond the call of duty. A great many people provided invaluable assistance at various stages of this book's conception, writing, and publication. Kimberley Cameron and her team deserve credit for getting the manuscript into the hands of the folks at Writer's Digest. There, Amy Jones, Kim Catanzarite, and an untold army of others helped hammer this book into final shape, doing so under unusual and challenging circumstances. Thanks to all the folks at Penguin Random House who helped ensure the book made it to press. Everyone at Writer's Digest, past and present—specifically Jessica Strawser, Ericka McIntyre, Taylor Sferra, Tyler Moss, Cassie Lipp, Tiffany Luckey—provided me a means, both through the magazine and writing conferences, to develop the ideas that ultimately evolved into this book. So too the many teaching and blogging outlets that have granted me a platform—specifically, Therese Walsh and everyone at Writer Unboxed; Gabriela Pereira at DIYMFA; Rob Hart and Renée Asher Pickup at LitReactor; Elaine Petrocelli and all the incredible folks at Book Passage; Susan Page and Paulette Shanklin at the San Miguel de Allende Writers' Conference; D.P. Lyle, Kimberley Howe, Taylor Antrim, Christopher Graham and everyone associated with the International Thriller Writers various writing programs; and Steven James, who graciously invited me to join him and Susan May Warren for his Character Conference in Atlanta. I also need to credit three exceptional fellow teachers and writers who have assisted and inspired me at various times: Donald Maass, Robert Dugoni, and James Scott Bell, all of whom abide by the credo: Keep learning. David Ivester no doubt will prove every bit as creative, dogged, and invaluable with this book as he did with my last, and deserves a word of anticipatory thanks for that effort. A word of thanks is long overdue for Arnold Ross, Archie Addison, Ranko Bojanic, Bogdan Baishanski, and all of my professors working with the Ohio State advanced undergraduate mathematics program when I was lucky enough to benefit from their guidance; they taught me what it means to be honest, demanding, and responsible to one's students, and continue to inspire me to this day. Finally, no account of indebtedness would be complete without inclusion of my wife, Mette, without whom yearning would lack all meaning.

About the Author

David Corbett is the award-winning author of the writing guides *The Art of Character* ("A writer's bible"—Elizabeth Brundage) and *The Compass of Character*. He has published six novels, including 2018's *The Long-Lost Love Letters of Doc Holliday*, nominated for the Lefty Award for Best Historical Novel. His short fiction has been selected twice for *Best American Mystery Stories*, and his nonfiction has appeared in *The New York Times*, *Narrative*, *Bright Ideas*, and *Writer's Digest*, where he is a contributing editor. He has taught at the UCLA Writer's Program, LitReactor, Book Passage, and at writing conferences across North America and Mexico, and is a monthly contributor to Writer Unboxed, an award-winning blog dedicated to the craft and business of fiction. www.davidcorbett.com

Table of Contents

PART TWO
Develop a Deeper Understanding

Introduction

←――――――――――――――――――――――――――――――――――→

More often than not, people don't know why they do things.

—William Trevor, "The Room"

THE METHODOLOGY OF THIS BOOK— MOTIVATION AS THE COMPASS OF CHARACTER

One hears it trumpeted at every writers conference, in every seminar and workshop, in every creative writing class: The fundamental question for every character—in every scene of every story—reduces to this: *What does she want?*

And yet, like all simple and straightforward truths, no sooner is this one stated than objections, rebuttals, and counterexamples emerge. How long does the reader have to wait before gaining so much as a glimpse of what Holden Caulfield actually wants in *The Catcher in the Rye*? And isn't it possible that the real motives for all of the characters in Harold Pinter's *The Homecoming* lie beneath so many strata of denial and deceit that they arguably don't exist?

Add to this the quote from William Trevor above, which suggests that people are often blind to why they act as they do, implying not only their intentions but their ends remain obscure as well. Worse still, all too often those seemingly most confident of their true desires prove to be wildly mistaken.

Oversimplifying the answer to that question—what does the character want—by limiting it to a single goal or objective typically generates facile, formulaic, unsatisfying results.

In *The Art of Character*, I put it like this:

> Readers and audiences shouldn't be vexed by a character's behavior, but they should never feel entirely comfortable either, or they'll be several steps ahead of the story at every turn. This may mean that at some level the character's motivation isn't yet clear—but will be clari-

fied as the story proceeds—or it may mean that the motivation is more complex than simple reductive explanations can justify.

Your ability to explain your character kills her. Whatever she does, the reader or audience needs to feel her actions arise not from this or that identifiable source, but from the whole of her personality, her wants and contradictions and secrets and wounds, her attachment to friends and family and her fear of her enemies, her schooling and sense of home, her loves and hatreds, her shame and pride and guilt and sense of joy—her character.

I stand by that. As my teaching of characterization has progressed, however, I have learned that writers need specific guidance on how to conceptualize and execute something that conjures "the whole of [the character's] personality," without getting lost in a swarm of conflicting details.

Strikingly, this has proved as true of accomplished writers as novices, with the former all too often trying to conjure complexity with an enigmatic phrase (or two, or three …), a tactic meant to reward the clever rather than the insightful.

I realized that all my students, beginner or accomplished, could benefit from a step-by-step process that clarified the task at hand and yet did so without trivialization, i.e., without reducing it to a simplistic or reductionist formula.

The methodology needed to be accessible conceptually to novices so they could wrap their minds around it and use it effectively, and yet open-ended enough so that their creativity wasn't stuffed inside a dogmatic box.

I also needed to make sure that, once learned, the process would continue to serve them for their entire careers, as their writing became more demanding and sophisticated.

The result has been the methodology presented in this book. Specifically, two foundational premises guide the material throughout:

1. Every individual faces a conflict between two basic impulses that are often irreconcilable: *the pursuit of the promise of life* versus *protection from the pain of life*.

2. Every individual possesses inner resources, some harmful, some beneficial, that often remain untapped until extraordinary circumstances force them to the surface.

These premises give rise to a methodology for approaching characterization that emphasizes deep-seated needs, internal as well as external conflict, and the lifelong search for a core sense of self in the face of certain death. That methodology can be summarized as follows:

1. The question of what a character wants can be broken down into four elements (which are discussed in detail in chapters one through six):
   - Lack
   - Yearning
   - Resistance: Weaknesses, Wounds, Limitations, External Opposition or Obligation, Moral Flaws
   - Desire

2. Characters, like the human beings on which they are based, possess an inner sense of when they are living up to who they are and how they should live, and when they are not. As the Buddhist monk Bodhidharma put it: "All know the way, few actually walk it." This goes beyond mere right and wrong to the very core of identity and what it means to exist. I call this response to the gravitational pull toward a more fully realized self and a more fulfilling way of life the Compass of Character.

   Like a physical compass, this native sense of self responds to a strong but unseen force, a fundamental sense of one's true nature. However, it can also be misled by other forces in the near at hand that pull it off course. What seems "true" may simply be, in the near term, gratifying, empowering, even ecstatic—pathologically so. It often takes a long while of being lost before an individual recognizes her error, and even if she redirects her search there is no guarantee the end point will ever be reached, if it even exists.

Once this fundamental understanding is mastered, the writer is better prepared to answer the questions that suggest themselves immediately after posing, "What does the character want?"

- Why does she want it?
- Why doesn't she have it already—what internal, external, and interpersonal obstacles hold her back?
- What is she willing to do and to risk in order to get what she wants—i.e., how badly does she want it?
- What deep sense of identity, meaning, or purpose does the object of Desire awaken?
- How does that deeper Yearning define who she is and the life she hopes to live?
- What will be lost if the character fails to succeed? How will this affect her newly awakened sense of self?
- Why now?

Connecting the question of want to the metaphor at the heart of this book—character as compass—we might reframe the issue of what the character wants as where she hopes to go, with the understanding this journey has both external and internal elements.

Desire implicitly suggests a goal, but if the goal is meaningful it also suggests a destination in the broadest sense. Once the Desire is gratified, the character will be in a new and different place—not just spatially (she may in fact have traveled nowhere in that sense), but in terms of how she sees herself, how she values her relationships, how she defines her life and interprets the world. And she will evaluate this new destination not just in its own terms but also with respect to how much closer she has come to the elusive sense of fulfillment that constantly beckons like true north but is never immediately at hand.

RECENT TRENDS IN STORYTELLING REQUIRE COMPLEX MOTIVATION

One of the more compelling reasons for this book comes from three increasingly prevalent trends in mainstream storytelling:

- The growing need to develop multiseason character arcs in long-format TV series.

- The burgeoning popularity of multivolume series in the fantasy genre, spurred in part by the success of George R. R. Martin's groundbreaking pentalogy, A Song of Ice and Fire, the source of the vastly popular TV series, *Game of Thrones.*
- An emerging trend in the crime genre, where series characters do not simply reappear book to book but evolve over the course of the protracted storyline.

Each of these phenomena necessitates a long-range view of character development, which in turn requires that characters be complicated and sophisticated enough to compel action and maintain interest over extended narrative arcs. It isn't just literary fiction that demands sophisticated characterization. It is fiction, period, regardless of the medium in which the story is told.

Obviously, it isn't just long-form fiction that benefits from complicated and sophisticated characterization, and the methodology contained in this book is by no means restrictive in this regard. Rather, this book seeks to show how to build from simple to complex character motivation so that anyone working in any medium can use its methodology creatively, capably, and productively.

One doesn't create meaningful complication merely by "adding more stuff," but rather by building from a sound foundation capable of contradiction, growth, transformation, and surprise.

Regardless of one's genre or medium, the need remains to provide characters who speak to our deepest understanding of what it means to be human—to experience the mysterious truth that we are in fact alive, to want our lives to mean something, to search for a way to make our actions matter—all in the shadow of a death we cannot escape.

This search for meaning and worth implicitly suggests a profound longing for a deeper, clearer understanding of who we are and how we should live. And every search implies a need for some sense of guidance: a compass. This book will show you how to conceive, create, and develop that compass within each of your characters, and how to bring those characters to life on the page.

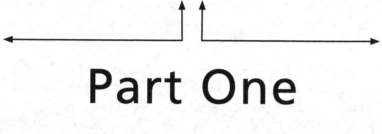

Part One

Developing a Technique

If you want to identify me, ask me not where I live or what I like to eat, or how I comb my hair, but ask me what I think I am living for, in detail, and ask me what I think is keeping me from living fully for the thing I want to live for.

—Thomas Merton, *My Argument with the Gestapo*

1

The Logic of Longing

←————————————————————————————→

> Happiness implied a choice, and within that choice a concerted
> will, a lucid desire.
>> —Albert Camus, *A Happy Death*

Simplicity is the essence of elegance, and the more we can ground complexity in a clear, coherent simplicity, the more our efforts, as they become more intricate, can hope to retain the elegance of truth.

The subject matter covered in this chapter will be addressed over and over in greater depth and detail in all the chapters that follow. Before that in-depth exploration occurs, however, we want to trace the outlines of our approach, the better to comprehend that depth and detail as it arrives later.

As I mentioned in the Introduction and as I will repeat throughout this book, desire drives story. But desire possesses various levels and crosscurrents, working in harmony and discord.

First and foremost, we need to distinguish between levels of want, and to do so we need to invent a nomenclature. From here forward I will use the following terms in the following ways:

- *Desire* refers to the character's willful pursuit of some concrete goal or ambition in the story. That goal may be internal—to be a more honest person, to give up drinking. It may be interpersonal—to mend or deepen a relationship. More often than not, however, it is external—save the miners, rescue the hostage, win the prize, find the way home—but even if it isn't, external factors invariably affect success or failure.
- *Yearning* refers to the deeper, life-defining need or longing that explains why and how badly the character wants to achieve that goal, anchored in the kind of person he longs to be and the way of life he hopes to live.

This distinction in terminology is arbitrary. It's just a device. But without it, one finds oneself swimming around in a terminological soup, constantly trying to figure out exactly which kind of want is at issue.

The four key elements of longing to explore when creating your main characters and significant secondary characters are:

1. Lack
2. Yearning
3. Resistance (Weaknesses/Wounds/Limitations/Opposition-Obligation/Flaws)
4. Desire

At its most fundamental, the interplay among levels works like this:

1. The character begins the story in a state of *Lack* that he may or may not recognize: a state of unfulfilled promise, malaise, boredom, disappointment, compromise, loneliness, isolation, lack of direction, absence of purpose or meaning, existential angst, even dread.

   More fundamentally he is not living up to his own reasonable expectations of who he should be, how he should live. He is in some way failing the fundamental challenge of his life, falling short of his ambitions, his dreams, his destiny.

   This is not just true of the unsuccessful. The great musician and songwriter Bruce Springsteen, known for the lyric "Everybody's got a hungry heart" (among many others), openly admits in his one-man play *Springsteen on Broadway* that he feels he has not lived up to his deepest ambitions. The Hall of Fame second baseman Bobby Doerr similarly once admitted in a late-life interview: "I never had the feeling I was good. I always had the feeling I had to do a little better." If this is true of those who personify great accomplishment and wide acclaim, how can it not be true of us? Not even monks are perfectly contented, for their compassion renders them fully aware of the world's suffering. The person who claims otherwise, is on some level, living a lie.

2. Lack is created at least in part by an unfulfilled *Yearning* that may be equally vague or undefined, at least at the story's start.

The Compass of Character

The individual's Yearning speaks to his sense of the promise of life—his *dream of life*, as it were—and often can most simply be identified with the kind of person the individual longs to be (his "fully realized self") and the way of life he hopes to live, embodied in the place he would most feel at home, the people he would most happily call his family or tribe, living the daily life he'd find ideal.

But Yearning is more than an image or a dream of the good life. It often demands great effort in service of seemingly hopeless goals, such as the call to honor and integrity in an environment defined by decadence, intrigue, and deceit.

There are also those whose Yearning shuns what the rest of us would call decent or noble or good. Instead they envision fulfillment in destruction, violence, predation, pain. Like a wolf in the wild, such an individual identifies fulfillment with the taste of blood.

Whether fully recognized at the start of your story or only clarified amid its intensifying conflict and the increasing risk of failure, loss, or disaster, implicit within the character's Yearning lies a compulsion, a calling, a sense of responsibility and ownership to that more complete sense of self and the way of life it defines.

This personal reckoning conjures the *willfulness* needed for the character to continue striving to fulfill his Yearning, to live up to its demands, to answer the call of destiny—or, more modestly, to live up to one's own promise, to see the job through, or, in the most expansive meaning of that phrase, to follow the compass of one's character.

3. The reason that the character's Yearning is unfulfilled is because some form of *Resistance* stands in his way, whether that comes from external oppositional forces or internal ones, or both. Either way, as yet the character lacks the means or will required to overcome that Resistance.

When the forces of Resistance are internal, the character's Yearning is blocked by a countering impulse of self-protection, a kind of psychological and emotional armor, a defense against the ridicule and pain of failure. This sort of recoiling from the demands of life is not without its advocates and is epitomized in sayings such as *Better to be a live dog than a dead lion* and *Better the trouble that follows death than the trouble that follows shame.*

Whether the forces of Resistance are internal or external, they can make Yearning feel foolish, impossible, terrifying, futile, or otherwise out of the question.

Resistance can take several forms:

- *Weaknesses*: laziness, cowardice, lack of confidence, cynicism, despair;
- *Wounds*: some loss or injury that has crippled the individual's ability to love, heal, or act decisively;
- *Limitations*: youth, old age, inexperience, lack of intelligence, poor health, poverty;
- *Opposition*: a countering external force, normally embodied in another person—dream-killing father, overprotective mother, undermining teachers, slacker friends, a snobbish society, an oppressive culture; or it may take the form of a demanding obligation, like the need to be a responsible parent or a caretaker for someone in need;
- *Flaws*: selfishness, deceitfulness, indifference, cruelty, greed, a willingness to manipulate others.

Note: These elements are not independent; on the contrary, they often act in concert, influencing and amplifying each other.

The term Pathological Maneuvers (chapter five) is used to define the attitude toward life and the habitual behaviors created by the combined influence of the various forms of Resistance.

The core internal conflict in your story can be defined as one between a need to avoid or minimize *the pain of life* versus the desire to embrace and pursue *the promise of life*. These needs should be viewed in their most expansive senses. Just as the promise of life speaks to more than mere pleasure to include such factors as meaning, significance, purpose, integrity, and identity, so too the pain of life encompasses more than just physical hardship, including such experiences as shame, guilt, loneliness, betrayal, abandonment, desperation, and meaninglessness.

4. The foregoing three elements address the character's background as the story begins. Then *something happens*—an opportunity arises or a misfortune strikes: the loved one appears, a body is found, the expedition is approved, the car breaks down in the middle of nowhere—and that triggers the *Desire* to respond or to act.

One of the fundamental requirements of a dramatically compelling and thematically unified story is the need to weave together the pursuit of the character's principle goal (Desire) with the fundamental longing it speaks to (Yearning).

In fact, Yearning both provides the motivation for the pursuit of the goal (by tapping into the reservoir of willfulness Yearning provides) and defines the stakes (by identifying what the character stands to lose in terms of self-worth, status, meaning, and purpose).

A WORD OF CAUTION CONCERNING TERMINOLOGY

The use of nouns to describe the various elements of character we've just discussed—Lack, Yearning, Resistance, Desire—creates a potentially misleading impression that these are concrete objects, even if of a uniquely spiritual, psychological, or emotional kind.

For those of an idealistic temperament—i.e., those who believe in a human soul or who agree with Plato's concept of ideal forms—this will likely cause few difficulties.

For those disinclined to believe in the objective reality of things like a soul, fate, destiny, even identity, such idealization can seem problematic if not plain wrong.

If that is your inclination, it might prove better to think of Lack as a state of mind, while Yearning, Resistance, and Desire are better conceived as impulses toward something rather than the something itself.

Taken this way, Lack is more adjectival than noun-like, referring to the manner or attitude with which the character faces her life at the story's outset: contented, bored, anxious, accepting, despondent, suspicious, rebellious, etc.

Yearning and Resistance have more of a verb-like quality, suggesting movement toward or away from promise or pain, fulfillment or safety. Yearning and Resistance are not so much states of being as ways of reacting to the psychological and emotional forces pulling the character in one direction or another.

So, too, Desire. Though it may be encapsulated in a concrete objective or goal, the real phenomenon is the impulse compelling pursuit of that objective or goal.

Whatever one's philosophical take on objective truth, the fact that characters can be mistaken about their goals, their longings, their limitations, and so on, argues for a certain fluidity in thinking about Lack, Yearning, Resistance, and Desire.

If conceiving of them as concrete objects acting like planets with their own unique gravitational fields works for you, by all means embrace that. If not, it may be better to think of your characters as being in the grip of these various conflicting forces, which oblige them to move, to feel, to respond, and to act in various, often contradictory, ways. Just as we breathe and feel thirst or hunger due to processes that ultimately reduce to the simple fact that we are alive, so to with Lack, Yearning, Resistance, and Desire—they are elemental aspects of human life, nothing more, nothing less.

This latter approach may feel vague or difficult to get one's mind around, especially at first, but its key benefit is that it captures the gnawing sense of uncertainty so common to human endeavor.

The choice as to which approach to use, however, as with so many aspects of writing, remains entirely yours.

EXERCISES

Choose two main characters from your current work in progress (WIP) and answer the questions below for each character.

- In every instance, answer the question for your protagonist. If you don't know as yet who your protagonist is, choose the main character who is most compelled to act during the story or who arouses the most empathy.
- For your second main character, choose your opponent if you have one. If you're writing a love story, choose the loved one. If you're not

writing a love story and don't have an opponent, choose another main character—an ally, a mentor, a parent, etc.—who interacts with your protagonist in a meaningful way.

With the understanding that we will be exploring these issues in much greater depth and detail in the ensuing chapters, for now identify as best you can for each of the two main characters you have selected:

- Lack
- Yearning
- Resistance (Weakness/Wound/Limitation/Opposition-Obligation/ Flaw
- Desire

If you need assistance, remember that the most direct way to explore these areas is to *answer these questions*:

- What is missing from my character's life? (**Lack**)
- What is my character's *dream of life*: the type of person he longs to be, the way of life he hopes to enjoy. How will being that person and living that life help mitigate his sense of Lack? (**Yearning**)
- What aspects of the character's personality contribute to her Yearning's remaining unfulfilled? (**Resistance**)

  - What *Weaknesses* does she possess?
  - What *Wounds* has she suffered?
  - What *Limitations* hold her back?
  - What external *Opposition* has she faced, and does she continue to face it? What *Obligation* has stolen her attention and energy from what she would prefer to do?
  - What moral *Flaws* does she exhibit?

How have any or all of these factors contributed to her focus on protecting herself from the pain of life rather than pursuing the promise of life?

  - What is the character's chief objective or goal in the story, and how will achieving it help gratify her Yearning? (**Desire**)

2

The Hole at the Heart
of the Matter—Lack

When he was dry, he believed it was alcohol he needed, but
when he had a few drinks in him, he knew it was something
else, possibly a woman; and when he had it all—cash, booze,
and a wife—he couldn't be distracted from the great emptiness
that was always falling through him and never hit the ground.

—Denis Johnson, *Angels*

[To] know oneself is, above all, to know what one lacks. It is to
measure oneself against Truth, and not the other way around.

—Flannery O'Connor, *Mystery and Manners: Occasional Prose*

I. THE ECHO IN THE EMPTY ROOM

One of the most fundamental realities of human existence is the sense,
however conscious or unconscious, that something is missing from our
lives. This sense of lack never leaves us and is to the psyche what hunger, thirst, and sexual craving are to the body.

This sense of something missing or incomplete is not solely the
provenance of the unsuccessful, lonely, or lost. Far from it. Even great
and successful individuals admit to a feeling of coming up short in what
they hoped to achieve. Not even wealth or fame can erase the sting of
unmet dreams.[1]

This deep inner void is addressed in virtually every religious and
philosophical tradition:

- Plato likened the soul to a winged creature capable of soaring toward pure Truth and craving that union. But all too often the soul's

---

1 See the discussion of Bruce Springsteen and Bobby Doerr in the context of Lack in
the preceding chapter.

wings, weakened through contamination with falsehood and mere opinion, keep it earthbound, where shadows are confused with the reality that casts them.

- Aristotle believed all things existed to fulfill their purpose, or *telos*, and the purpose of man was to strive to live in accord with reason, the better to flourish and achieve his unique individual destiny, a state he called "eudaimonia."
- Augustine identified original sin as the cause of man's Lack, the inheritance of Adam and Eve's banishment from Paradise. The soul exists in a state of painful, "restless" exile from the beatific vision, to which it instinctively and desperately hopes to return.
- In Hinduism, the soul (Ātman) is trapped in the cycle of karmic reincarnation. This creates a perpetual hunger or longing for liberation. The only escape is through unification of the soul with Brahman, the universal self and transcendent reality of the universe.
- Buddhism attributes this sense of Lack to our experience of the Non-Self, i.e., the absence of any individual soul or identity. The fact that there is nothing behind the ego or personality creates profound anxiety, part of the overall suffering (*dukkha*) that forms the first of The Four Noble Truths. Terrified at this inner sense of nothingness, we create a sense of selfhood or identity and try to anchor it in physical reality. This inevitably leads to a vain desire for power, wealth, sexual fulfillment, comfort, or acclaim, which is like trying to slake one's thirst with salt water.
- Confucianism is more of an ethical system than a faith system, but in identifying the five key virtues that define harmony, it automatically implies the disharmony that characterizes ordinary life. (This is equally true in other ethical systems, both secular and religious, such as Stoicism and Epicureanism. Their emphasis on virtue implicitly assumes a preexisting inclination toward vice.)
- Similarly, Ralph Waldo Emerson's concept of "the infinitude of the private man" recognized not only the impoverished state of most men but also the great promise of self-transformation if the indi-

vidual looked deep within himself in times of suffering and found "the god within."

- Emerson's disciple Friedrich Nietzsche premised his concept of the *übermensch* on the idea that man, living in a world without God or absolute truth, needed not only to create his own values but to imagine an ideal self toward which he could strive; only then could he overcome his current self, so often afflicted with weakness and doubt and self-pity, an effort that would require lifelong struggle.
- The American Pragmatist tradition, from William James through John Dewey to Richard Rorty, denies the reality of Platonic essence and instead looks to Darwinian evolution as the proper view of human life—i.e., we are in a constant, inescapable state of growth toward an uncertain but hopefully better future.
- The philosopher Martin Heidegger identified anxiety as the fundamental aspect of our existence, rooted at least in part in the fact that we can never achieve "truth" outside our individual cultural, biological, and individual biases, and that lack of foundation creates a sense of inescapable unease. He specifically defined existential guilt as the awareness of all we are not.
- Sigmund Freud and Alfred Adler considered neurosis the fundamental condition of mankind, caused by the inescapable internal conflicts man is born with. All humans seek escape from the anxiety and sense of inadequacy neurosis inflicts, an escape psychoanalysis tries to provide, even though it can never be totally successful.
- Carl Gustav Jung considered the self essentially divided between conscious and unconscious personalities, and referred to this unstable lack of integration "the undeniable common inheritance of all mankind."[2] The fundamental task of man was synthesis of these opposites, a lifelong process he called "individuation."

Regardless of how you interpret it, this fundamental sense of Lack is a key definitional attribute of what it means to be human. We are at all times aware of a certain sense of being incomplete.

---

2 *Man and His Symbols*, conceived and edited by Carl G. Jung, Aldus Books, 1964.

As a casual review of the examples above should reveal, there are two main ways of categorizing this sense of incompleteness.

- We feel incomplete because our lives are defined by the call of an objective identity, destiny, truth, or soul—i.e., the idealized sense of self and way of life we associated with Yearning in the previous chapter. Lack is caused by this sense of a search in progress, i.e., Lack is created by our unfulfilled Yearning.
- We feel incomplete because that is our fundamental nature, rooted in intrinsic feelings of inadequacy, confusion, and dependence that begin in infancy and continue through adulthood as we try to define our place in the world. Here, Lack is not the effect of unfulfilled Yearning, but rather its cause. Our ideas of who we want to be and how we want to live are fashioned by our desire to escape the anxiety that defines our incomplete lives, and often evolve over time given the vagaries of experience.

Either way, there is a cause-and-effect relationship between Lack and Yearning. Which is cause, which effect, largely depends on how one views human existence. But it also often seems to be the case that Lack and Yearning have a more symbiotic, yin and yang, feedback-loop relationship; which one serves as cause and which effect depends on what stage of life the character is in, what challenges he faces at a particular time, or other circumstances.

We will explore this in greater depth and detail in the following chapter in our discussion of Yearning, but it's important to note the issue here because it is a frequent point of confusion.

EXERCISES

- Return to the two characters from your current WIP (the same two you used for the previous chapter's exercises). Specifically, return to your previous definition of their Lack. How does the foregoing discussion alter your understanding of what is missing from their lives? How aware are they of what it is that feels missing?

- From the list of philosophical and religious interpretations of Lack and Yearning, which, if any, most closely resembles your own? How is that understanding revealed in your characters? Do your characters have such an understanding? (Do they perhaps have distinct understandings—from you or each other?)
- For one of the characters, imagine his Lack as the effect of his unfulfilled Yearning—i.e., imagine specifically the kind of person he wishes to be, the way of life he hopes to live. How aware is he of these things, i.e., how clearly does he sense his own Yearning? How does that affect his Lack, i.e., his feeling that something is missing from his life? How do you imagine he will eventually discover what it is he truly wants—who he wishes to be and how he hopes to live?
- For the other character, imagine she does not possess such a clear-cut notion of her Yearning, but rather just a sense of being incomplete, inadequate, unfulfilled, or wishing to escape the life of deprivation and fear she has so far known. What would be the most immediate step she would take to lead what she believes would be a better, more gratifying, less anxious life? How will that be the first step in creating a life that truly feels worth living? Is that step in your story? If not, why not?

II. PROJECTION AND CONTENTMENT— HOW LACK REVEALS ITSELF IN SIMPLE CHARACTERS

First, by "simple character" I do not mean to suggest someone beneath the dignity of discussion, exploration, or dramatization. Quite the contrary.

What E.M. Forster in *Aspects of the Novel* referred to as "flat" characters (versus "round" ones), and James Wood in *How Fiction Works* designated as "transparent" characters (in contrast to "opaque" ones), are capable of serving significant dramatic roles, and often are hardly as simple (or flat or transparent) as they might seem.

The inner life of such characters is by no means nonexistent, and thus they may well have profound inner conflicts, and possess a sense of Lack, Yearning, Resistance, and Desire much like any other character. For one reason or another, however, their internal struggles are minimized or managed, and their compulsion to act is often motivated not from within but by events in the external world.

Alternatively, they feel no compulsion to act at all, and either enjoy a sense of contentment or have gained a hard-won acceptance of themselves and the world.

THE TRAVELING ANGEL—EXPERIENCING LACK THROUGH THE OUTER WORLD

A descendent of the knight errant, the saintly pilgrim, and the wandering bard, the character type commonly referred to as a "traveling angel" roams from place to place (or merely situation to situation), solving problems with a unique skill set, then moving on. This approach is typical of:

- Westerns (i.e., the plains gunman, the Lone Ranger, the High Plains Drifter);
- Detective stories and thrillers (e.g., Agatha Christie's Hercule Poirot and Miss Marple, Dashiell Hammett's *Continental Op* and Sam Spade, Raymond Chandler's Philip Marlowe, Ian Fleming's James Bond, Lee Child's Jack Reacher, and so on);
- Tales of the samurai and *ronin*.

The romantic or sentimental version of the traveling angel is exemplified by characters such as:

- The English Mary Poppins (who is "practically perfect in every way");
- The French Amélie (who is often overcome by "an urge to help mankind");
- The Japanese Tora-san (a plump, clownish itinerant peddler who "dreams of doing grand deeds").

To the extent such characters feel a Lack, it usually takes the form of compassion or a "will to justice," a sense that the suffering and injustice of the world cries out to them in a unique way, compelling them to right wrongs, heal wounds, repair relationships.

These characters typically possess a solid sense of identity and purpose. However, this doesn't mean they are devoid of loneliness, doubt, regret, or other internal issues. In fact, absent such internal issues, the characters can seldom become as fascinating as they need to be to make this story-type compelling. The traveling angel is not an Everyman suffering the journey through Vice and Virtue. He is a bona fide hero with a unique personality. It's just that his internal issues, however complex or poignant, remain largely unaffected by the story's events. He is there to help others, then ride into the sunset.

THE CONTENTED CHARACTER

A second character type for whom Lack seems unproblematic is the untroubled or "happy" character, whose life seems in order, whose grievances are few or nonexistent, and who feels that the promise of life, in her case at least, has been largely rewarded.

Such a state of tranquility is often largely relative, of course. Whatever internal Lack she may feel—falling short of who she wishes to be, living the way of life she hopes to live—is minimal, or at least manageable. She has come to accept herself and her circumstances with little internal doubt or turmoil.

It's important to mention here that *such a character makes a lackluster protagonist unless something external seriously disrupts, undermines, or threatens to destroy the tranquil world in which she abides, or the untroubled sense of self she possesses.* This will require her to pursue and establish a new equilibrium, and depending on the story type this may result in a totally new understanding of herself or her world, if not both.

The struggle for that new equilibrium may be largely external, such as in thrillers or disaster stories. In such stories, the character's happiness and the virtues underlying it are not mistaken or false; rather, they are tested by an exterior force capable of taking that sunshine away.

Alternatively, if the previous state of tranquility was premised on a misunderstanding of the world or a false sense of security, then the new equilibrium will also require a reexamination of the character's sense of self—what error of judgment or misguided belief created that mistaken contentment? What new state of wisdom or awareness will be necessary to return to some semblance of order?

The issue from a dramatic perspective is the need to understand that though the character may feel no conspicuous Lack at the outset of the story, she will as soon as the disruptive force upends her world. She will also discover that the skills and disposition that suited her in her previous state of relative bliss will no longer serve her well. The story will concern how she develops a new understanding and acquires her new skills—or doesn't, to the destruction of her or some part of her world.

THE SADDER-BUT-WISER CHARACTER

There are, of course, seemingly tranquil characters whose state of well-being has come at some cost—mature individuals, whose shortcomings and failures have not crippled or stifled them.

Such characters, through the struggles they've faced and the disappointments they've endured, have gained a genuine, unsentimental acceptance of themselves and life that neither lets them off the hook nor debilitates them with regret. They have learned firsthand that existence is a contact sport and the good die young.

In contrast to the happy individual discussed above, the sense of well-being exhibited by this type of character has come at a price, and they are more defined by a hard-won wisdom than contentment.

In stories where characters of this sort serve as a protagonist, the character's eventful past creates echoes that must be revisited and once again silenced or dealt with in the course of the story. In this sense, he resembles the so-called happy character, in that his life of forbearing acceptance will be disturbed by some external force, and the story will address how he finds a way out of that turmoil, both internally and externally, and either returns to his previous stoicism, redefines it, or embraces something new.

Frequently, one encounters such characters in a secondary role, such as mentor or ally, rather than as protagonists. Consider for example Jasper Palmer-Smith in P.D. James's *The Children of Men*, played by Michael Caine in the film adaptation. Once an Oxford professor (a political cartoonist in the film), he now lives like a hermit in the woods with just his dogs and stroke-paralyzed wife for companionship. However, he proves a crucial ally to the hero, Theo Faron (Clive Owen), providing invaluable information to allow Theo's escape with Kee (Clare-Hope Ashitey), the first pregnant woman on earth in the last twenty years. Jasper also bravely, stoically, even cheerfully accepts death as the natural consequence for his loyalty. Only someone aware of life's tragic dimension and the price to be paid for virtue could be capable of such self-sacrifice.

EXERCISES

- Does your WIP feature a character who is a traveling angel—i.e., a character who travels place to place or situation to situation to right wrongs, battle the wicked, tend to the brokenhearted, repair relationships, or otherwise lend a helping hand? If so, how do external circumstances speak to his deep-seated will to justice or sense of compassion?
- Does your WIP feature a character who is happy or contented with her life at the story's outset? What changes upset the order of her world? How does she change due to the struggles and conflicts she faces over the course of the story?
- Does your story feature a character whose tranquil life has been obtained after long travail, suffering, setbacks, and disappointments? Is he a protagonist or a secondary character? If a protagonist, how is his psychological equilibrium tested by the story's events? If he is a secondary character, how does his hard-won self-acceptance aid one or another of the major characters?

III. URGENCY, ANXIETY, AND DENIAL— HOW LACK REVEALS ITSELF IN MORE COMPLEX CHARACTERS

For a great many characters, not to mention people in the physical world, Yearning and Lack are problematic. If acknowledged, they reveal the inadequacy of the individual, his inability to live up to his own ideals or fulfill his dreams, and the basic impoverishment of his life.

It's an unfortunate truth that people in fact go to great lengths to dampen their awareness of what they truly want from their lives and expect of themselves. This is what Henry David Thoreau referred to when he wrote, "The mass of men lead lives of quiet desperation."[3]

From the perspective of dramatization, the question we need to ask is, How do we portray what is essentially an absence—worse, an absence of which the character may be on some level unaware, or even deliberately trying to ignore or deny?

The response lies in recognizing that it's not the absence, per se, that we portray, but its effect on the character, and the manner with which he tries to manage, dismiss, or mitigate it. In other words, we show the *behavior* that reveals that something is amiss. (We will deal with this question in greater detail in chapter five, when we address what I refer to as Pathological Maneuvers—i.e., habits of behavior formed in the attempt to circumvent the pain of life.)

WHEN THE CHARACTER IS AWARE OF HIS LACK: URGENCY—LOVE AND OBSESSION

The most common story type in which a character is or becomes aware of a sense of Lack early on is the love story. No sooner do Romeo and Juliet encounter one another at the masked ball than they sense what is missing from their lives: each other.

In such stories, the dramatic problem is relatively straightforward. The entire plot will be premised not on the awakening of the character's Yearning but its relentless pursuit in the face of seemingly insurmountable odds presented by whatever force is keeping the lovers apart.

Most modern love stories are not so simple, however, especially in the West, where exterior barriers to romance—family, religion, culture, laws against adultery or divorce—have been minimized if not eliminated. What keeps the couple apart in most contemporary love stories is the lovers themselves—specifically, their own internal issues

---

3 He most likely did not add, "and die with their songs still inside them," as is often claimed. However, that's not just poetic, but apt.

concerning worth, attractiveness, lovability, commitment, duties to others, and so on.

In such stories, Lack creates Yearning for the romantic connection, but the characters must resolve their inner issues and face both themselves and each other honestly before the bond between them can genuinely thrive.

Beyond the realm of romance lies another story type where the character is fully aware of what is missing from the outset. Consider these examples:

- In *Oedipus Rex*, Oedipus understands that a curse has brought a plague upon the city of Thebes. Once the Oracle informs him that the reason for the plague is that someone killed the king and seduced the queen, Oedipus feels compelled to find the miscreant and bring him to justice, unaware that he himself is the culprit.
- In *Treasure Island*, Long John Silver has long been searching for a way to find Captain Flint's treasure, and once he learns that Billy Bones's map has been found, he does everything in his power to insinuate himself into the crew of the *Hispaniola* in order to join the search for the buried gold.
- In *Moby-Dick*, Ahab responds to the loss of his leg at the hands of the whale with a near-maniacal obsession with killing the beast.
- In *The Great Gatsby*, Jay Gatsby believes that stealing Daisy from her husband, Tom Buchanan, will be his entrée to the world of legitimate status that has so far eluded him, despite his wealth.

Notice how, in each of these cases, the character feels an urgent, blind, even obsessive need to eliminate or mitigate the sense of Lack. This is caused by a misunderstanding of what can genuinely fill the inner emptiness Lack creates. Their obsession blinds them.

This kind of story logic is not limited to kings, pirates, ex-rumrunners—or lovers. *Virtually all characters, once they become aware of what they Lack, choose a mistaken means of addressing it.*

This is because the events of the story are a learning process, and the characters have yet to internalize the lessons they will encounter as the story progresses.

Rather, they will try to solve the problem presented by their sense of Lack with the limited or misguided understanding of themselves and their lives that they possess at the story's outset. (We will cover this in greater detail in chapter eight, *Folly's Footsteps: Misguided Desires and Misbegotten Yearnings*.)

ANXIETY: THE SOUL'S ALARM THAT SOMETHING IS AMISS

In some stories, the character is not yet clear on what is missing and only gains that awareness in the course of the story. The character may understand that it is love or success or excitement that's missing, but she has no concrete grasp as yet of how to change that, or if change is even possible.

Like the lovers and obsessive characters discussed above, they do indeed gain a better awareness of their sense of Lack, but that awareness may not be present in any clear form at the story's outset.

They may wake up in the morning only to be greeted, as their dreams fade away, by thoughts of obligations unmet, duties unfulfilled, promises betrayed—if not open condemnation for the lesser souls they have allowed themselves to become, rather than the greater ones that once seemingly defined their futures.

When we encounter characters of this type in stories, they often exhibit an agitated boredom, impatience, restlessness, even anger, craving something they cannot yet define. Their inner voice may vary from self-scrutiny to self-doubt to self-condemnation, depending on how well things are going at any particular moment and how adequately they seem to be maintaining.

In some cases the character may feel a stifling indifference to life, revealed in a state of lassitude, emptiness, or malaise. The classic example of such a character is Holden Caulfield from *The Catcher in the Rye*.

DENIAL: NUMBNESS, REPRESSION, AND WHISTLING PAST THE GRAVEYARD

Another strategy for dealing with one's sense of Lack is to live in a state of denial. Characters who resort to this approach have perfected their oblivion to what is truly missing from their lives, crafting a psychic suit of armor against their own misgivings and self-doubt. This can demonstrate itself in several ways:

- A kind of psychic numbness (often enhanced by drugs or alcohol).
- A blithe state of cheerily "whistling past the graveyard." (Note the difference between this and the happy character discussed in Section II above.)
- Adherence to a creed or belief system, or membership in a movement that provides meaning from outside, drowning out internal doubts and questions.
- A kind of adamant distraction, where what is important is considered so pointless or out of reach that the character actively tries to blot it from his mind, busying himself with pleasure, thrills, work, or just the noisy bother of life, the better to drown out the haunting silence within.[4]

Regardless of how Lack expresses itself—or is suppressed—it reveals an underlying anxiety that lies at the heart of the human condition, which we either allow ourselves to feel (or cannot help feeling) or do everything in our power to deny or silence.

Put differently, every day we have a choice between an authentic anxiety or an inauthentic belief that all is well. As the Norwegian playwright Henrik Ibsen put it in *The Wild Duck*, "If you take the life-lie away from an average person, you take away his happiness as well."

The principal takeaway: It is in the character's *attitude* toward his daily life, toward others, toward his own limitations and idiosyncrasies, that even a character who is oblivious to his Lack or actively trying to ignore it will nevertheless reveal its manifestations.

EXERCISES

Return to two characters from previous exercises. If one or the other is unaware or in denial of their Lack, describe how what's missing from

---

4 In *Either/Or*, the Danish philosopher Søren Kierkegaard refers to such an individual as the "busy man," who uses his constant state of activity to deflect an honest reckoning of himself and his life.

The Compass of Character

their lives is revealed in their attitude toward their daily activities and the people around them. (Put differently, describe how each character is living "a life of quiet desperation.")

- For one, make her unaware of her Yearning. How does her Lack reveal itself? In laziness, emptiness, a day-to-day funk? A lack of direction or motivation? A state of acquiescence?
- For the other, make him in denial of his Yearning. How does his sense of Lack reveal itself here? A state of psychic numbness, possibly from drink or narcotics? Forced optimism? Devout adherence to a creed? Compulsive distraction?

If applying these techniques feels forced, ask yourself why. How else might the character reveal her Lack?

IV. THE SPECIAL CASE OF LACK INDUCED BY TRAUMA OR TRAGIC LOSS

Characters who have suffered some nightmarish shock often live in a constant state of avoidance and dread. Examples include:

- victims of rape or torture or profound, prolonged psychological or sexual abuse;
- survivors of terrible accidents or disasters;
- combat veterans;
- those who suffer from a pitiless, disfiguring, or debilitating disease;
- those who have nursed a loved one through such an illness, especially one that was long and ultimately terminal.

Fear, isolation, insomnia afflicted with intrusive nightmares, and substance abuse for the sake of psychic numbness often typify such lives.

Even if the aftermath is not that severe, or the individual manages to gain some control, the "lizard brain" never forgets. A low-grade hum of fearful anticipation, lying at the threshold of consciousness, remains all too common.

What I have just described is commonly known as Post-Traumatic Stress Disorder (PTSD), which typically has its genesis of one or more incidents of shattering fear, often tinged with profound shame. There is a related disorder, however, referred to as Moral Injury.

Moral Injury is typically found in those who have been involved in counterinsurgency operations, where the combatant-civilian distinction is often vague, even fluid. One can also find it, however, in police officers, journalists, aid workers, or anyone who has heard about, witnessed, or personally taken part in an atrocity or any incident that profoundly calls into question the individual's sense of morality, justice, meaning, or humanity. Here the precipitating cause of the disorder is not fear but an offense to the conscience that is so life-changing it destroys the individual's sense of the world as a safe, just, or meaningful place.

For individuals who have suffered either PTSD or Moral Injury, the idea of a "dream of life" often lies so far out of reach that Yearning feels not just impossible but irrelevant. The link between the character's Lack and her original, more expansive Yearning is broken. Simple normalcy, freedom from fear, a feeling of safety, some semblance of justice or humanity—would suffice in and of themselves. A life of quiet desperation, or quiet anything, would be a profound relief.

Despite the modern terminology, such characters are hardly new to the scene. George Eliot's *Silas Marner* features just such an individual. Betrayed by his best friend, falsely accused of theft by his own small religious community, abandoned by his bride-to-be, Silas flees to a town where he's unknown, only to be falsely accused again, this time for witchcraft when an herbal remedy he offers a sick old woman actually works. In the wake of this relentless series of unjust reversals, he retreats into bitter solitude, taking solace only in the gold he earns from his weaving.

In his short story "Lobster Night," Russell Banks tells of a skier named Stacy who'd once had Olympic ambitions but saw them vanish one night at age seventeen when she was struck by lightning. She felt like she'd been shot in the head, and though she's tried to put the episode behind her, all she has to do is the say the word "lightning" and it comes back with agonizing vividness, along with the fear that it might happen again.

The only people who say lightning never strikes twice in the same place have never been struck once.

EXERCISES

Is there a character in your WIP who has experienced any of the types of trauma identified in this section, or anything similarly devastating? How would you describe their state of Lack? How does it affect their behavior and attitude toward life? Try to envision this answer in a scene or scenes. What is the best they can hope for in their current day-to-day lives—what does that look like? How might that change in the course of your story? What prompts that change?

V. WHEN THE CHARACTER'S OBLIVION TO HIS LACK IS ABSOLUTE

Earlier in this chapter, we discussed cases when a character responds to the sense of something missing with a blithe, superficial indifference that I likened to "whistling past the graveyard." This assumes, of course, that at some level, however tenuous, the character detects the anxiety—the grave—he is trying to suppress, ignore, or wish away.

But what of those instances when the character seems devoid of even that dim an awareness?

One can find such knot-headed characters in stories as widely different as James Joyce's "Two Gallants," Flannery O'Connor's "The Barber," and James Lee Burke's novel *Wayfaring Stranger*, in which certain Texas oil men "take pride in their ignorance."

Just such a character sometimes appears in the role of the Fool, which comes in a variety of incarnations, from benevolent to bothersome.

In Jerzy Kosinski's *Being There*, Chance the gardener is mistaken for a sage when his utterly banal and vacuous statements are taken for secret profundities.

Another variation is found in the Captain Mainwaring comedies and others of its kind. Like the traveling angel, this character type perpetually feels obliged to solve some perceived problem (which often is nowhere near as serious or solvable as he imagines), but his pompous, stodgy, imperious, or "principled" personality only makes the situation worse, and others are obliged not only to solve the problem on their own but all too often bail the hero out.

Two distinct explanations for this kind of obtuse behavior suggest themselves:

- The character's denial of his Lack is simply more vehement than we've previously discussed. He may, like Captain Mainwaring, project his sense of something wrong onto the outside world, with an obsessive need to fix it rather than look within for the problem's true source. In such an instance, he will have to be shocked into recognition through events in your story—i.e., probably by being forced to recognize there really is something he doesn't have that he desperately wants. This quite likely will also involve re-assessment of who he is, who he cares about, and what matters to him. Such a character could well serve as a main character and even a protagonist.
- The character is constitutionally unaware of what is missing from his life, whether from a personality disorder such as narcissism, a state of impervious self-satisfaction, or simple ignorance. Absent the lightning strike of disaster, someone lacking insight is impervious to change. And a character incapable of change makes a poor protagonist—unless, like Chance in Kosinski's *Being There*, he's a "holy fool," and like a traveling angel inspires those around him to change, while experiencing nothing of the kind himself.

The point: If you find yourself creating such a character, you have to decide which of the foregoing alternatives—vehement denial, personality disorder, or abject oblivion—explains his seeming unawareness of what is missing from his life. That will determine whether the character is a protagonist that's capable of change, an opponent (like the flagrantly racist barber in the eponymous Flannery O'Connor story), or a secondary character.

EXERCISES

In your current WIP, is there any character you believe might fail to be aware of his Lack in any meaningful sense? If so, how do you account for that oblivion: vehement denial? Personality disorder? Projection of his Lack onto the outside world? Impervious self-satisfaction? Utter oblivion? What role does the character play in your story? How does your answer regarding the nature of his unawareness correspond to the role he plays in the story?

VI. SYMBOLIC REPRESENTATION OF THE CHARACTER'S LACK

Although the character's sense of Lack can be portrayed through his attitude or behavior—whether that attitude or behavior is anxious, indifferent, contentedly unaware, or something else—it is often wise to find a symbolic representation, which can be returned to as the story progresses.

Examples include:

- Hester Prynne's scarlet letter, representing both the sanctimonious hypocrisy in which she's condemned to live and her subversive defiance of it.
- The green light at the end of Daisy's East Egg dock that Gatsby can see from his lawn across the water. The light mirrors not only the love he lacks but the legitimacy he craves.
- The ducks in Tony Soprano's pool, which represent his need for family, both the one defined by business and the other rooted in blood.

Each of these symbols provides an iconic representation of what the character lacks and longs for that can be used throughout the story—and most importantly at the end—to portray whether the character's sense of emptiness remains unchanged or has found relief in one form of fulfillment or another.

Alternatively, as mentioned previously, the character's sense of Lack can be represented in a distinct pattern of behavior that he exhibits at the beginning of the story. That behavior may change as he struggles through the conflicts he faces or not—and that change or lack of change will be represented by a return to a situation that echoes the opening scenes: Does the character behave differently in that situation now, or not?

Consider these two examples:

- In *A Streetcar Named Desire*, Blanche Dubois drapes scarves over the lampshades to soften the light, which symbolizes her fear of the harsh reality that she is growing older and thus losing her sexual allure, which has been her chief source not just of pleasure but of power. At the end of the play the lights are all too bright as Stanley rapes her. In the following scene, when Blanche submits to the "kindness of strangers" who take her away to an asylum, we understand that from this point forward Blanche's only hope to escape the harsh light of reality is madness.
- In *Breaking Bad*, Walter White begins the story in a series of dreary humiliations—waking up to exercise mindlessly on his stationary bike while his pregnant wife sleeps, teaching chemistry to a roomful of uninterested teenagers, working at the car wash after work for extra money. Over the course of the ensuing five seasons, Walt will transcend those humiliations in the form of Heisenberg, the most notorious meth cook in the Southwest, who tells his wife: "I am not in danger, Skyler. I *am* the danger."

EXERCISES

- For any two characters you have used in response to the previous Exercise questions, try to come up with a symbolic rendering of the character's Lack. What is it? How do you see the character's understanding of that symbol changing—or not changing—as the story moves forward?
- Alternatively, create some sort of unique habitual behavior that embodies how the character has responded to what is missing from his life. How do you envision that behavior changing (or not) by your story's end?

The Compass of Character

SUMMARY OF MAIN POINTS IN THIS CHAPTER

- One of the fundamental aspects of human experiences is the sense that something is missing from our lives. This is called Lack.
- There are two basic ways of conceptualizing Lack:

  - It is the effect of our unfulfilled Yearning and exists in some fundamental way prior to our awareness of it.
  - It is the fundamental aspect of our lives, created by the sense of inadequacy, dependence, and fear we experience early in life.

- Seemingly "simple" characters who do not feel a particularly intense sense of Lack fall into three categories:

  - Traveling angels.
  - The contented character.
  - The mature, "sadder-but wise" character.

- More complex characters typically express their sense of Lack in their attitude or behavior, which is usually typified by urgency, anxiety, or denial.
- Characters who have suffered extreme or prolonged trauma often feel such profound Lack that their Yearning has been stunted.
- Characters who seem utterly oblivious to their Lack fall into two categories:

  - Those in a state of particularly fierce denial (i.e., they can possibly serve as a protagonist).
  - Those who possess no insight into this aspect of their lives (i.e., they likely would make a poor protagonist).

- A particularly effective way of representing the character's Lack is to choose a symbolic representation of it, or to present a distinct habitual pattern of behavior the character has adopted to deal with it.

3

The Heart of the Matter
Itself—Yearning

Various stories you read may leave you a little cold, distanced—
you may admire, maybe you have a kind of "smart" reaction—
but nothing resonates in the marrow of your bones, and the
reason is that the character's yearning is not manifest.
—Robert Olen Butler, *From Where You Dream:*
The Process of Writing Fiction

"It hurts my head to think about. It's stupid how much I want this."
Finally Vince reaches out and grabs her broken arm. "Look:
don't ever feel stupid for wanting something better!"
They're both a little surprised by the force of his answer,
and Vince knows he's also talking to himself. They stand across
from each other, staring, until Vince lets go of her cast and looks
away, embarrassed. "So tell me about this house."
—Jess Walter, *Citizen Vince*

I. THE PULSE OF STORY, THE SOURCE
OF WILLFULNESS

No other subject addressed in this book is so central to dramatic portrayal as the one we are about to discuss: Yearning. That is the reason
for this chapter's length and level of detail. Take it slow. Read carefully. Mastering this topic alone will improve your writing considerably.

As the preceding chapter indicates, Lack and Yearning are often two
aspects of the same phenomenon. Where Lack is defined by absence
and a sense of something missing, Yearning is the drive to fill that void.
In its simplest formulation, Yearning can be thought of as the need to

make the individual's *dream of life* come true: the hunger to become the person she longs to be, to realize fully the way of life she hopes to live.

Yearning is the source of the character's willfulness, without which nothing meaningful gets done. It reflects a longing that is never fully satisfied; rather, it pushes the individual onward throughout his or her life.[1]

It shapes the urgency that drives her refusal to quit, compromise, surrender, die.

It defines the stakes by articulating the *meaning* of what she desires, and how it defines both herself and her life, without which existence comes to resemble at best a pointless exercise, at worst a living death.

Even if life has battered and broken the character's soul, Yearning's echo will remain, a harsh reminder of what might have been, or the stubborn call to try once more.

Don't be misled, however, by the word "dream." Yearning is a harsh mistress, often requiring extreme effort in pursuit of a seemingly quixotic or hopeless imperative. It motivates lost causes as well as victories. It drives villains as well as heroes.

The comedian and actor Robin Williams, in describing his technique for getting to the heart of a portrayal, remarked, "Once you find that deep deep deep deep secret, the thing that drives him, you'll understand the character." He added that you will instinctively know once you've found that secret. This points to several insights:

- Yearning is often obscured, a "secret"—to the character himself if not the reader or audience.
- That secret creates an urgent drive—toward what? That too may be unclear, at least at the story's start.
- Recognizing that secret requires an intuitive engagement with the character, not an intellectual analysis.

Like Aristotle's term *eudaimonia*, loosely translated as "flourishing" or "fulfillment," Yearning is meant to encompass not just the individual's sense of reward or happiness, but his unique purpose and goal in

---

1 The Norwegian metaphysician and author Peter Wessel Zappfe remarked in his essay "The Last Messiah:" "Whenever a goal is reached, the Yearning moves on."

life and his ability to live in accordance with it. The great Russian poet Anna Akhmatova, in her poem "Why Then Do We Not Despair," referred to this ineffable willfulness as "something not known to anyone at all/but wild in our breast for centuries."

However, Yearning does not point faithfully and irrevocably toward goodness, certainly not in the short term. The underlying drive that animates Yearning serves a greater purpose than virtue: Selfhood. And that goal requires unification of all the elements of our psyche—Ego and Shadow, anima and animus, conscious and unconscious, virtue and vice.

In fulfilling the demands of unity, one's rise toward heaven cannot skip past a descent into hell. The compass that steers us toward *something more* can direct us toward nobility or savagery, depending on whatever seemingly worthy objective—or harrowing ordeal—suddenly appears before us.

And that is the point. Yearning is more than a mere misty longing for who we might be, how we might live. It calls to us relentlessly from within, urging us on: *You're more than this. You serve something greater. You must.*

Just when or how it is formed remains an open question: Are we born with it, like a soul or a destiny? Or do we create it during the struggle of life? Is it some combination of the two? Are the answers to these questions universal, or unique with each individual?

Regardless, it compels us to act in service of something deeper, something greater than our everyday affairs, and remains a continuous presence and influence throughout our lives. Though it may adapt to the unforeseeable twists and turns of circumstance, Yearning never stops demanding that we try harder, reach deeper, give more. And in that way it never stops reminding us that something is missing, we are less than we expect of ourselves, our lives remain incomplete.

Its demands can feel so relentless, intimidating, or impossible that we may try to deny them, ignore them, bargain them away. And yet, like the condemning whisper of a guilty conscience, a rejected Yearning's call never falls completely into stillness, except perhaps in our waning years, when the mask we place on death begins to slip away, and we're forced to face the whole of our lives honestly, at which point our hearts turn toward acceptance, or ossify in regret.

EXERCISES

Given the summary nature of this introductory section, we will forego specific exercises here in favor or more uniquely targeted ones later in the chapter.

II. LACK AND YEARNING—CAUSE VS. EFFECT

One of Yearning's most mysterious qualities is that it need not be conscious. In this regard it acts much like hunger, thirst, the sex drive, the need to breathe.

Though it may indeed be unconscious for at least part of the story, Yearning gains its most significant influence when it rises from the unconscious and becomes not just apparent but undeniable.

This may happen all at once or by degrees. It may come too late to change the course of events, as happens in tragedy. If it doesn't happen at all, you have the sort of character we discussed in the previous chapter, whose ignorant oblivion to his Lack (and thus his Yearning) remains absolute. As noted there, such characters tend to make poor protagonists, unless your intent is comic. (This is another of those "rules," however, daring to be defied, though that challenge is best left to more accomplished writers.)

In any event, as noted in the previous chapter, Lack and Yearning often resemble two sides of the same coin—one is the sense that something is missing, the other the compulsion to fill that void.

This sometimes causes confusion, and part of that confusion results from how these two elements, Lack and Yearning, interact. To recap briefly how we put the matter in the previous chapter, there are two ways to conceive of Yearning and where it comes from:

- We feel incomplete because our lives are defined by the call of an objective, even transcendent identity, destiny, truth, or soul—i.e., Lack is created by our unfulfilled Yearning.

- We feel incomplete because that is our fundamental nature, rooted in intrinsic feelings of inadequacy, confusion, and dependence that begin in infancy. Here, Lack is not the effect of an unfulfilled Yearning, but rather its cause.

We will explore these distinct methodologies in the following two sections. For now, however, note how Lack and Yearning, just like pursuit of the promise of life and protection from the pain of life, serve as countervailing forces throughout our existence.

Yearning as cause speaks to a faith in the promise of life, whereas Lack as cause places avoidance of the pain of life at the helm. Accordingly, it is not hard to see that the latter, when used for purposes of motivation, may ultimately feel insufficient or lackluster, since its principle goal is merely an escape from suffering or misfortune, and not some greater state of self-fulfillment. This is why, even when this method is used for a character, some underlying issue of identity, purpose, meaning, or a connection to others must also be at stake.

The identity taking shape within the individual represents not just an idea of self but a longing for fulfillment of what that sense of self represents: a moral code, a way of life, a dream of happiness, a sense of belonging and home. It can be misguided or mistaken, led astray by pipe dreams, false prophets, easy money. It can be malformed by deprivation, extreme suffering, betrayal, and other bitter misfortunes. It can be disfigured at birth by a personality disorder such as narcissism or psychopathy. But the sense of identity that Yearning feeds remains in a constant state of evolution and flux, adapting to outer circumstances and inner demands, constantly straining for that ineffable state of grace that will define true happiness, fulfillment, and self-justification.

EXERCISES

Take two main characters from a current Work in Progress (WIP).

- For each, identify as best you can their Yearning: their longing to fulfill a certain dream of life—the kind of person they want to be, the way of life they hope to live.

- For one, conceive of that Yearning as an intrinsic sense of identity or destiny. For the other, imagine the character's Yearning developing from feelings of inadequacy, confusion, and dependence, and a longing to escape those feelings. (Note: If you do not as yet feel confident in the subject material to answer these questions, you can wait for the exercises that follow after the next few sections.)
- Take a moment to reflect on the inner strength, the sense of purpose, the willfulness, and the determination each character possesses. If one seems weaker in this regard than the other, explore why.
- How might you intensify the longing each character feels for something better?
- What might happen in either character's life to damage or redirect that longing, i.e., what terrible misfortune might force them to redefine their dream of life?

III. YEARNING AS A CALLING, SELF, SOUL, OR DESTINY

> There is always one moment in childhood when the door opens and lets the future in.
> —Graham Greene, *The Power and the Glory*

As mentioned previously, one way to think of Lack is to understand it as the effect upon the individual of an unfulfilled Yearning—i.e., Lack *is caused by* Yearning's presence, influence, or call, and the awareness that this longing remains unfulfilled.

Lack frequently appears in just that way in our stories. The character feels Lack most poignantly when he understands just what it is that's missing from his life, and realizes that this absent element serves to define who he believes himself to be, what kind of life he thinks is worth living, and what it will take to change.

In this interpretation, the object of the individual's Yearning—his idea of his true identity, and the way of life he dreams of living—exists to some degree *prior to* the Lack in some fundamental way. In this conception, it is often regarded as a calling to destiny, a psychic image of the Self, a *daimon*[2], or a soul. The character may only see it "as through a glass darkly," but it is there, waiting to be discovered, and made manifest.

This is not merely a western concept, as evidenced by the rite of passage rituals of many Native American tribes. These initiations marked the transition from youth to adulthood, and in some cases began quite early in life, as with the Ojibwa, who introduced them to children as young as four or five, though many tribes waited until puberty. Regardless of when they were conducted, these ceremonies typically included a formal vision quest, during which, through severe deprivation or hardship, typically endured in isolation, sometimes accompanied by the ingestion of hallucinogenic agents, the initiate experienced a unique manifestation of the animal or totem that would become his or her personal Manitou, or guardian spirit. This Manitou would not merely symbolize the initiate's adult identity but provide counsel on how to live. These visions had a social aspect—they had to be affirmed by tribal elders as genuine—but otherwise the notion of a spirit guide bears a strong resemblance to the concept of a personal *daimon*.

The strength of this approach is the definite and compelling sense of self it conjures, the certainty of purpose, the depth of willfulness. Once such a Yearning is recognized for what it is, it cannot be ignored except through a willful "resistance to the call."[3] It stands in the mind and heart like a beacon of identity and purpose. The character diverts his glance at the risk of surrendering what it means for him to be alive.

One weakness of this approach is that it can seem fanciful, antiquated, sentimental, or mystical in the wooliest sense. However, this may result from poor execution rather than faulty conceptualization.

Another weakness lies in how the concepts of fate and destiny often appeal to an autocratic temperament. Fascism famously promotes a view of history that defines freedom in terms of surrender of individual

---

2 I use the word "*daimon*" in its classic sense, referring to a kind of psychic twin—a motivating presence that first appears in one's youth as a core image or experience that will come to animate, guide, and inform the individual throughout her life.
3 See Vogler, Christopher, *The Writer's Journey: Mythic Structure for Writers*, Michael Weise Productions, 3rd Edition (2007).

will to some unseen, unknowable, and overpowering force, typically embodied in the state, the nation, or the race.[4]

YEARNING AS CALLING IN GENRE FICTION

One typically finds the formulation of Yearning as a calling in myths, heroic adventures, action stories, and certain tales of romance. It can also be lampooned in satire or black comedy in the form of a great fool blind to his presumptions.

For other examples, consider:

- The benevolent "traveling angel" who instinctively senses the loneliness and unhappiness in others, and feels compelled to offer the special comfort only a stranger can provide.
- The detective, who understands that the job of justice is never done. Like Sisyphus with his boulder, he knows all too well that the conclusion of one case only heralds the arrival of the next.
- The cyborg or android who senses in his nature the absence of some critical factor, which for lack of a better term he thinks of as his humanity.
- The soldier-of-fortune, who sees in combat the true human condition, stripped of pretense, false innocence, and hypocrisy, and so is always in search of the next war zone.
- The lover, whose loneliness reveals itself in a longing for someone who "sees me as I really am," which in turn creates the magnetic force that brings him and the loved one together.

A casual glance at these examples will reveal that they typify the characters of genre fiction, and it is precisely in genre fiction that this understanding of the relationship between Lack and Yearning is most commonly found.

However, there is no rule obliging genre characters to adhere to this formulation, any more than there is such a rule for any other kind of fiction.

---

4 See for example Erich Fromm's *Escape From Freedom* (1941).

There is also nothing intrinsically slight, specious, or clichéd in this understanding of Yearning and Lack, only in its execution on the page.

This view of Yearning as a calling or an objective core identity harkens back to a pre-Renaissance understanding of man and his place in the world, a view which has experienced a new lease of life in certain quarters in the aftermath of modernity's giving rise to two world wars and the Holocaust. The twentieth century was not kind to materialism, skepticism, and relativism, though it also did not convincingly refute them.

Jungian analysis and Positive Psychology, plus a renewed interest in the philosophers of antiquity (Aristotelian virtue ethics in particular), speak to a return to the view that life possesses direction and meaning and that selfhood requires a search for purpose and identity.

THE SENSE OF CALLING IN DISTINGUISHED INDIVIDUALS

The view of Yearning as a calling, often experienced early in life, is also frequently observed in the biographies of distinguished individuals. For a few noteworthy examples,[5] consider:

- The philosopher R.C. Collingwood, at the age of eight, upon opening a copy of Kant's *Ethics* in his father's library, felt an overwhelming sense of the importance of the words; a disgraceful recognition that he had no clue what they meant; and a sense of personal importance to this moment, a sense of destiny he could only define with the words, "I must think."
- At the age of two, Judy Garland, born into a theater family, saw a performance of the Blue Sisters, three girls aged five to twelve. When the youngest stepped forward for a solo, the young Judy (then known as Frances "Baby" Gumm) sat mesmerized. When the song was over, she turned to her father and asked, "Can I do that, Daddy?" Her sister Virginia recalled that this moment revealed to everyone that Baby Gumm already knew exactly what she wanted. When her father obliged his youngest daughter's wish and allowed

---

5 For additional examples, see Hillman, James, *The Soul's Code: In Search of Character and Calling*, Random House (1996).

her to sing "Jingle Bells" all alone at a subsequent performance, the crowd went wild, demanding numerous encores, until she literally had to be dragged from the stage.

Both of these examples point to a core self-image or experience that provides the kernel of Yearning that will come to animate and elucidate the individual's life. But it's not merely an impression of who the individual hopes to be. There is also an irresistible sense of personal mission: *This is who I am. This is what I was born to do.*

This is not a one-time affair. This sense of calling shadows the individual's life. That shadow reveals itself in effects: motivation, resistance to compromise, faithful persistence regardless of circumstances, even if this requires improvisation and adaptation to unforeseen reversals and detours.

WHAT EXACTLY DO WE MEAN BY GREATNESS IN A CHARACTER?

As compelling as these biographical examples may be, however, a somewhat obvious objection suggests itself almost immediately: They concern famous or exceptional people. How does this translate to the more commonplace individuals who populate so many of our stories?

First, one should resist the idea that using examples of greatness to inspire the rest of us is some kind of snobbish plot. We are seldom inspired by the ordinary or the mediocre, but that shouldn't be confused with pretense or arrogance. It's not fame or status that stirs us but excellence, integrity, beauty, courage, truth. These virtues do not belong to a single social or economic class. But they are indeed confined to a special group of persons—those who demonstrate *character*.

And why should we shrink from portraying great individuals anyway? Not even the many anti-elitist *-isms* of the past half century have managed to ban completely from storytelling the lives of the exceptional.

Winston Churchill alone has found himself incarnated in film and TV on an average of more than seven times *per year* over the last decade. Long-format TV has embraced the Tudors, the Borgias, the rulers of ancient Rome, and Queen Elizabeth II among many other eminences. Hilary Mantel famously fictionalized Ireland's most reviled villain, Oliver Cromwell. And the increasingly popular genre of epic fantasy could arguably be described most simply as the conjunction of magic and myth with medieval history, with its fondness for royalty, knights, saints—and dragons.

We also can hardly benefit from dismissing the numerous characters who come to their stories already "wondrous and strange:" Achilles, Odysseus, Antigone, Oedipus, Medea, Lear, Othello, Macbeth.

One needn't resort to royal bloodlines for such characters. All that's needed is a commitment, however troubled or haphazard, to greatness of heart or moral responsibility, whether the character comes in the form of detectives like Harry Bosch or Jane Tennison, the White House staff members of Aaron Sorkin's *The West Wing*, or the runaway slaves Cora and Caesar in Colson Whitehead's *The Underground Railroad*.

As long as at least some stories reach for historical or monumental scope, seeking to inspire—or to caution against reckless ambition—there will be room for outsized characters, whether they come from real life or the imagination.

To say that a sense of calling or destiny motivates such characters is simply to recognize that vanity, ambition, greed, and the need for adulation can only take one so far. They will not prove up to the test of genuine greatness, which requires a profound sense of personal identity and integrity as well as responsibility to one's cause, especially in the face of punishing opposition.

DESTINY AS A CALLING TO CHARACTER OR VOCATION

Independent of whether one believes or not in such things as fate or purpose: *What we mean by destiny is not a call to greatness but to character.*

For an example of this in fiction, consider Gustave Flaubert's "A Simple Heart." The servant Félicité lives what can only be described as an ordinary life, made unique in only two ways: the generous selflessness of her love, which she offers regardless of recompense, and the rigid simplicity of her religious devotion, rooted in a literal interpretation of things so profound that, when she sees a similarity between her pet parrot and the image of the Holy Ghost in the local church's stained glass window, she ultimately identifies one with the other.

That is not the stuff of international fame, royalty, or Nobel prizes. But it does speak to a life lived in accordance with a firm sense of personal identity.

Ironically, this same sense of calling often results not from a commitment to oneself or an individual vision of life but from a commitment to others, as in recognition of a profound sense of duty. One can find this kind of selflessness in dedicated members of the armed services, religious orders, social movements, and a variety of other professions from medicine and law to teaching, police work, and nursing. What is a personal vocation if not a calling?

Even if the call to a given profession is a recognition of individual purpose, not a social conscience, the point isn't the work per se but the devotion to excellence. Cabinetmakers, glassblowers, carpenters—anyone who finds in work or life a summoning to do the best he can is answering a call.

An informative example of this in fiction appears in the Jack Irish novels of Peter Temple. The protagonist, Jack Irish, was once an up-and-coming defense lawyer—until his wife was murdered by an unhinged client. All but broken in spirit, Jack nonetheless regains a finger-hold on life by serving as a kind of legal troubleshooter, skip tracer, and debt collector, as well as a sidekick to the professional gambler Harry Strang. But the person who genuinely saves him, serving as his most profound moral and spiritual guide, is the cabinetmaker Charlie Taub, a German taskmaster who never settles for anything less than perfection. From Charlie, Jack relearns what it means to care about something profoundly. He not only accepts the older man's withering criticism as a form of penance, he gains an appreciation for the inherent natural beauty of fine wood and devoted craftsmanship. This provides, if not exactly a calling, at least a path toward self-reclamation, a direction toward wisdom and acceptance.

A CAUTIONARY WORD ON OVER-SIMPLIFICATION

Even though we have made a reasonably sound argument against modernity's suspicion of Yearning as a calling, a certain circumspection is nonetheless still called for.

Tying a character's actions to a single motivating factor—fame, pleasure, money, revenge—tends to diminish the character in the reader's or audience's eyes. Absent some sort of larger or more complex meaning, such motivations feel trivial, no matter how relentless the pursuit.

The same is true of Yearning. If it feels encapsulated too conveniently in a neat little package earmarked as the character's "destiny," it cannot help but feel contrived. Rather than serving to reveal a heroic sense of purpose, it will feel like a cheap trick, or a descent into sentimentality.

One way to avoid such reductionist oversimplification is to recognize the symbolic nature of the image or event that evokes the sense of calling. Symbols by their nature are complex, multi-facted, even contradictory. Such a sophisticated representation, the intensity of its effect, the daunting nature of its likely consequences, and the demands it places on the character—demands that will require responsibility, persistence, courage—all mitigate against the potentially simplistic effect of tying the character's behavior to this single, life-defining cause.

The key point is to observe that, if one conceives of Yearning in this way, as a calling, it means that the individual, at some single point in her life or at various points, recognizes a fundamental truth about herself, and understands that a certain way of living is so crucial to her identity that failing to live up to it would mean a profound betrayal of who she is. Deny her calling, and she lives a lie.

EXERCISES

Return to your WIP and choose two of the main characters you've selected for work in previous exercises. Ask the following questions:

- Does either character feel a sense of calling in her life? If one or the other doesn't, why not? What guides or motivates her actions in the absence of this sense of calling?

- When did that calling occur? (If it hasn't happened yet, but will happen in the course of your story, what do you foresee causing that sense of calling to become clear, undeniable?)
- What form does the calling take?

    - An early childhood experience or image that galvanizes a sense of direction or purpose?
    - A sense of vocation to the clergy, the military, a social movement?
    - A sense of excellence in their chosen profession?
    - A "calling to character," i.e., a distinct sense of self, personal dignity, or moral clarity.

- How does the calling help identify the kind of person the character wants to be and the way of life she hopes to live?
- If writing within a genre, how does the calling serve the particular premises of that genre? (For example, how does the sense of calling inspire the detective's "will to justice" or a doctor's "devotion to care"? If your character is a traveling angel, how and when did they come by their sense of calling to be of service to others?)
- How do you intend to overcome the possibility of oversimplifying Yearning by anchoring it to a sense of calling? (Hint: look to the complex symbolic nature of the image or event that defined the calling, the intensity of its effect, the grave nature of its likely consequences, and the demands it places on the character.)

IV. YEARNING AS A NATURAL OUTGROWTH OF LACK

Nothing of me is original. I am the combined effort of everyone I've ever known.

—Chuck Palahniuk, *Invisible Monsters*

Not everyone finds notions such as soul and destiny and "psychic twins" convincing—for example, those who lean toward a more materialist explanation of human life and experience. For such persons, another interpretation presents itself.

We exit the womb small, naked, and screaming. We are immediately and entirely dependent on others, who may to our infant minds resemble benevolent giants—or treacherous, devouring monsters.

Even as our awareness of ourselves and others matures, we remain in a state of dependence and inadequacy because, as children, we cannot provide for ourselves, we lack any real power to change our lives, and our mental faculties are evolving.

Very early in the child's life, however, a tenuous sense of self emerges, if for no other reason than the child is given a name and is treated uniquely in connection with that name. This is how the child begins to understand who she is and how she must behave to get what she needs and wants.

The greater share of our personalities are formed during this period. How could we not experience a profound sense that something is missing? Autonomy, safety, understanding, independence, romance, adventure, identity—all lie elsewhere, in the years yet to be lived.

Come adolescence, the unique sense of personality becomes more defined, and a sense of individual purpose or ambition begins to take shape. This often arises from both internal reflections and outward encouragement. The strength of this individual sense of identity, which also includes moral prerogatives and emotional longings, combined with its ability to withstand conflict, doubt, temptation, and struggle is what we typically refer to as an individual's *character* in the non-literary sense. And it does not ossify in youth and never changes thereafter. On the contrary, throughout life it adapts to circumstances—not just good fortune but failure, loss, the awareness of death—and reshapes itself to suit ambition to reasonable expectation while still retaining a larger sense of what might be.

In this way it's not Yearning but Lack, the sense of being incomplete, that forms the ground on which our lives are built. Yearning is created, not all at once or even completely, but provisionally, step by step, as we navigate our lives. It shows us where we want to go to escape where we have been.

We are not born with Lack and Yearning in any transcendental way. We acquire them through the grind of life. To borrow a phrase from Yeats, they are forged "upon the anvil of the world."

FASHIONING AN IDENTITY THROUGH EXPERIENCE—THE SELF AS SOCIAL CONSTRUCT

We are influenced throughout life—even in the womb, and especially in infancy and childhood when our reliance on others is near absolute—by people on whom we depend, whose love we seek and whom we love in return.

Later in life we will find others who inspire us, and whom we wish to impress and emulate. This series of relationships provides an avenue toward psychological and emotional growth. We hope to solidify personal bonds we find particularly meaningful, expanding and deepening our connection to those who enrich our lives, with the hope of living up to their example.

It may well be that, if I come to sense a soul or "psychic twin" or *daimon* within me, it is just a collection of impressions gathered from traits belonging to the various individuals who have encouraged and inspired me, traits I now wish to emulate—my father's implacable calm under fire, my mother's generosity and humor, my coach's insistence on mental toughness, my favorite professor's meticulous honesty. Patch them together, you get someone I would gladly be, or at the very least could live with.

Or, in the words of Virgil: "We make our destiny by our choice of the gods."

This again roots Yearning's quest for identity, purpose, and meaning squarely in the individual's experience of Lack, for it is my fear of displeasing or disappointing these others, of not living up to their expectations, of being rejected, scorned, or abandoned by them, that motivates me to achieve.

And yet anyone who has attempted this strategy, of seeking fulfillment purely through pleasing others, has realized at some point what a dead end it presents.

However homely and insipid the old bromide "To your own self be true," its truth is undeniable. One is far more likely to irritate someone by slavishly seeking their approval as one is to please them. Fondness, respect, love, admiration—these are gifts, not rewards. We do not and cannot genuinely "earn" them. They are freely given by others—and can be withheld, or taken back.

All of which returns us to the notion that this impression I have of the kind of person I want to be, the way of life I hope to live—the dream of life animating my Yearning—is at some point unique to me. It defines my integrity and my commitment to a moral vision and a conception of personal excellence: my character.

Even if you resist the idea that, "Each person enters the world called," you cannot deny that the near universal experience of men and women includes at least in part a craving for something better, something more—and that translates internally into a longing to be a more complete person, living a more meaningful life, however the individual defines such things.

THE POWER—AND THE LIMITATIONS—OF VIEWING LACK AS CAUSE OF YEARNING: CREATING NECESSITY FROM POSSIBILITY

The strength of this more naturalistic approach is that it feels more down to earth and manageable. It makes the motivating forces readily identifiable, and tangibly explains their power over the individual. The reader will have little problem seeing why the character is driven to do what he does: *He wants something better than he's known to date.*

It is also consistent with the increasingly materialistic understanding of existence that has pretty much won the ideological day since the Enlightenment, as well as Compensation Theory in psychology.[6]

---

6 Compensation Theory argues that the drive to flourish is grounded in childhood, adolescent, or early adulthood experiences of loss, deprivation, humiliation, scorn, bullying, abandonment, loneliness, and so on. Poverty inspires a need for security, shame a need to prove the mockers wrong, abandonment a need for trustworthy love—or safe, reliable solitude.

The Compass of Character

It is not without its limitations, however. One key weakness of the materialistic, compensatory understanding of Yearning is that it does not by necessity conjure the willfulness required of a truly compelling protagonist. (At its most single-minded, it is more naturally inclined toward conjuring adversaries, opponents, villains—those who are embittered, enraged, or goaded by their misfortunes and keen on the kind of "living well" that defines the best revenge.)

Although I may have an understanding of who I would prefer to be and my ideal lifestyle, that doesn't automatically spur me to pursue either. There is no calling to destiny or claiming of my fate, no intrinsic demand that I own or take responsibility for who I want to be and how I want to live. Such things remain possible—but not necessary.

For this reason, protagonists conceived in this way can often feel ambivalent, lackluster, or torn, meandering through their stories instead of truly taking hold of their opportunities and refusing to let go. In the words of the playwright Edward Albee, such people "spend too much time living as if they're never going to die. They skid through their lives. Sleep through them sometimes."[7]

If my most profound longing is merely to find the safest place possible, how will I muster the determination to act selflessly, or to endure great hardship or even suffering in the name of some ideal? Why not, to whatever degree possible, look for the easiest way out?

Some such protagonists only click into gear with a literal or figurative gun to their heads. Some only respond when the thing compelling them to act—the loved one, the bag of money, the killer, the mountain—is staring them in the face.

The task with such characters, then, is figuring out how to put that gun to their heads or force the object of desire directly in their path—to make their better selves and better life not just possible but *necessary*—and make the inner need for it so profound no amount of resistance or opposition can defeat the character's effort to obtain it.

That willfulness may spring from their intrinsic nature or hard experience, but it must be there. Backstory exploration will prove crucial

---

7 Richards, David, "Edward Albee and the Road Not Taken," *New York Times*, June 16, 1991.

with such characters, for you will need to understand why, when faced with great adversity, they do not surrender but instead redouble their efforts.[8] You will not have recourse to destiny or fate, only the character herself. What made her capable of understanding the stakes and refusing to quit, where others in her place might lack that capability, choose the easier way out, even curl up in a ball—or turn and run?

The answer often lies in one of two aspects of her life:

- In the struggle to overcome her misfortunes, whether in the past or in the course of the story, she has come to develop a concrete sense of conviction that now defines her, and which she feels she cannot betray without sacrificing something crucial that she has learned about herself and her life. *Such a strong sense of self often only arises once the character has experienced the profound disorienting loss that death represents, or is forced to confront some other fundamental life-altering truth about the world, others, or herself.* In facing such a shattering, inescapable truth, the character comes to understand that the chances to live up to one's ambitions and ideals are not limitless. It's now or … when? It is in such "dark moments of the soul" that the stakes of identity and Yearning can become truly seared into consciousness.
- She has developed a deep connection to one or more other characters, whose protection from loss, pain, or danger she sees as a personal responsibility.

Obviously, these two possibilities are not mutually exclusive, but often work in concert.

Absent the character possessing such a newfound sense of identity or meaningful interpersonal connections, the risk is that nothing great or life-defining will crown whatever success she manages to accomplish. She will have survived, dodged a bullet, lucked out. If that does not somehow change her life—if her sense of self and her relationships with others remain the same despite that ordeal—you need to ask yourself why. Even those who narrowly escape disaster

---

8 We will look at techniques for the exploration of backstory to establish willfulness in chapter five.)

through no great effort of their own tend to reappraise their good fortune, if not their life.

For an example, consider Juliet Armstrong in Kate Atkinson's novel, *Transcription*. At age 18, her mother dies, leaving Juliet alone and adrift. As war approaches she seeks work with the government only to find herself enlisted by MI5 as a transcriber of secretly recorded conversations with British Fascist sympathizers. The work is tedious and boring, and a possible romance with a coworker founders due to his closeted homosexuality, but bit by bit she proceeds deeper and deeper into the world of espionage, learning to assume false identities and play a role for the sake of gaining information. The "gun to her head" is not just the war and the distinct possibility of defeat at the hands of the Nazis, but living up to the expectations of her superiors. If not exactly a calling the work is gratifying and engaging. Five years after the war's end, she begins to face repercussions of her work she failed to foresee, and begins to realize that even false identities have real consequences, even as, while lying in hospital after being struck by a car in a crosswalk, she feels a certain bemusement at the dreamlike unreality of it all.

Here we see the absence of any intrinsic or transcendental sense of destiny or Self prompting the choice of vocation or life path. There is no grand ambition driving Juliet; rather, she is drawn along by circumstances that become increasingly compelling as war approaches. Juliet grows into her own identity even as she assumes others, like an actress. Nevertheless, the sense of urgency created by the war and the pressure to live up to what her superiors expect of her in the crucible of world conflict creates the drive to fulfill her obligations as best she can and live up to the demands placed on her. Her identity is molded by her experience, but absent the intense pressure of the war, she might easily have continued drifting along, missing her mother with no sense of direction to her life.

Another shortcoming of this approach echoes back to a remark made in the preceding section: linking a character's actions to easily identifiable causes often tends to diminish the character in the reader's or audience's eyes. There always seems to be more at issue than getting even, finding safety, hooking up.

This limitation is particularly noticeable in the approach that seeks to identify a single "backstory wound" or "black moment" that alone explains whatever difficulties the character is experiencing in the present. If only life were so simple that the healing of one wound or overcoming one misfortune could lead to health, happiness, and a new car in the garage.

This problem can be mitigated by grounding the character's Lack in more than one misfortunate experience. Poverty, for example, seldom involves the mere absence of money. It reverberates through the child's entire life, his ability to read and succeed at school, his health and ability to join others in activities, his status among others, his expectations of himself and his life, his faith in others and "the system." (We will address this more global approach to backstory in chapter five.)

The same can be said for virtually any truly transformative state of deprivation that might be seen as a motivational experience. It's not just one moment of hardship that spurs the character's Yearning. Rather the constellated experiences associated with his misfortunes shape a distinct and demanding notion of who he wants to be and how he wants to live.

EXERCISES

Return to your WIP and choose two of the main characters you've selected for work in previous exercises. Ask the following questions:

- Is the character's Yearning rooted in a desire to overcome some sense of vulnerability, dependence, or deprivation rooted in his past? What concrete events caused that sense of vulnerability, dependence, or deprivation?
- How does the character's Yearning, by helping define the kind of person he wants to be and the way of life he hopes to live, provide purpose and direction to his life in light of his previous misfortunes and hardships? How do his relationships to others he loves and admires shape his dream of life—the kind of person he longs to be, the way of life he hopes to live?

- When does the character's Yearning come into sharp focus: at the beginning of the story, the end, somewhere in between? Does that sharper focus happen suddenly at some critical moment, or does it emerge gradually?
- How does Yearning engender the character's willfulness— specifically, how does it inspire him to rise above a mere desire to avoid the pain of life and instead live up to the greater notion of himself he has come to recognize, or exhibit selfless courage on behalf of others?

V. WEIGHING AND BALANCING THE TWO APPROACHES

You are more authentic the more you resemble what you have dreamed you are.
—Pedro Almodovór, *Todo Sobre Mi Madre*

He allowed himself to be swayed by his conviction that human beings are not born once and for all on the day their mothers give birth to them, but that life obliges them over and over again to give birth to themselves.
—Gabriel García Márquez, *Love in the Time of Cholera*

Both of the foregoing approaches—the view that Yearning results from an innate sense of calling versus the view that Yearning emerges in the course of weathering the experience of life—have their advantages and disadvantages. You need to take a moment to reflect on which approach feels most natural and true to your own view of life, for that is the place from which you write.

That said, don't deny yourself the opportunity to create characters who see the matter differently than you do. The debate between materialism and idealism has not been decided despite more than 2500 years of effort. You will not make an irrecoverable mistake by favoring one view over the other. But neither will those who disagree with you, including your characters.

Also and perhaps more importantly, in the foregoing discussion we have hinted at a possible reconciliation between the two approaches that can lead to a single, coherent vision of how Lack and Yearning interact, and how Yearning takes form in a way that can inspire profound willfulness and selflessness.

We've already noted several times how Lack and Yearning often appear to be two sides of the same phenomenon, and they share a dynamic relationship. They are not static, independent properties of the individual's nature; rather, they influence and shape each other throughout the individual's life. On the one hand, a sense of emptiness begs for fulfillment; on the other, the unfulfilled longing conjures the sense of emptiness.

A character whose Yearning has been formed not merely by his life's misfortunes or sense of possibility for something better but forged in the fire of mortality by a tangible experience of death—either in one's own life or the life of a friend, family member, loved one—understands the ultimate stakes of her dream of life. Death is there to snatch that dream away forever, and that can occur at any moment. With this understanding of the stakes, the character has access to the profound wellspring of willfulness and connection to others mentioned above as necessary for a truly motivated protagonist.

Finally, the two approaches may differ in concept but in the end bear a distinct resemblance in execution.

If a character whose Yearning has grown out of his Lack in the natural evolution of his life nonetheless feels it intensely, if it provides a sense of purpose or identity, and points toward a state of fulfillment, a better way of life, it will matter little whether that newfound sense of purpose and a better life did in fact arise from his life's experiences or is in fact objectively innate and was there all along, waiting to be discovered. The entire point of this exercise is to offer characters a sense of clarity and willfulness that permits them to believe in the merit of their task and to act decisively—even if, as it turns out, they're profoundly mistaken.

Furthermore, the concept of Yearning as being rooted in a firm sense of calling or destiny or guided by a *daimon* is not incompatible with a sense of its evolving through the experience of life. The point isn't whether it is truly objective or not, whether it is formed at birth or bestowed by nature or by God, but rather the instinctive naturalness with which the individual senses its verity—*this is truly, undeniably me*—and the intensity with which she responds to it.

The key isn't where Yearning comes from in any objective sense, but in how the character becomes aware of it, takes it to heart, and acts upon it.

Consider as an example Eleanor Roosevelt, who suffered a childhood characterized by repeated loss of loved ones and cruelty at the hands of a tutor. She responded not only through acting out—lying, theft, violent fits of temper—but in cherishing a story she told herself on a day-by-day basis, until it became more real to her than life itself. In that story her dead father was alive, she was the mistress of his elaborate household, and she joined him on his worldwide travels.

This example points to a clear sense of identity forged at least in part by hard experience, but it also reflects a concrete image beckoning Eleanor toward a unique dream of life. Such a dual genesis of Yearning may in fact be the true human condition. Once again quoting Peter Wessel Zapffe's "The Last Messiah": "The human yearning is not merely marked by a 'striving toward', but equally by an 'escape from.'"

Similarly, a personal vocation typically doesn't take the form of a thunder-strike on the road to Damascus. Rather, one grows into it as the nature of one's own character and the realistic prospects of the life ahead become clear.

Consider Robbie Turner in Ian McEwan's *Atonement*. The son of Grace Turner, a servant who lives on the grounds of the Tallis estate, Robbie has been raised with the gracious financial support and personal sponsorship of Jack Tallis, the head of the upper-crust family. That sponsorship has permitted Robbie not only to obtain a good education but to attend Cambridge, where he excelled. In trying to determine what career to pursue, he has evaluated the various options afforded him. He has pursued landscape gardening, but this now seems no more than a "bohemian fantasy, as well as a lame ambition." His Cambridge studies focused on literature, and though he did well the prospect of pursuing it further seems little more than "an absorbing parlor game." Rather, his "practical nature and frustrated scientific aspirations" have led him to an "exercise of will"—he has chosen to study medicine. "He would take lodgings in a strange town—and begin." Above and beyond the instinctive appeal of this vocation is the fact he made the decision on his own, rather than having it proposed by "an ambitious headmaster," a "charismatic teacher," or his patron, Jack Tallis, all of whom have proposed other avenues. He feels he is finally his own man: "his adult life had begun."

Others who see in their vocations a unique individual calling—nurses, soldiers, clergy, teachers, farmers—observe a similar path in weighing options and choosing, ultimately settling on the life path that seems to both suit their temperament and skill set and speak to their individual notions of who they are and what they want from life.

Not all such callings take the form of a single professional career, of course. Consider these two examples:

- Josephine Baker—born into abject poverty, pawned off to work for and sleep with older men, kept naked because dresses cost too much—set up a stage with box benches in a tenement basement, and forced her young friends to watch her dance. She became famous as an exotic and erotic dancer in 1920s Paris, with a closetful of dresses, a truly international star. But she also refused to perform for segregated audiences (thus her exile from the U.S.), became active in the French Resistance to the Nazis in World War II, joined the Civil Rights movement in the U.S. under Rev. Martin Luther King, Jr., and raised nearly a dozen orphans of mixed race. Her Yearning involved more than merely an escape from poverty—it revealed itself in a lifelong refusal to bow to oppression and a determination to fight not just for her own freedom and dignity but that of others.
- From an early age, the future Irish revolutionary Thomas Francis Meagher exhibited a gift for language as well as an impish, defiant, anti-authoritarian streak. Born into a wealthy merchant Catholic family, he rankled at the brutality of English rule, especially the fact so many Irish had to emigrate—"compelled to surrender the land of

their love and pride"—simply to survive. Arrested and exiled to Tasmania for his part in the 1848 Rebellion, he escaped captivity and fled to the United States, where he quickly rose to prominence as an orator. Forbidden forever to return to Ireland, he confessed that he felt an as yet-undefined sense of destiny in his adopted homeland. That sense of destiny quickened to life when, in the early months of the Civil War, he formed the Irish Brigade, five regiments of Irish immigrant recruits hoping to prove their worth as Americans by fighting for the Union. Under Meagher's command, they fought with conspicuous bravery and suffered brutal casualties at the battles of Antietam, Chancellorsville, and Fredericksburg.

Neither of these individuals led a life defined by a single, clear trajectory or career path. Rather, at various junctures of their lives, they responded to a sense of calling that came with urgency, clarity, and a sense of necessity, and adhered to a certain moral prerogative.[9]

In some ways the distinction between the two approaches in question bears a resemblance to the nature versus nurture debate, with the same indefinite conclusions. Even if the vast majority of behavior is instinctual or rooted in unconscious motivation, we cannot escape the fact that, from the perspective of how we live our lives, if choice is not objectively real the illusion of choice is, and we are obliged to live our lives making decisions and suffering consequences, and this is equally true whether we have a unique calling or whether we fashion our identities through the gauntlet of experience.

The bottom line: sooner or later in life, a unique sense of self with distinct ambitions and longings emerges, and it both bears elements of an intrinsic identity and demonstrates an adaptability to external circumstances. We remain true to a core persona, however vaguely

---

9 Also note that, as far as we know, both individuals experienced their sense of calling only after suffering or witnessing some grave deprivation. It is unclear whether their Yearning was at least in some sense affected or even forged by these experiences, or whether their response to deprivation was predetermined by some essential aspect of their natures preexisting within them at birth. From the perspective of dramatic portrayal, the question may also be irrelevant.

perceived or expressed, while responding to the various positive and negative experiences of life.

Whether it quickens to life with great clarity in childhood, or requires more time or a life-changing incident to materialize, sooner or later Yearning becomes more than just a question of what is possible; it defines what is necessary, responding to an underlying sense of urgency, gravity, passion. Even if we shrink from or reject entirely its demands on us.

EXERCISES

Return to two main characters from your WIP that you worked on in the exercises relating to the cause-and-effect relationship between Yearning and Lack earlier in this chapter, i.e., one who has felt his Yearning as a sense of calling or vocation, and the other one whose Yearning has emerged naturally from his sense of Lack, i.e., his sense of who he wants to be and the way of life he hopes to live is rooted in overcoming the deprivation and dependence he has felt in his life.

- As before, compare the two characters—specifically, weigh how deeply each character feels the impetus to pursue that greater sense of self and richer way of life. Then answer:
  - Where does that willfulness come from? At what point in the story does each become aware of it?
  - Does one feel his willfulness more strongly than the other? How can you tell?
- How clearly does each perceive his Yearning? How different are those perceptions and the clarity with which they're recognized?

VI. HOW YEARNING DEFINES THE STAKES

Yearning does not exist in a vacuum—or merely in the breast of your character. It reveals itself in action—what the character does, why he does it, and what meaning he attaches to success and failure.

As the character goes after whatever exterior goal, objective, or ambition exists in your story—i.e., as he pursues his Desire, as we defined it in Chapter One—he encounters conflict. If the story is structured to maximize its dramatic impact, that conflict intensifies in the form of increasingly worse frustrations, setbacks, roadblocks, failures—rejection, betrayal, or abandonment by friends and allies, intensified resistance or open attacks from adversaries, even outright disaster.

The struggle to continue pursuing the Desire despite the mounting conflict—and the increasing risk and reality of failure—forces the character to ask: Why continue? Why not surrender, compromise, turn back?

The answer lies in his awareness of his Yearning. Either through the urgent demands of the calling that has set the character on this path, or through his struggles to gratify the Desire—facing the prospect of failure, disgrace, ruin, even annihilation—the character becomes aware of the deeper need, the core longing that he has imperfectly grasped before. Or, if he has in fact been aware of it previously, he now at last realizes the inescapable intensity of it, the *necessity* of it.

This awakens him to the stakes. A character's Yearning speaks to what he believes his life is truly about: *the kind of person he longs to be, the way of life he hopes to live.* If he turns his back on that, now that it's become painfully clear, he's basically giving up on himself and his life. He must accept the truth of his Yearning or die—psychologically, emotionally, morally, professionally, or physically.

This is how to create stakes that are truly profound—not through increasingly daunting action sequences, feats of daring, or ever-expanding peril.

Recognize that whatever outer goal or ambition the character pursues in the story somehow speaks to this deeper, implacable, life-defining need: his Yearning. He has tried to escape it, silence it, bargain with it, but that option is now gone forever. He must live up to it now, or understand that the rest of his life will be characterized by the shame of that failure. How can he live with himself once he's given up on himself?

For a real world example of what we're talking about, consider the great Italian poet, Dante Alighieri. He confessed that what saved him during his darkest hours of despair and dissolution was the rediscovery of his love for Beatrice, long dead. He realized that their love was the greatest source of joy and truth in his life, and if he did anything that might shame or degrade himself before her eyes, he would consider that a terrible sin. Her memory embodied his Yearning, and failing to honor that memory would risk his very soul. In this way her image guided him out of the darkness into which his life had descended.

Even if your story emphasizes external struggle—such as in mysteries, thrillers, adventure tales, horror stories—the character's outer actions speak to some inner longing or need, and in no small way define his identity.

As we shall see in chapter seven, exterior struggles often concern justice, survival, adventure, or freedom. The character's Yearning, therefore, should be anchored in—though not simplistically reduced to—some deep-seated need to see justice done, to survive at all costs, to answer adventure's challenge, to be free at last.

This does not absolve you, however, from asking the more fundamental questions:

- Why does the character feel these particular needs (and not others)?
- How do these needs define who he is and how he wishes to live?
- How do they lend meaning to his life?
- Are these needs simply intrinsic to his nature—i.e., part of the call to a particular destiny—or are there experiences in his past that forged them, intensified them?
- Is it possible both circumstances apply—i.e., that his Yearning was vague or weak or misunderstood until the outer Desire called him to action, at which point, little by little, his understanding of himself, his life, and what that it all means at last began to clarify?

There are of course individuals—and characters—who fail this critical test. At some point in the past or within the story itself, they buckled under and failed. When the calling of character beckoned, they could not reach any deeper within themselves to summon the willfulness necessary to make one more effort. They live ever after with the knowledge that when their dream of life lay seemingly within reach, they could not grab hold.

Perhaps they have made peace with that failure, and become sadder-but-wiser, or they live in a state of persistent anxiety or stubborn denial, as we discussed in chapter two when discussing Lack. But the truth remains that the failure was life-defining. The character cannot look into a mirror—or his heart—and not see who he might have been.

EXERCISES

Return to two of the characters from your WIP that you've been developing during your progress through the material. For each of them ask:

- How is the external struggle in the story forcing them to confront the prospect of failure?
- What deep needs or longings have the struggle awakened? Specifically:
  - Why does the character feel these particular needs?
  - How do these needs define who he is and how he wishes to live?
  - How do they lend meaning to his life?
  - Put differently: How would failure create a crisis of identity or purpose?
  - How would failure evoke a profound sense of shame for having not lived up to the fundamental challenge of the character's life?

VII. YEARNING'S INEFFABLE NATURE

The quest for the self has always ended, and will always end, in a paradoxical dissatisfaction.

—Milan Kundera, *The Art of the Novel*

Can the character's understanding of who he is, what he lives for, how he wishes to spend his life in the face of certain death, all be summed up in a single pat phrase, no matter how evocative that phrase? To come home. To be free. To find true love.

Consider this passage from a journal entry by Mary Fulton Holliday, a cousin of the famous western gambler and gunman Doc Holliday:

[I] want to see the world. I want to know and to see what lies beyond these time-worked farms, the life beyond these mountains. It's not idle curiosity, but the desire to see and know what others are doing, and to look into the minds and hearts of men. All is riddle to me now, so I want to find the answer. There is no one in this community who can tell me. All I know [is] from school books, weekly papers, and our own library. I want to accomplish something, and here we seem to live only for the day. I want to live beyond the day, and what would a life be without experience? It is hard to tell you what I feel, it is a feeling without a name.[10]

You could identify the longing expressed in this passage by the phrase "see the world" or "live life to the fullest," but you can feel immediately how inadequate those seem. Yearning is more organic, complex, and ineffable than that, and speaks not just to external experience but identity and meaning.

However, that doesn't mean it can't be realized in a symbol, an image, or some other impressionistic representation.

For an example, return once again to Dante and Beatrice. It would be impossible to sum up in a single pat phrase what her image in his memory meant to the poet, but it personified everything true and noble that he expected of himself. It called him to his greatness—a greatness he himself never believed he truly or completely lived up to.

Or consider Gatsby's green light, Ahab's white whale—these stand for so much more than their mere physicality represents. When Gulliver returns from his travels, he is so disgusted by the pettiness of mankind he takes solace in his horses, who remind him of the noble equine race of Houyhnhnms he met in his final voyage.[11]

For a more contemporary example, consider Lou Berney's *November Road*. Charlotte Roy at age eleven defies the advice of her friends' parents to stay in the shallows on the town side of the Redbud River where they swim during the hot prairie summers. Instead, Charlotte, the strongest swimmer among her friends, wills herself against the

---

10 Quoted in Karen Holliday Tanner, *Doc Holliday: A Family Portrait*, University of Oklahoma Press (1998).

11 Just as a symbolic representation of Lack is often useful (as discussed in the preceding chapter), this same symbolic rendering can represent Yearning. In fact, this is often its most successful representation.

The Compass of Character

current to the far side, where she then sprawls in the sun, daydreaming about skyscrapers in New York City, Hollywood premiers, African safaris, "wondering which of many delightful futures awaited her." That experience of strength defines her sense of promise and gives her confidence that whatever dream of life awaits her, she is up to the task.

As we will see in additional references to this novel throughout this book, especially in the next chapter on Resistance, life proves far more daunting than eleven-year-old Charlotte can foresee. She finally makes the decision to break free—leave her alcoholic husband and the "quaint, safe, friendly" but suffocating life she has come to accept in the small town of Woodrow, Oklahoma. She needs to find "a place where it wasn't so hard to tell the past from the future."

During a phone call while on the road to Los Angeles to stay with her sister, Charlotte tries to justify herself to her husband, and finds she cannot explain what future she hopes for, merely that she knows she is not the person she wants to be. "Maybe I'll never be," she tells him, "but I need the chance."

Her Yearning is undefined but no less intense for that—she knows it involves something new, something greater than she has allowed herself to accept for herself, and it may involve her love of photography, her talent for which she has allowed to lie dormant for years. Regardless, her best chance of fulfilling that inchoate Yearning lies west, as it has for generations of the restless, the ambitious, the hopeful, driven by a dream of a better life.

Another example appears in *News of the World* by Paulette Jiles. Captain Jefferson Kyle Kidd discovered his calling as a foot messenger during the Indian Wars under General Andrew Jackson. That image, of enduring danger to bring news to others, often running barefoot through uncharted forests, stays with him as he pursues a career as a printer. After his wife's death and his daughters' marriages leave him a solitary widower, he becomes a traveling reader, reciting news articles from around the world to audiences in remote outposts in post-Civil War Texas and Indian County. In his final role as messenger, he transports a ten-year-old white girl, abducted by the Kiowas at the age of six then "rescued" by the U.S. cavalry, to her relatives outside San Antonio. At least, that's the plan, until Captain Kidd recognizes that blood relation alone does not guarantee a rightful place for the girl, and decides this newfound "message" deserves a more compassionate and honorable address.

In *The Art of the Novel*, Milan Kundera reveals that this approach is not unique to the psychological novel. He explains that he conceives of his characters not in terms of their past but in terms of their existential problem, which in turn requires each character to possess an *existential code* comprised of key words that reflect that fundamental problem. For Tereza in *The Unbearable Lightness of Being*, that code consisted of the words body, soul, vertigo, weakness, idyll, Paradise. For Tomas it was simply lightness and weight (to reflect the lack of gravity to existence). Kundera uses these existential codes to capture the fundamental concerns at the heart of his characters' lives the way other writers use symbols or images. The character's Yearning is to break the code, solve the existential problem.

In our discussion of the *daimon* above, we noted how it often appears as a core image or a transformative experience that appears early in life, and which shadows that life ever after. That core image or experience is never simple, but open-ended, allowing for the interpretive improvisation that experience will oblige.

Trying to confine Yearning within a pat phrase or ready-made concept, such as "home" or "freedom" or "justice" or "love," will only diminish it—and the character—in the reader's or audience's estimation, unless those concepts are open-ended, inviting complex interpretation.

Which is why it is often wise to imagine Yearning through a symbol, and might even be evoked by a work of art or a piece of music—something that speaks to your intuition and the deeper levels of your imagination.

Although music figured in various significant ways in how Anthony Burgess depicted the character of Alex in *A Clockwork Orange*, it was Beethoven's "Ode to Joy" that captured best the essence of how he not only justified but idealized his life of "ultra-violence."

This kind of symbolic, imagistic conceptualization of Yearning allows for a deeper, more intuitive, less logical or reductionist understanding of the character. It takes you beneath the clamor of words to the character's essence.

But it can also seem too amorphous to serve simple story needs. We'll address how to solve that problem in the following section.

EXERCISES

- For two of the characters you have been working on in previous exercises, and for whom you have developed an understanding of their Yearning, try to envision a symbolic rendering of it. If using a work of art or a piece of music helps, by all means use it. Take a moment to reflect on the end result. Do you feel a deeper connection to the character's Yearning? If not, why not? Do you feel that a concept such as Home, Freedom, True Love, or Honor is sufficient for your purposes?

VIII. BRINGING YEARNING DOWN TO STORY SIZE

The life of a character should be an unbroken line of events and emotions, but a play only gives us a few moments on that line—we must create the rest to portray a convincing life.
—Constantin Stanislavski, *An Actor Prepares*

The above quotation from Stanislavski points to a problem every writer faces when creating characters: How do I balance the broader understanding of the character's life with the specific demands of the story? How do I reflect the fullness of my characters' existence when I have only these few episodes at my disposal? This problem is no more apparent or demanding than when dealing with Yearning.

In every story, some aspect of the character's incomplete nature, some element of the life he hopes to live, is tangibly at stake, and thus capable of destruction or fulfillment—otherwise the story has nowhere to go.

First, understand that the character never fully gratifies this deeper Yearning. Just as Lack is unquenchable, so Yearning remains elusive and unfulfilled, constantly adapting to new circumstances, until our lives are over. Returning to a line from "The Last Messiah" quoted earlier in this chapter: "Whenever a goal is reached, the Yearning moves on."

However, your character will get nearer to fulfilling that more expansive, elusive Yearning in the course of the story, and you need to identify what that interim destination will be. I call that interim destination a Yearning Horizon. It will define how, due to the events of the story, the character has become at least a little more aware and capable of being the person she secretly wants to be, living the life she knows she should live.

I always ask how, at the end of the story, my characters have become at least a little braver, more honest, and more loving—or not. And if not, why? The courage may be wobbly, the honesty bitter, the love rocky, but those virtues are the milestones I mark on the character's journey to a life she believes is more worthy, authentic, and gratifying than the one she was living on page one.

For an example, consider Kem Nunn's 2014 novel *Chance*, adapted for television in 2016.

The protagonist is a consulting psychiatrist named Eldon Chance. He seems to be a perfect representation of the kind of character whose Yearning is rooted squarely in his Lack—meaning that to understand what he longs for, you first need to catalog the numerous failures in his life, and then invert them.

During medical school in Boston, he became so obsessed with a fellow student that she fled to San Diego to escape, only to have him follow; he was arrested and involuntarily committed, a stain on his past he has yet to completely erase. (This is why he does not treat patients, but merely serves as an advisor to lawyers and other officials seeking an independent opinion concerning a given individual's mental state.)

His marriage has recently imploded, due at least in part to his seemingly intrinsic passivity and indecisiveness, a habitual reaction to the obsessiveness that almost ruined his life. Though still close with his teenage daughter, she is demonstrating "stalking" tendencies similar to those he exhibited when young and he does not know how to help her.

From that mound of wreckage, how might we construct Dr. Chance's Yearning? We can imagine, given his early and continuing involvement with the field of medicine, that central to his identity is the notion of healer, and his inability to act on this deep-seated impulse forms one of his life's great regrets. This need to heal also animates at least in part his desire to be a good father to his daughter.

But above and beyond the need to heal is the longing to engage life fully, not merely to observe and render an opinion. His fear of regressing to an obsessive state has held this larger longing in check. His clinging to accepted morality, and staying within the strict bounds of what is commonly considered legal and permissible, save him from straying back into his own worst impulses.

So one might define his Yearning as to be a man capable of caring for and protecting others, engaging with them and the world in an active, decisive, forceful way, without fear that by doing so he will regress into self-destructive, obsessive fixation. A lonely man, he also wishes to love and be loved—honestly, openly, fearlessly.

Enter Jaclyn Blackstone. The wife of an abusive homicide detective, she possibly suffers from dissociative personality disorder—or is feigning this disorder to justify other deceptions.

Dr. Chance is assigned to refer Jaclyn to a new therapist when hers dies, and quickly reverts to old ways. His desire to help her and get her away from her abusive husband quickly turns to first professional then romantic obsession.

Given the danger posed by her husband, he enlists the help of a young man named D he meets through a furniture broker. D possesses numerous combat skills and a firm belief in the intrinsically subjective nature of moral lines. He provides Dr. Chance fighting and survival tips that enhance his sense of capability and power.

At the end of the story, we realize Dr. Chance still has a long way to go. He's made a decisive step toward being the man he wants to be, living the life he hopes to live, but that journey is far from over. In fact, it has merely entered its next phase.

Put differently, he's reached the horizon line defined by the story, but another automatically beckons.

In creating and developing your own characters, don't neglect Stanislavski's admonition. Recognize that the actions in your story represent only part of a life, and the longings that motivate the character reflect only a portion of a much more complex Yearning, which resists simplistic definition or compartmentalization into distinct and tidy categories, no matter how useful that compartmentalization may prove as you narrow your focus to write.

EXERCISES

- Given your understanding from previous exercises of Yearning for two of your main characters, what ambitions or goals in the actual story point toward short-term gratification of that Yearning, i.e., provide a "Yearning Horizon" for the character?
- How does the character come closer to being the person he wants to be, living the way of life he hopes to live—or fails to do so—given the events of your story?

IX. NO MAN IS AN ISLAND: THE ROLE OF OTHERS IN THE CHARACTER'S YEARNING

> Who knows what true loneliness is—not the conventional word, but the naked terror? To the lonely themselves it wears a mask. The most miserable outcast hugs some memory or some illusion.
>
> —Joseph Conrad, *Under Western Eyes*

In identifying Yearning as the longing to be the kind of person the character hopes to become, to achieve the way of life he dreams of living, we risk making one of the fundamental errors of characterization: Imagining the character in isolation, rather than living among others.

As should be obvious from the example of Dr. Eldon Chance explored immediately above, it is the rare individual whose idealized life does not include companions, family, and other loved ones.

Loners and outcasts, of course, can make for fascinating characters. And yet their status as outsiders is defined with respect to others, i.e., with respect to the community of which they are not a part. Their isolation may be chosen, it may in fact be an essential aspect of what they expect of themselves and how they hope to live, but that doesn't magically wipe the rest of the world off the planet—or from their minds and hearts.

Earlier, we addressed the folly of defining one's happiness on the basis of what others want. Integrity, authenticity, and dignity form crucial elements to self-fulfillment and happiness. None of them, however, can guarantee that one will be loved. Some of the greatest stories, in fact, are premised on the conflict between one's own sense of honor, truth, and what is right, and what others would demand—especially loved ones.

But the need for connection is so fundamental, so engrained from infancy when we are so dependent on the care of others, that believing anyone can honestly idealize a life devoid of human contact is living a solipsistic fantasy. Ask Ebenezer Scrooge.

The question is never *how* the character is alone but rather *why*, and what value he places on regaining a place among others. What are his terms? Are they self-selected or imposed by others? If the latter, what will it take to be invited back inside the social circle? Which circle would that be? Who would decide if he's welcome or not? How much does he trust, respect, or love the person or persons who hold his return in their hands?

Even the most devoted loners don't shun completely the society of others.

Michael Connelly's Detective Harry Bosch, whom Connelly created specifically to be an outsider like the classic PI heroes of the genre but working on the inside with the police, shuns and alienates many of his associates, but not all. He chooses his connections carefully, while focusing most of his emotional attention on his daughter.

Thoreau famously kept three chairs in his cabin for guests, and if more than that number arrived they took the conversation outdoors. He soon discovered that he had more company once he chose to live alone than he had when residing in town. He did not resent these visitors. On the contrary, he admitted that these social interruptions not only didn't disrupt his self-communion but in fact broadened it.

One might argue that the Desert Fathers, the Irish wayfaring monks, and other pilgrims on a solitary spiritual path refute the contention that all people seek the company of others. And yet such individuals do not seek to be alone for the sake of solitude itself, but to employ that solitude to enhance their communion with the will of God.

Outcasts present a special case, since they have not chosen their isolation, but have had it imposed on them.

In the cases where physical deformity has made them hideous to others, such as Quasimodo, the "Hunchback of Notre Dame," and Joseph Merrick, the "Elephant Man," not only has their desire for human connection remained intact, its pursuit and fruition comprise the most affecting aspects of their stories.

In cases where moral transgression has made the character an outcast, there are a variety of ways to depict that status.

Hesther Prynne is the moral outcast par excellence. Forced to wear her shame embroidered on her dress, resented by the other women in her village for her beauty and pride, and banished to a cottage on the edge of town, she nonetheless finds solace in her daughter, Pearl, and never stops loving the girl's father, Arthur Dimmesdale, to the point of making sure that, upon her death, her grave resides beside his.

Blanche DuBois, whose drinking and sexual improprieties have driven her from her hometown, tries to find refuge with her sister, Stella. When that leads to brutalization by Stella's husband, Stanley, Blanche turns to the "kindness of strangers."

Even if utter, self-imposed exile or isolation takes place, that doesn't by necessity render impossible a longing for human contact. If the character feels regret, he may still long for some sort of return to the community that has banished him, even if that no longer is possible. Returning to the quote from Joseph Conrad at the top of this section: "The most miserable outcast hugs some memory or some illusion." And should his heart harden completely through indifference or bitterness, that doesn't mean he yearns for the life he's been given, merely that he's come to accept it.

The foregoing examples should make it clear that even those characters who seemingly live apart nonetheless cannot sever their ties with others completely, nor do they honestly wish to. There remains in every human heart the longing for connection, no matter how pitiless the circumstances that have rendered it unlikely or impossible.

How much more important, then, is connection for those who haven't been exiled, excommunicated, or abandoned? For this vast majority of characters, Yearning by necessity includes the hope of loving and being loved, of friendship, camaraderie, belonging.

The person such a character hopes to be is intrinsically one worthy and capable of love, trust, companionship. And the way of life she dreams of living cannot be imagined without others included within it.

Expanding this notion of connection, don't neglect those characters whose vision of themselves and their preferred way of life includes their community, city, country, world. This expansiveness of spirit and moral concern typifies genuine greatness, and there are perhaps no nobler characters in fiction than those who humbly accept the mantle of leadership, be they human or Hobbit.

As appealing as the lonesome cowpoke may be, particularly to a certain subset of American readers, he is no more real than the unicorn. Even wanderers travel town to town. And the most fervent hermit remains aware that someday a stranger may appear at his door.

EXERCISES

- For two of the characters from your WIP that you have addressed in previous exercises, identify the other individuals that are necessary for the character's Yearning to be fulfilled—which comrades, friends, family members, lovers?
- If the individuals envisioned in the character's Yearning are unknown or indistinct—the love not yet met, the person who might forgive—identify why that uncertainty exists.
- How is the person the character hopes to be worthy and capable of love, trust, companionship?
- How is the way of life she dreams of living enriched by the others within it? Does he also feel an obligation—a calling—to the larger community, city, country, mankind?

- If the is character is a loner, drifter, or outcast, identify the circumstances that cut her off from human society. What might conceivably draw her back within the circle of friendship or society?

SUMMARY OF MAIN POINTS IN THIS CHAPTER

THE PULSE OF STORY

- In its simplest formulation, Yearning can be thought of as the individual's drive to fulfill her "dream of life:" the person she longs to be, the way of life she hopes to live. It concerns not just the external facts of the individual's life but her connection with others and her very identity.
- Yearning can also be thought of the inverse of the Lack. What's missing from the character's life (Lack) is the fulfillment of his Yearning.
- The character's Yearning is the source of the her willfulness, without which nothing meaningful gets accomplished. It defines the stakes by articulating the meaning of what she desires, and how it defines both herself and her life.

TO BE BORN IS TO BE CALLED

- The character's Yearning can be thought of as a calling, represented by a *daimon*, a kind of psychic twin—a motivating presence that first appears in one's youth as a core image or experience that will come to animate, guide, and inform the individual's life.
- As the personification of the character's Yearning, the *daimon* issues the call of destiny, the need to fulfill the demands of one's soul. It does so with passionate intensity, and remains throughout life as both goad and guide along the journey to the fulfillment of that destiny.
- However, destiny is not just for exceptional or eminent individuals. *Destiny is not a call to greatness but a call to character.*

YEARNING AS NATURAL REACTION TO THE LACK

- An alternative conception of Yearning is that it only takes shape in the course of life's struggles.
- In some versions of this approach, the drive to excel—or simply survive—is grounded in experiences of deprivation, and anchors Yearning in the individual's sense of Lack, which is grounded in experience, not essence.
- In this interpretation, the idealized person the individual hopes to become may be fashioned from a collection of impressions gathered from others whom the individual has found inspiring or otherwise impressive, and seeks to emulate.
- This can prove useful in characterization, because it is so concrete, and makes the motivating force readily identifiable.
- However, that is also the major shortcoming of this view. Linking a character's actions to easily identifiable causes tends to diminish the character in the reader's or audience's eyes. This problem can be mitigated by grounding the character's Lack in more than one misfortune, or understanding the extensive breadth of a single misfortune's effects. Similarly, you can identify his idealized self not through one person who inspired him but several, and molding their various influences together into the person he wishes to be.
- Another weakness of this approach is the risk of rendering the character incapable of mustering the willfulness needed to overcome truly dramatic challenges. The better self and better life defined by her Yearning remain a mere possibility, not a necessity. This can be overcome by having the character develop a deeper sense of self or purpose through the course of her ordeal—in particular, through an encounter with mortality—or by providing her with meaningful emotional bonds to others.

WEIGHING AND BALANCING THE TWO APPROACHES

- Whether one conceives of Yearning as innate or emerging in the course of life's struggles, it always represents a sense of direction toward a better self, a richer way of life. That sense of a better self and way of living is what is meant by the Compass of Character.
- Regardless of approach, this Compass of Character at some point of the story must be strongly felt, providing both willfulness and clarity of purpose, or you risk having the character appear aimless, lackluster, weak-willed.

HOW YEARNING DEFINES THE STAKES

- The struggle to continue pursuing the outer objective in a story despite the mounting conflict forces the character to ask: Why continue? Why not surrender, compromise, turn back? The answer lies in the character's Yearning.
- Through facing the prospect of failure, ruin, even annihilation, the character becomes aware of the core longing that he has imperfectly grasped before. Or, if he has in fact been aware of it previously, he now at last realizes the inescapable intensity of it, the *necessity* of it.
- This awakens him to the stakes. A character's Yearning speaks to what he believes his life is truly about: *the kind of person he hopes to be, the way of life he longs to live.* If he turns his back on that, he's basically giving up on himself and his life.
- Whatever outer goal or ambition the character pursues in the story must somehow speak to this deeper, implacable, life-defining need: his Yearning.

YEARNING'S INEFFABLE NATURE

- Trying to confine the character's Yearning within a pat phrase or ready-made concept, such as "home" or "freedom" or "justice" or "love," will only diminish it—and the character—in the reader's or audience's estimation.

- It is therefore often wise to imagine the character's Yearning through an image, a work of art, or a piece of music. This kind of symbolic, imagistic conceptualization of Yearning allows for a deeper, more intuitive understanding of the character. It takes you beneath the clamor of words to the character's essence.
- Just as a symbolic representation of Lack is often useful (as discussed in the preceding chapter), this same symbolic rendering can represent Yearning, given the symbiotic, cause-and-effect relationship between the two.

BRINGING YEARNING DOWN TO STORY SIZE

- Recognize that the actions in your story represent only a part of a life, and the longings that motivate the character reflect only a portion of a much more complex Yearning, which resists simplistic definition or compartmentalization into distinct and tidy categories, no matter how useful that compartmentalization may prove as you narrow your focus to write.
- Identify the "Yearning Horizons" that define the climax of your story—i.e., the partial fulfillment of the character's Yearning that he strives for and manages to accomplish—or not.

NO MAN IS AN ISLAND: THE ROLE OF OTHERS IN THE CHARACTER'S YEARNING

- Do not neglect the inclusion of others—lovers, friends, family, community—in conceiving the character's Yearning. The person such a character hopes to be is intrinsically one worthy and capable of love, trust, companionship. And the way of life she dreams of living cannot be imagined without others included within it. Not even loners, outsiders, and outcasts truly yearn for a life of utter isolation.

4

Why the Character's Yearning Remains Unfulfilled—Resistance

<del>←————————————————————————→</del>

To conquer fear is the beginning of wisdom, in the pursuit of truth as in the endeavor after a worthy manner of life.
—Bertrand Russell, *Unpopular Essays*

Nor did it escape him that the conclusion he'd come to about her—that it was simply *being* Nicki that came between her and what she wanted—was the same conclusion Paula had reached about him last night.
—Richard Russo, "Interventions"

In the preceding chapter, we explored the various ways characters come to define themselves by how they identify and pursue their dream of life. Now we will address the forces always at work to limit, stifle, even kill that dream, i.e., the forces of Resistance.

Whereas Lack and Yearning share a symbiotic, quasi-cause-and-effect relationship, Yearning and Resistance are in perpetual conflict, the one conjured by the promise of life, the other the pain of life. That conflict, especially to the extent Resistance inhibits the character's pursuit of his Yearning, creates or intensifies the feeling of Lack the individual suffers due to his unfulfilled ambitions and longings.

Those ambitions and longings remain blocked by a countering impulse of self-protection, a kind of psychological and emotional armor, a defense against the ridicule, pain, and doubt that accompany failure, which have combined to make the individual's dream of life feel foolish, impossible, terrifying, futile, or otherwise out of the question.

In other words, these three forces—Lack, Yearning, Resistance—are all interconnected, though the exact nature and mechanics of those connections differ.

As already noted in chapter one, Resistance can take several forms:

- *Weaknesses*: laziness, cowardice, lack of confidence, cynicism, despair, etc.;
- *Wounds*: some loss or injury that has crippled the individual's ability to love, heal, or act decisively;
- *Limitations*: youth, old age, inexperience, lack of intelligence, poor health, poverty;
- *Opposition/Obligation*: a countering external force, normally embodied in another person—dream-killing father, overprotective mother, undermining teachers, slacker friends, a snobbish society, an oppressive culture; or it may take the form of a demanding obligation, like the need to be a responsible parent or a caretaker for someone in need;
- *Flaws*: selfishness, deceitfulness, indifference, cruelty, greed, manipulation.

These elements are not independent; on the contrary, they often act in concert, influencing and amplifying each other, as we will see in several examples below.

As you develop your characters, it's also important to resist the impulse to inflict every form of Resistance upon them, heaping on the psychological miscues, moral burdens, and emotional baggage out of some misguided instinct for completeness. Some characters will lack a Weakness or a Wound or a Flaw; what does or doesn't apply will emerge as you creatively imagine each character's backstory.

That said, let's explore each of these elements individually in greater detail.

I. WEAKNESSES

The ancient moralists saw virtue not merely as an inclination but as a habit that needed to be nurtured and developed throughout one's life, practiced like a skill such as musicianship or artistry, because the vices—Weaknesses—that tended to hold us back were so insidious, tempting, and inherent to our nature.

This leads us to several immediate observations:

- Weaknesses are either innate to the individual's personality or somehow become ingrained in the course of his experience and psychological, emotional, or moral development.
- They are dispositions, i.e., inclinations toward certain behaviors rather than overt actions in and of themselves. However, if allowed to develop into habits of mind, they tend to inhibit the character's willfulness, conviction, inner strength, or belief in himself.
- They are difficult to overcome, and require either lifelong vigilance or a shock to the system to do so.

An inventory of some of the more common human shortcomings we commonly refer to as Weaknesses brings the point home. Begin with the Seven Capital Vices: pride, greed, envy, rage, gluttony, lust, and sloth, and add the following:

Cowardice
Denial
Insecurity
Cynicism
Despair
Apathy
Indulgence (drink, sex, drugs)
Irritability
Impulsiveness

One might add as well a craving for constant stimulation, excitement, risk taking, or danger. In essence, *any addictive behavior is evidence of a Weakness*. And those who work with individuals suffering from addiction identify a profound sense of personal shame as a key element of the addictive personality. In terms of characterization, this means that merely identifying a character as an addict often seems at best a half-measure without also identifying the episodes in his backstory that created that crippling sense of shame. (We will discuss how to conduct that exploration in chapter five.)

Take a moment to reflect on your own life. Think of occasions when you hoped to achieve something truly significant but fell short because one or more of the foregoing qualities contributed to your inability to reach your goal, or alienated others whose assistance you needed or could have used.

Making this sort of moral inventory of one's own Weaknesses can be an unpleasantly sobering but ultimately beneficial exercise, for in identifying these shortcomings a commensurate virtue always presents itself.

Vice/Weakness	Virtue/Strength
Cowardice	Courage
Denial	Acceptance
Insecurity	Self-assurance
Cynicism	Purposefulness
Contempt	Compassion
Despair	Hopefulness
Apathy	Engagement
Indulgence (drink, sex, drugs)	Moderation
Irritability	Goodwill
Impulsiveness	Restraint

What virtually all of the strengths or virtues point to is an element of mindfulness and discipline, qualities that do indeed reflect a mature self-awareness rather than youthful impetuosity. However, even a causal look at human affairs, let alone one's own life, reveals that vice is hardly restricted to the young.

The need to minimize the pain of life is perfectly understandable. The problem arises when one uses the excuse of pain avoidance to exempt oneself from pursuing a meaningful life. As Camus remarked, "There is always a philosophy for a lack of courage."

As with ourselves, so with our characters. The following examples demonstrate the point:

In Lou Berney's *November Road*, Charlotte Roy has lost her self-confidence in the wake of her father's early, inexplicable death and her mother's retreat into fearful isolation. Where Charlotte was once a confident swimmer, she now feels "life's currents were more treacherous than she'd thought." She heads off for the University of Oklahoma in Norman at age seventeen only to become so overwhelmed and lonely after just six weeks that she packs up and returns to her safe, friendly, dull life in tiny Woodrow.

In Henrik Ibsen's *A Doll's House*, Nora Helmer submits to her husband's infantilizing patronization for the sake of the security he provides to her and her children. Only when his nakedly narcissistic self-interest is exposed does she see how she has allowed herself to be deceived and demeaned.

It's not just destructive inclinations that can create a Weakness; seemingly benign, even virtuous ones can have a similar impact.

I worked as a private investigator in the second trial of Larry Layton, one of the Peoples Temple gunmen at the airstrip where representative Leo Ryan and four others with him were killed. I know firsthand the accounts of many Temple members, survivors who joined with a sense of overly optimistic idealism, only to see it end more tragically than any of them imagined possible. History sadly offers many such examples of social, religious, and political movements inspired by exactly such idealism that devolved into bloodshed, genocide, and terror. That need for a pure, innocent utopia—rather than the difficult work of building a just society—is one of humanity's greatest collective Weaknesses, and as yet its appeal for a certain kind of individual has shown few if any signs of diminishment.

EXERCISES

As with previous exercises, select two main characters from your WIP and ask:[1]

---

[1] We will return to the issue of exploring the character's backstory with greater specificity in the next chapter. Though your answers here may turn out to be only preliminary, give them your best effort regardless.

- Which of the Seven Cardinal Sins or other Weaknesses identified in this chapter, if any, do they possess? Are they innate to the characters' natures, or did they come by these Weaknesses in the course of their experience? If the latter, identify what specific experience(s) led to the development of the Weakness.
- Which virtues do these Weaknesses point to? How or why do your characters lack in these virtues, or possess them to an insufficient degree? When if ever did the characters first become aware of this lack? What has held them back from developing these virtues?
- How is the Weakness you've identified for each character holding them back from pursuit of their Yearning, i.e., their dream of life?
  - Specifically, how is your character's Weakness undermining his sense of optimism, self-confidence, or self-worth?
  - Alternatively, if your character's Weakness is a form of naivete or idealism, what confrontation with harsh reality creates a shock to the system that "shatters her illusions"? Is that confrontation in the past, or does it occur in the timeframe of your story?

II. WOUNDS

> I know what it means to lose the one you've counted with your future.
> I know how it feels to have the future stripped from you.
> —John Larison, *Whiskey When We're Dry*

Anyone who has lost a loved one unexpectedly or prematurely to death; suffered a devastating betrayal or heartbreak; or experienced some other severe, life-altering setback knows the emotional tailspin, the despondency, the sense of pointless emptiness that can ensue.

Death especially forces us to ask the basic questions of existence: Why am I here? What am I supposed to do? What will it matter if death can snatch it all away so arbitrarily and so utterly? Not only do the questions arise, but all too often the answers feel wanting, if they appear at all.

Lost love can have an equally devastating impact, prompting many of the same questions, due to the seemingly worth affirming, even redemptive nature of romantic or filial love. A serious breakup, whether with a lover or a friend, terminates more than a connection with someone. It can feel like a judgment: *I don't deserve to be that happy.* And the question we often ask ourselves becomes: *What is wrong with me?*

Even more embittering is betrayal. Few things have a greater capacity to shatter one's faith in others. Learning to trust again in the aftermath of being set up for a fall, lied to, or played for a fool often seems impossible, depending on the level of intimacy one shared with the person responsible.

Such confrontations with the abyss can stop a person cold in her pursuit of a meaningful life, let alone a dream of life. Wounds represent a fracture in the fabric of existence as it has been understood up until the devastating experience. The shocking reality of annihilation, loss, and deprivation; the inevitable sense of disorientation and meaninglessness that tragic loss creates; and the seeming hollowness of all entreaties to resume faith in life's worth, all contribute to a complete rethinking of what it means to live, to dream, to hope, to care.

In Paulette Jiles's *News of the World*, six-year-old Johanna Leonberger is the sole survivor of a Kiowa raid on her family's ranch. The Kiowa spare Johanna and raise her as one of their own, to the point she forgets the English language and considers the tribe her family. When she is ten years old, however, the U.S. cavalry informs the Kiowa they must return Johanna to her surviving relatives, an uncle and aunt the girl does not know. The tribe obliges; they cannot afford to antagonize the armed soldiers who have turned the tide of the war against the Indians. For the second time in her young life, Johanna is ripped away from the world and people she knows. As she travels south with Captain Kidd, the man charged with her transport, she longs to escape and return to the tribe; the prospect of being unloaded on relations she has never met holds no appeal whatsoever. She comes to understand, however, that return is impossible. Her life seems empty of meaning, and all she can do is surrender to an indifferent fate.

Some Wounds, especially profound ones, heal slowly if at all. When a sense of personal responsibility or guilt is present, it can also be nearly impossible to obtain (or in some cases accept) forgiveness.

In Kate Atkinson's novels featuring Jackson Brodie, the ex-soldier-cum-private investigator lives in the shadow of an unshakeable sense of guilt created by the murder of his sister and the subsequent suicide of his older brother, who felt responsible for the sister's death because he was supposed to pick her up at the bus stop the night she was killed. Even though Jackson is not responsible for either death, he remains haunted by both, and feels a particular inclination to help women in jeopardy. He also tends to fall into unfulfilling romantic relationships, the intimation being he suffers from an ongoing need to punish himself.

Ian McEwan's *Atonement* is premised on the need to find some way to make up for a devastating error that one of the main characters, Briony Tallis, committed when she was a young and impressionable girl. That error led to the arrest and imprisonment of Robbie Turner for an attempted rape he did not commit, an imprisonment that ultimately led to his enlistment in the army and his death at Dunkirk. Also destroyed was Briony's sister, Cecilia, who was in love with Robbie. Ceci deserts the family, becomes a nurse in London, and is killed during the Blitz. Briony is never able to atone for what she did, except through the novel she writes late in her career, in which she tries, however feebly, to give Robbie and her sister one small moment of the happiness she stole from them.

We cannot leave this topic without returning to a subject we addressed briefly in chapter two in the section "Lack Created by Trauma or Tragic Loss": Post-traumatic Stress Disorder (PTSD) and Moral Injury. Their effects on Yearning are discussed sufficiently in the earlier chapter, so I will not revisit them here, except to point out a particularly powerful and innovative fictional representation.

In the 1993 film *Fearless*, based on the novel of the same name by Rafael Yglesias, who also wrote the script for director Peter Weir, the story concerns two survivors of a horrific plane crash, each of whom deals with the tragedy in a distinct way. Max Klein, a prominent architect whose pre-crash personality was typified by cautious anxiety, immerses himself in what is known as "pink cloud syndrome," where he ecstatically embraces each moment of life in a way he never did before—it is an unconscious, short-term strategy of denial doomed to fail.

In contrast, Carla Rodrigo, whose two-year-old baby died in the crash, cannot forgive herself and finds no solace in her faith or her family. A trauma counselor working for the airline, unable to reach either of these survivors, decides to introduce them in the hope they might somehow heal each other. Although Carla's reaction to her terrible loss—where her dream of life is shattered—is by far the more familiar approach one sees in fiction as well as in life, the great power of the story is the recognition that Max's exuberant denial is also a reaction to the loss of his dream of life, especially its most central feature: safety.

EXERCISES

- With the understanding, again, that we will return in the next chapter to the issue of exploring the character's backstory to discover Wounds and other forces of Resistance, choose two main characters from your WIP and make at least a preliminary effort to identify one or more episodes in the character's past that reveal:

  - The death of a cherished loved one.
  - A devastating breakup.
  - An embittering betrayal.
  - The crushing loss of a key career opportunity.
  - Some other severe, life-altering setback.

- Describe the aftereffects of those Wounds on the characters. Specifically, explore how the Wounds inhibit each character's belief in her dream of life or sap her willfulness in its pursuit.
- How does each character answer these questions in the aftermath of their wounding?

  - Why am I here?
  - What am I supposed to do?
  - Why will it matter?
  - What's wrong with me?

- How do they respond when others try to tell them to "pick themselves up and dust themselves off" or "smile while their hearts are breaking" or offer some other conventional truism in response to what they are experiencing?

III. LIMITATIONS

Unlike Weaknesses, which bear a taint of moral fault, Limitations are constraints beyond the individual's direct control that nonetheless inhibit her capacity to pursue the life she wishes to live.

Limitations can create both internal and external barriers to the pursuit of an individual's Yearning. We are referring here to the former instance, i.e., those cases when the individual herself allows her condition to hold her back. When the restrictions are imposed by others, not the individual herself, this is a form of External Opposition, which we will cover in the next section. It is often the case that both forces, internal and external, combine to impose whatever impediments the individual faces.

Examples of Limitations include the following:

- Youth/Inexperience
- Advanced Age
- Poor Health/Injury
- Physical Abnormality
- Mental Illness
- Homeliness
- Lack of Intelligence

Let's discuss each of these in a bit more depth.

YOUTH/INEXPERIENCE

How many of us spend our early years pining for that moment when we are no longer "too young"—too young to do this or that; too young even to try such a thing; too young to know about such matters; too young to understand what is necessary; too young to understand the consequences, let alone endure them. Our bodies are not strong enough, our minds are not developed enough, our experience of the world remains insufficient, etc. And yet the fact we resent and defy such decrees testifies to the strength of our Yearning, our dream of life, our longing for something better.

In Katherine Anne Porter's *Old Mortality*, the sisters Maria and Miranda Gay suffer at the start from not one but two Limitations: youth and being female in the American South at the turn of the twentieth century. The girls' family members, being particularly sensitive to scandal given the escapades of a spirited renegade aunt, ensure that the girls' youth and femininity remain strictly confining, to the point that the girls live in a state of constant, bemused observation, unable to do much of anything except be seen and not heard. Only one of the sisters, Miranda, ultimately breaks free of this stifling atmosphere, and not until the age of eighteen, when she learns the truth about her family. The renegade aunt did not die romantically or tragically from some cruel disease, but from an overdose, which was her way of escaping the family's pernicious greed and vanity.

It wasn't just turn-of-the-century mores that proved so confining in the South—jump ahead a half century and we discover in the "tired old town" of Maycomb, Alabama, a certain Jean Louise "Scout" Finch in *To Kill a Mockingbird*. Scout feels constrained not so much by her gender—her status as tomboy goes largely if reluctantly unchallenged—but by her age, especially as it affects her ability to do much beyond observe the goings-on around her (in between scrapes with boys who irritate her).

When youth is presented as a main character's Limitation, it is almost always in some way overcome in the course of the story—that is, for all intents and purposes, the point. The unchanged youngster makes a poor protagonist, unless one's intent is comic or satiric. Consider, for example, Miranda Gay's sister, Maria, who never appears to question the family conceit but instead simply vanishes into the suffocating circle. Child characters that remain stifled throughout the story in the pursuit of their Yearning because of youth or inexperience are best consigned to secondary roles, as examples of what can happen when the opportunity of experience is forsaken.

ADVANCED AGE

Just because one grows up doesn't mean Limitations related to age disappear. They return with a vengeance once the enfeebling effects of the years take their toll, both physically and mentally. Where the young feel the promise of life always beyond reach in some indefinite future, the aged see it fading into the mists of memory, with only the certainty of death lying ahead.

When advanced age forms the chief Limitation for a major character, creating the primary barrier to achieving one last chance at the dream of life, the story almost always provides an opportunity that affords the character that chance, even if that opportunity turns out to be illusory, Pyrrhic, or short-lived.

In the short story "Here on a Visit" by Edward Cannon, twice adapted for film under the title *Going in Style*, three retirees—Joe, Al, and Willie—face the demeaning reality of old age in America, which largely amounts to pinching pennies, loneliness, and boredom. If only to break the stifling monotony, Joe proposes they rob a bank. The men feel they have nothing to lose; they're prisoners, behind bars or not. The heist does indeed upend their world, even though "forever" has a much shorter time span than usual.

POOR HEALTH/INJURY

The issue of sickness in fiction has a long pedigree, especially from the nineteenth century forward. In her seminal examination of the subject, *Illness as Metaphor*, Susan Sontag demonstrated how physical health has often been used to portray certain characterological inclinations. For example, those suffering from tuberculosis were thought to have delicate sensibilities and thus be acutely sensitive to art, literature, and poetry; cancer patients, on the other hand, were thought to be introverted, fatalistic, taciturn loners.

The use of illness in fiction goes far beyond tuberculosis and cancer, of course, but that isn't really the point. We aren't concerned with the use of illness merely to add an element of poignancy or special urgency.

Here our focus is on those instances when illness or serious injury has forced the character to redefine the kind of person she wants to be and the way of life she hopes to live. Such characters can be protagonists, opponents, or secondary characters, but the key point is that their dream of life has suffered a serious detour due to their poor health.

In stories that use illness or injury in this way, what the character initially hoped for in life has been seriously sidetracked by some critical degradation in their health. We typically meet them at a stage in their life where their disease is already part of the fabric of their personality, presenting not only a physical but a psychological Limitation on what they believe is possible. The story will often involve how an incident or change in circumstances presents them with a challenge or an opportunity to transcend the limiting effects their disease or injury has had on them up until then.

An iconic example is Laura Wingfield in Tennessee Williams's *The Glass Menagerie*. The childhood polio that afflicted her has not only crippled her physically, giving her the distinctive limp that renders her unattractive to "gentlemen callers," it has also made her a virtual shut-in, haunted by fearful anxiety concerning the outside world. Only the imagined personalities of the glass figurines she has collected enliven her reclusive existence. Her only hope of developing a new, tangible dream of life outside the small apartment she shares with her overbearing mother and desperate-to-leave brother, Tom, lies in rescue, which is what makes the appearance of Tom's friend Jim so compelling. This is Laura's chance to return to the world. What will happen?

It isn't just main characters who suffer from health issues, of course. Literature abounds with secondary characters whose illness or injury significantly impacts both the story and the other characters, from Beth March in *Little Women* to Ralph Touchette in *Portrait of a Lady* and beyond. In each instance, the character's illness does more than impair their own pursuit of their Yearning; it reacquaints the main character with the importance of pursuing her own.

PHYSICAL ABNORMALITY

A pronounced physical defect can also sidetrack the character in his pursuit of the promise of life.

Tyrion Lannister in the Game of Thrones series is the dwarf son of a warrior king, and he lives in the shadow of his more fearsome, conspicuously masculine kinsmen. When we first meet him, he has come to accept his role as royal disappointment and contents himself with whoring and Herculean wine consumption. But as events unfold, and he withstands a variety of misadventures, betrayals, and attempts on his life, he earns the right to regard himself in far more dignified terms. And he no longer takes to heart the demeaning opinion others form at a glance.

MENTAL ILLNESS

Another extreme variant of physical illness or injury is mental illness, though it presents something of a special case. Characters so disabled by psychological or emotional impairment as to be unable to formulate a clear or realistic dream of life lie beyond our intentions here.

Here our concern is those instances when mental illness serves as a Limitation, i.e., a force of Resistance inhibiting the character's pursuit of her Yearning. In such cases, there needs to be some prospect of mental health toward which the character can realistically aspire.

Such a character is Carrie Mathison on the Showtime TV series *Homeland*. A CIA case officer with remarkable skill, unique talent, and a fearless, indomitable disposition, Carrie also suffers from bipolar personality disorder. In her manic episodes, she often sees connections that others do not. However, as her mania progresses those connections not only multiply but edge into delusion. The pressure and intensity of the work as well as the anxiety it creates sometimes exacerbates her illness, to the profound concern of her sister and father. Absent medication, she is at risk of full-blown psychosis requiring electroconvulsive therapy. The tightwire act she is forced to execute between performing the job she was "born to do" and trying to manage the danger it presents given her condition, creates a continuous thread of tension through every episode.

HOMELINESS

It might seem like small beer to bring up mere unattractiveness after discussing cripples, dwarves, and the insane, but stories abound with those who have had to refashion their dream of life around the fact they are never anyone's first choice to dance. Equally plentiful are accounts of how such wallflowers adjust—either by refusing to take no for an answer, recognizing what it is that actually makes them attractive, or finding some other avenue to hope and happiness.

Jane Eyre comments often on her plainness, and doubts she could ever be attractive enough to win the affection of the man she loves, Mr. Rochester. Her hopes fall even further when Rochester brings home to his Thornfield manor the striking Blanche Ingram. Shockingly, Rochester proposes not to Blanche but to Jane, whose inner beauty wins the day—for a while, at least.

In Alfred Hitchcock's *Vertigo*, when Midge realizes Scottie no longer fancies her, she tries a number of strategies to lure him back. First, she becomes his confidante, hoping that warmth may eventually lead to heat. When Scottie's obsession with the mysterious—and beautiful—Madeleine intensifies, Midge paints a portrait of herself similar to one Madeleine visits every day, which only alienates Scottie further. Finally, when Scottie suffers a nervous breakdown due to his guilt over Madeleine's death, Midge makes one last effort, assuming a maternal role, but that too fails. Her dream of marrying Scottie and sharing his life will remain unfulfilled.

When homeliness is a character's Limitation, they still have resources at their disposal—inner virtue, pluck, creativity—but the truth typically remains that at least sometime in their life they simply weren't attractive enough, or believed they weren't, and that awareness held them back from pursuing or obtaining something they truly wanted.

LACK OF INTELLIGENCE

Sometimes it's not that the individual isn't attractive enough to dream big, but rather he's just not smart enough.

The crime genre is literally overflowing with characters whose ambitions far outpace their wits—it might even be said that their lack of intelligence accounts for their choice of profession, shaping their understanding of where their talents lie and what they deserve from life.

It isn't just men who fall into that trap.

In Jess Walter's *Citizen Vince*, Beth is a prostitute trying to earn her real estate license. Vince suspects that the broker sponsoring the effort is just winding her up for free sex, but Beth has begun to obsess on the prospect, and realizes both that she wants it more than she's wanted anything before and is terrified she's not smart enough to pull it off. The dream is right there for the taking if only …

EXERCISES

- Review the various characters you have already planned to include in your WIP. Do any of them possess one or more of the Limitations identified above, or some other Limitation not identified? How does that Limitation specifically inhibit her pursuit of her Yearning? To the greatest extent possible, try to envision your answer in a scene that exemplifies the general state of her frustrated dreams for a better life.
- If none of your characters possess a Limitation, select two in particular—they can be main characters or secondary characters—and consider providing them with one. Evaluate how this affects their portrayal. How does this alter their behavior? How does it affect the behavior of those around them? How does it change the general trajectory of the story?

IV. OPPOSITION/OBLIGATION

Whereas the effects of Weaknesses, Wounds, and Limitations upon the character's Yearning result from their *internal* influence on her ability to pursue her life's ambition, here we turn to *outside* factors that serve to constrain her dreams.

As noted in the opening to this chapter, this countering external force is normally embodied in another person, and the examples provided included dream-killing father, slacker friends, an oppressive culture, and so on, as well as the need to be a responsible parent or a caretaker. For the writer, this offers a somewhat obvious advantage—it lends itself directly to dramatic portrayal in scenes involving other characters.

Although these factors are external, they often become internalized as well, and can turn into a Weakness such as despondency or lack of confidence, once again revealing how the various forces of Resistance often interact and influence each other.

Here are some of the most common Obligations or sources of Opposition:

- Parental Influence
- Teachers, Clergy, and Other Authority Figures
- Peer Pressure
- Care for Another
- Class/Social Standing
- Minority Status

Let's discuss each of these briefly in turn.

PARENTAL INFLUENCE

Parental influence can constrain or distort an individual's Yearning through negative effects such as cruelty, cynicism, and overly harsh criticism, or through positive ones such as coddling, overprotectiveness, or an excessive willingness to forgive, especially where the latter distort the individual's ability to endure the natural setbacks of any honest, active life.

Returning to Charlotte Roy in Lou Berney's *November Road*, whom we discussed above with respect to Weaknesses—in the wake of Charlotte's father's death, her distant and timid mother, though still loving, has become overprotective while at the same time cocooning herself in an isolating anxiety so profound it infects Charlotte's own sense of confidence and willingness to take risks or stand out in any way.

Of course, it's not just a desire to preserve a parent's affection or the need for their protection and support that can have such an effect. Fear of scorn, anger, even abandonment all too often play a role as well.

Perhaps the most poignant example is also one of the most famous: Colin Craven in *The Secret Garden*. After the loss of his wife shortly after she gave birth to Colin, Mr. Craven cannot bear to look at his son. In the wake of that stifling rejection, amplified by the malevolent influence of Mrs. Medlock, the head of the manor's servants, Colin has become a lonesome, bedridden boy. He believes he suffers from a rare spinal disease that prevents him from walking and that he will eventually become a hunchback. Only through the intercession of the story's young heroine, Mary Lennox, and the influence of his dead mother's garden, which Mary has brought back to life, does Colin come to realize that his condition is all in his mind.

TEACHERS, CLERGY, AND OTHER AUTHORITY FIGURES

It's not just parents who can sidetrack the young people in their care. Any influential adult potentially has that power.

Teachers in particular can have a profound effect, due to the day in, day out nature of their contact and their role as providers of necessary information.

In Muriel Spark's *The Prime of Miss Jean Brodie*, the titular character selects six of her ten-year-old students at an Edinburgh girls' school to be members of a special group she calls "the Brodie set." She proceeds to inculcate them with her intensely held convictions, including her fascination with fascism, constantly impressing upon them the significance of her having selected them as her coterie. Although each of the girls to some extent succumbs to Miss Brodie's thrall, only Sandy, her presumed favorite, actually surrenders her own sense of direction and promise to the older woman's influence, though in an odd and fascinating way. She has an affair with the married man who is secretly in love with Miss Brodie, largely to better understand the mind that harbors that love, then adopts the man's Catholicism, becomes a nun, and fingers her former mentor as a fascist sympathizer at the outset of World War II.

As with certain teachers, so too with certain members of the clergy. In Emer Martin's *The Cruelty Men*, the priests and nuns who oversee the Catholic Church's industrial schools make sure to denigrate and shame and brutalize the boys and girls in their care on a daily, even hourly basis. Their treatment is so relentless that many of the children come to see themselves as worthless human beings.

PEER PRESSURE

It is not just elders who can exert external pressure on an individual's pursuit of her dream. Friends, siblings, and "the gang" can as well.

In the TV series *Breaking Bad*, Jesse Pinkman tries to move beyond the self-destructive behavior and influences that have led him to the brink of suicide, particularly in the aftermath of the overdose death of his girlfriend, Jane. His user and dealer cohorts, however, including longtime pals Badger and Skinny Pete, have different ideas, and insist he not only continue to party hearty but stay in the game so they themselves can enjoy the "fat stacks" of the drug business.

CARE FOR ANOTHER

How many dreams have been forestalled by parents honoring their duties to their children, or by children returning the favor later in life by accepting the care of an aging parent?

In Rick Riordan's mythology-adventure novel *The Red Pyramid*, Julius Kane, a master of ancient magic, conceals his powers while assuming the more staid façade of Egyptologist, doing so to protect his children from malevolent forces his magic might conjure. Explaining his decision to suppress his powers to his daughter, Sadie, he tells her that one of his most difficult duties as a father was to realize that his own dreams, goals, and wishes were secondary to his children's.

In the same way parents self-sacrifice, so too do children. In the film *Rachel, Rachel,* based on the novel *A Jest of God* by Margaret Laurence, Rachel Cameron is the middle-aged sister left behind to look after her aging, clueless, acidly sweet, impossible-to-please mother. She remarks to her best friend, "I'm in the exact middle of my life," by which she means that whatever dream of life she once possessed has been surrendered, and if she does not act soon to rekindle it, the rest of her days will amount to little more than one long lonely slide into death.

CLASS/SOCIAL STANDING

The entire Naturalist school in American literature arose in response to what its adherents considered a sentimental, prudish, middle-class bias in the Realism of writers such as Henry James and William Dean Howells, where the individual captained his own life without any great interference beyond his own nature. Influenced by the work of such post-Enlightenment thinkers as Marx, Darwin, and Freud, the writers Frank Norris, Stephen Crane, Eudora Welty, Theodore Dreiser, and Richard Wright, among others, felt committed to portraying men and women of the lower classes to demonstrate how their lives were determined by overwhelming economic, social, biological, and psychological forces. Despite the modern trappings of their thought, their vision aligned with the ancient understanding of man struggling for dignity and selfhood against the forces of fate.

Poverty, sex, race, and class in particular animated many of these writers' works, along with their various consequential effects: poor health, wretched living conditions, substandard education, minimal social connections, and the desperation such circumstances foster. We will take up race and sex in the next section on Minority Status, and confine our discussion here to poverty, class, and social standing.

What concerns us here is the question of how such factors as poverty and class and social standing have undermined the individual's faith in his own dream of life. The literary record is rife with examples, from *Moll Flanders* to *Les Misérables* to *Hard Times* to *Germinal* to *Maggie: A Girl of the Streets* to *McTeague* to *Ethan Frome* to *Sister Carrie* to *The*

Grapes of Wrath, and beyond. In each of these stories the grinding, degrading hardship of poverty and utterly bleak prospect of an entire life spent scraping for money shapes what kind of person the characters believe themselves to be, and the way of life they might realistically hope for, often resulting in a leap for whatever brass ring avails itself, with the predictably tragic results.

And as social standing so often finds its basis in one's financial circumstances, the two influences often intertwine. One of the greatest novels to explore this interweaving of money and status is Edith Wharton's *The House of Mirth*.

Its protagonist, Lily Bart, comes from a well-positioned New York family, and she has the reasonable ambitions of a young woman of her station, especially one as beautiful as she is—to continue socializing with her wealthy and well-connected peers, to marry well, and to age in relative comfort. Her father's fall from financial grace, however, has put her in a very unfavorable position money-wise, living on the sparse allowance meted out by her parsimonious Aunt Julia. Making matters worse, she has a bit of a gambling problem, though this is her only real vice; her problems are far more dictated by her belief in love, which motivates her refusal to marry simply for money, and her daring rebellion against the restrictive, sanctimonious conventions of her social peers. Lily struggles to live up to what she believes is a meaningful, fulfilling life, only to discover time and time again that the combination of her meager finances and the resulting fall from social grace that entails, exacerbated by the vindictive attacks by those who take pleasure seeing her "put in her place," all conspire to snuff out her dreams.

MINORITY STATUS

The plight of those with minority status in a culture where the majority actively resists their desire to be recognized as equals bears a certain resemblance to the misfortunes of the poverty-stricken underclass, with the exception that one can earn money and conceivably raise one's station. One cannot become a race or sex that one is not, and the often-tragic struggles of those who try to "pass" only underscores the issue.[2]

What we are concerned with here are those persons confined within a minority—whether premised on sex, race, immigrant status, or some other arbitrary trait—that makes them a target of social pressures that render pursuit of their dream of life difficult or even impossible.

The underlying factor in such prejudice is the presumption that the majority can dictate not just a minority's way of life but their very identity. This reveals itself in a number of behaviors—demands to dress or talk in a certain fashion, failure to recognize cultural traditions outside of the majority's, an insistence on speaking the majority's language—and is epitomized in the phrase so often uttered when members of a minority group dare to resist such attempts at coercion: "Who do they think they are?"

Perhaps the most obvious novel to exemplify the issue of race, especially as a social force that distorts and deforms the individual's sense of who he is and how he might live, lies squarely within the Naturalist tradition: Richard Wright's *Native Son*. Bigger Thomas lives in poverty and is dependent on his white employer to provide for his family. He hates whites for enjoying the kind of life he would like to have, and he hates himself for feeling that way. At the novel's end, after he has had the chance to talk with his defense attorney concerning the reasons he committed his various crimes, he gains a deeper understanding of the future he wanted and the man he hoped to be. He comes to recognize the intractable forces that prevented him from realizing those dreams, as well as the rage that his condition engendered.

As for the issue of women needing to adjust their ambitions to accord with society's conception of who they are and how they should live, look no further than Jane Austen's repeated portrayal of women dependent on marriage as the sole salvation from a life of penury. We saw the

---

2 A female-to-male transgender individual can, of course, hypothetically eliminate her minority status as a woman by submitting to the procedures necessary to transform her into a man, but this does not change the problem of her minority status as a transgender person in a majority culture that by and large does not wish to confront the profound questions regarding sexual identity raised by her existence.

theme addressed as well in our discussion of Wharton's *House of Mirth*, written almost over a century after *Pride and Prejudice* and *Emma*.

In the twentieth century, as women have entered professions previously dominated by men, the pushback has been particularly aggressive. The character of DCI Jane Tennison in the BBC *Prime Suspect* series, written by Lynda La Plante, provides an exemplary fictional representation. Tennison has struggled for years within the macho culture of Greater London's Metropolitan Police Force. At every step of the way, her progress has been impeded, undermined, or sabotaged by men threatened by her skill, intelligence, and determination. Over the course of the series, she rises to the rank of detective superintendent, allowing the audience to witness firsthand the incredible obstacles placed in her path at every step of the process, and the ferocity, focus, and sense of purpose required to overcome them—as well as the damage to her private life that struggle has caused.

EXERCISES

- As with the exercises in the preceding section regarding Limitations, review the various characters you have already planned to include in your WIP. Do any of them face any of the forces of Opposition identified above—or others not identified? Are any of them burdened with Obligations that dominate their lives? How do those Obligations or forces of Opposition inhibit their pursuit of their Yearning? Which other characters present that Opposition or Obligation? As before, try to envision your answers in scenes that dramatize the inhibiting influence of the other character acting in Opposition or creating the Obligation.
- If none of your characters face an external Opposition or Obligation, select two in particular—they can be main characters or secondary characters—and consider providing them with one. Evaluate how this affects their portrayal, once again asking specifically: How does this alter their behavior? How does it affect the behavior of others around them? How does it change the general trajectory of the story?

V. FLAWS

The last force of Resistance we will consider is unique in two very important ways.

First, whereas Weaknesses, Wounds, Limitations, and Opposition/Obligation serve principally to harm the character herself, Flaws are moral in nature and concern how the individual is not only harming herself but inflicting pain on others.

This can be seen in the specific types of Flaws we identified at the beginning of this chapter: selfishness, deceitfulness, indifference, cruelty, greed, manipulation. The harm done to the character herself largely results from the payback she receives for the damage she inflicts on others. In addition, she often suffers from the general distrust, aversion, or outright contempt of others who know of the damage she has caused, leaving her isolated and friendless.

Second, Flaws are particularly prone to be influenced or caused by other forces of Resistance. Although there are indeed individuals who possess an intrinsic inclination to harm or manipulate others—Cathy Ames in John Steinbeck's *East of Eden*, for example, described as having a "malformed soul," or those with a distinct personality disorder such as psychopathy, narcissism, or Machiavellianism—the great majority of harmful behavior can find its roots in the way the individual acts upon or responds to his Weaknesses, Wounds, Limitations, Obligations, or Opposition from others.

A few examples, several of which we've already discussed, should bring the point home:

- Miss Jean Brodie's arrogance—a Weakness—inspires not just her fascist sympathies but her willingness to manipulate her students and treat her lovers with cruel indifference.
- When the white whale severs Ahab's leg at the knee—a Wound—the captain's obsession with revenge soon becomes so extreme it blots out everything else, including any concern for the lives of his men.
- Blanche Dubois's experience of repeated deaths among her family members—a Wound—exacerbates her own anxiety over grow-

ing older and thus losing the one source of power over men she has possessed in her life, her sexual attractiveness. The anxiety feeds her alcoholism—a Weakness—as well as her predation on younger and younger men as sexual partners, leading to the liaison with one of her high school students that makes her a pariah in her small hometown.

- In *Midnight Cowboy*, tuberculosis and disfigurement—Limitations—combine in the harsh urban terrain of New York to create Ratso Rizzo's reliance on conning the gullible to survive.
- In *Native Son*, the daily degradations of racism—Opposition—fuel the blinding rage that leads Bigger Thomas to murder.

In each of these examples, the character's impetus to inflict harm is rooted in some other form of Resistance keeping them from fulfilling their dream of life. If you want to create a moral Flaw in a character, one approach is therefore to look to one of these other areas of Resistance and examine how the Weakness, Wound, Limitation, Obligation, or External Opposition might create such a state of rage, fear, bitterness, resentment, or hopelessness that the individual finds a way to justify abusing others.

Another way to create a Flaw in a character is to take a virtue and push it to an extreme:

- The character's love for someone or something is so profound and self-identifying that the thought of losing it elicits shattering terror and dread, so that any means taken to preserve or protect that love becomes justified.
- The character becomes so obsessed with justice or the truth that he steamrolls—or railroads—others in his pursuit of it. As with the foregoing example, the seemingly noble end justifies any means.
- She is so certain of her moral rectitude she's blind to her own bad acts.
- His loyalty obliges him to turn a blind eye to the immoral acts of others—worse, to join in their efforts or help conceal the wrongdoing.
- Her courage or ambition leads to recklessness or callousness.

- His lust for life leads to self-involved excess at the expense of others.

Daphne du Maurier's *Rebecca* offers a classic example of how this works. Mrs. Danvers remains so steadfast in her devotion to the late Mrs. de Winter—who was stunningly beautiful, bold, and glamorous—that she cannot contemplate accepting a replacement, especially the anxious, mousy nobody her master, Maxim de Winter, has brought home. Mrs. Danvers preys on the various insecurities of the new Mrs. De Winter to the point that the young bride loses all hope of ever measuring up and even, at the older woman's whispered urging, contemplates suicide.

The point, of course, isn't to populate your stories with characters intent on bad behavior. Rather, it's to recognize how the tendency to harm others is often rooted in other behaviors that seem to be harming only the individual herself. This underscores the way that a moral Flaw is often part of a larger *pattern* of interconnected tendencies that is holding the character back from fulfilling her Yearning.

One last approach to the interconnection of virtue and immorality deserves mention, and that is *The Fall* by Albert Camus. One of the greatest, subtlest, and most widely misunderstood novels ever written on the subject of consciousness and conscience, the story features narrator Jean-Baptiste Clamence, the self-professed "judge-penitent," who goes from a state of seeming generosity and altruism to realizing how much his supposed selflessness was really motivated by a vain desire for recognition. This leads to a moral crisis and gradual deterioration of his circumstances, in which he tries to ruin the stellar reputation he has created. Because others find the false persona he has manufactured more in tune with their preferences than his true nature, this effort fails. He deserts his previous life and embarks on a course of debauchery, since "no man is a hypocrite in his pleasures," but doing so only leads to a state of exhaustion. During the war, which he tries to escape by fleeing to Algeria, he gets elected "pope" of a North African concentration camp with the power to determine who receives food and water and who performs which work details. Ultimately he "closes the circle," completing his fall from virtuous hypocrite to honest monster by stealing water from a dying man.

For Camus, moral flaws did not arise from virtues pushed to extremes or the embittering effect of Weaknesses, Wounds, Limitations, and so on, but rather testified to the state of guilt intrinsic to the human condition. This immorality cannot be overcome. The best we can hope for is to face it honestly, accept judgment, and offer what penance we can.

EXERCISES

- Review your responses to the previous exercise questions concerning Weaknesses, Wounds, Limitations, and Opposition/Obligations. How might the forces of Resistance you've identified create a state of rage, fear, bitterness, resentment, or hopelessness that prompts the individual to lash out at others?
- Alternatively, select a character from your WIP and explore how a virtue the character possesses might be pushed to such an extreme that it actually serves to harm others.
- How does the character's flaw affect his ability to achieve his core objective in the story? Is correction of the flaw necessary to achieve that core objective? If not, why not? How will readers respond to your character if he remains immoral at the end of your story?

VI. THE INTERPLAY AMONG FACTORS— AND THE OVERRIDING ISSUE

As stated earlier, and repeated in the preceding section, forces of Resistance often act in conjunction with each other—influencing, enhancing, even creating one another. They are part of a pattern of behavior that the character has developed over time given the events in her past that have most indelibly influenced her need to protect herself from the pain of life.

In the next chapter we will examine how to explore the character's past to uncover these factors. For now, it is important to begin to look for these interconnections and understand how a character's behavior is not comprised of discreet influences but a web of interrelated ones.

Returning to an example we've used above, Charlotte Roy in Lou Berney's *November Road* first suffers a devastating loss when her otherwise young and healthy father dies unexpectedly from a heart attack (Wound). The shock sends her distant and timid mother into an emotional tailspin; she becomes overprotective, encouraging Charlotte to avoid taking risks or distinguishing herself in any way (External Opposition). That effort exacerbates Charlotte's own deteriorating self-assurance—once a confident swimmer, she now understands life has treacherous, unforeseeable crosscurrents. She feels so overwhelmed on the campus of the University of Oklahoma that she lasts a mere six weeks before retreating to the safety of her small-town home (Weakness).

The trauma of her father's death ripples out into other aspects of Charlotte's nature in life-altering ways, so much so that the pain of life eclipses the promise of life, and her protective impulses gain the upper hand. It will not be until she fears that her daughters may be succumbing to a diminished sense of their own fortunes that she wakens from this cocooning numbness and realizes she has to save them—and herself—by once again embracing the promise of life. She does this by grabbing her daughters and getting out, leaving behind the slowly suffocating existence—and alcoholic husband—she has blindly accepted up to that point.

In the next chapter, we will investigate in greater depth ways to explore the character's backstory in an effort to unearth these protective impulses and their causes. It remains crucial, however, to keep our focus on the balance between the two principle but opposing drives generating all behavior—the longing to fulfill the promise of life (Yearning) versus the need to protect oneself from the pain of life (Resistance). Every individual lives in a state of tension between these two countering impulses—and this tension is typically how the character experiences her Lack.

The action of the story, generated by the characters' internal, external, and interpersonal goals, will at every point be buffeted by these two underlying forces, which is why we have devoted so much time and attention to them at the outset. From this point forward, we will explore not only how these forces have emerged from the character's past but how they continue to influence the course of events through the story's narrative arc.

EXERCISES

- Go back through each of this chapter's sections and review your responses to the exercise questions. Choose two characters, hopefully major characters, on whom you've applied the lion's share of your attention. Itemize your responses where you have identified their:

  - Weaknesses
  - Wounds
  - Limitations
  - Opposition/Obligations
  - Flaws

- Look for ways the traits and behaviors you identified actually influence, enhance, or even create one another. Take a step back and look at that *pattern of behavior* as a unique element of character in and of itself. (This will be the first step in understanding what we will refer to in the next chapter as "pathological maneuvers.")

VII. GIVING THE RESISTANCE ITS OWN DAIMON

In the previous chapter on Yearning, we discussed the concept of a *daimon* guiding the character's understanding of his identity, his life's course, his destiny, his fate. This spirit guide typically takes the form of a core image, experience, or symbol that shadows the individual throughout his life. It often reveals itself most tangibly in its effects: motivation, resistance to compromise, persistence regardless of circumstances, even if this requires improvisation and adaptation. When resisted, it creates psychological and even physical symptoms: malaise, depression, despair, a propensity to illness.

Even if you're resistant to the idea of a spirit guide of *daimon*, we have already addressed how the use of a core symbol, image, or experience to represent the character's Lack and Yearning can be a useful technique. So too with Resistance.

In fact, the Greeks believed not only in a positive *daimon*, which they referred to as *agathodaímōn* ("noble spirit"), from *agathós* ("good, brave, noble, moral, lucky, useful"), but also a negative *kakodaímōn* ("malevolent spirit"), from *kakós* ("bad, evil").

Here we are not so much concerned with its evil aspects as its counterproductive ones—those aspects of its influence that enhance the forces of Resistance.

Just as the positive *daimon* will encourage the virtues that assist the individual in the pursuit of her Yearning, so too a negative *daimon* will enhance the effects of the character's Weakness, Wound, Limitation, Flaw, and so on.

In *The Art of Character*, I discuss the notion of a Ghost, which is either a character or a collection of experiences that represent the character's problems with his past. Those problems may very well be embodied in a single character, and it is often a character who provided the greatest force of Opposition: absent dad, fearful mother, vindictive teacher, etc. But the combined effect of all the forces of Resistance may take on a particular personality in the individual's mind—the backbiting critic, the mocking naysayer, the inescapable bully. By "putting a face" on the Resistance in this way, you can help both writer and reader envision the various forces that are holding the character back in one complex but unified conceptualization.

These are two particularly classic examples of where this is done well:

- Laura Wingfield's glass menagerie, which symbolizes her retreat into fragile fantasy rather than face the real world.
- Alcohol for Blanche Dubois, which she uses to numb her awareness of her advancing age and the loss of her sexual power; drink also enhances the blissful "mystery" conjured by her scarf-draped lamps.

EXERCISES

- Again, choose two of your main characters from your WIP. As in the last chapter where you attempted to find a symbolic representation of each character's Yearning, do so again but now with respect to the forces of Resistance holding her back. (Hint: Before beginning, look at all the forces of Resistance aiding the character in her protection of herself from the pain of life. Think of how they enhance and contribute to each other. Now try to imagine a single person, experience, or symbol that encapsulates most, if not all, of those various influences.)
- Go back to your symbolic rendering of each character's Yearning and compare it to this new symbolic rendering of the Resistance. Do they reflect each other in some way? If so, how? If not, could you perhaps come up with a different rendering that permitted a more symbiotic relationship between the two competing symbols? Could you perhaps find a single rendering that embodied them both?

SUMMARY OF MAIN POINTS IN THIS CHAPTER

INTRODUCTION

- Whereas as Lack and Yearning share a symbiotic, quasi-cause-and-effect relationship, Yearning and Resistance are in perpetual conflict, the one motivated by the promise of life, the other the pain of life.
- Resistance can take several forms.
  - *Weaknesses*: laziness, cowardice, lack of confidence, cynicism, despair, etc.;
  - *Wounds*: some loss or injury that has crippled the individual's ability to love, heal, or act decisively;
  - *Limitations*: youth, old age, inexperience, lack of intelligence, poor health, poverty;

- *Opposition/Obligation*: a countering external force, normally embodied in another person—dream-killing father, overprotective mother, undermining teachers, slacker friends, a snobbish society, an oppressive culture; or it may take the form of a demanding obligation, like the need to be a responsible parent or a caretaker for someone in need;
- *Flaws*: selfishness, deceitfulness, indifference, cruelty, greed, manipulation.

- These elements are not independent; on the contrary, they often act in concert, influencing and amplifying each other.

WEAKNESSES

- Three principle characteristics distinguish Weaknesses.

  - They are either innate to the individual's personality or somehow become ingrained in the course of his experience and psychological, emotional, or moral development.
  - They are dispositions, i.e., inclinations toward certain behaviors rather than overt actions in and of themselves.
  - They are difficult to overcome and require either lifelong vigilance or a shock to the system to do so.

- An inventory of the most common human Weaknesses begins with the seven cardinal sins—rage, greed, gluttony, lust, envy, sloth, pride—and proceeds to such shortcomings as cowardice, despair, cynicism, apathy, and selfishness.
- Any addictive behavior is evidence of a Weakness, but it also speaks to a profound sense of personal shame.
- For every Weakness one can name, there is usually a corresponding strength or virtue—courage for cowardice, compassion for contempt, generosity for selfishness, and so on.
- Although avoidance of the pain of life is not intrinsically destructive, it can be when it turns into a Weakness, i.e., a habit or disposition that makes it difficult or impossible for an individual to muster the willfulness or self-confidence to pursue the promise of life.

- More "positive" Weaknesses such as naivete and idealism can lead the character into shocking confrontations with harsh reality that also often shatter the individual's belief in herself or her life's ambitions.

WOUNDS

- The psychic and emotional Wounds that prove most dramatically valuable in fiction—i.e., those that inhibit the character's belief in her dream of life or that sap her willfulness in its pursuit—usually concern some severe, life-altering setback, resulting in an emotional tailspin, despondency, or a sense of emptiness or lack of meaning.
- Such Wounds include:
  - The loss of a cherished loved one unexpectedly or prematurely to death.
  - A devastating breakup.
  - A cruel betrayal.

LIMITATIONS

- Limitations are physical or psychological qualities beyond the individual's direct control that nonetheless inhibit his capacity to pursue the life he wishes to live. They are different from Weaknesses in that they typically bear no taint of personal fault.
- Examples of Limitations include:
  - Youth/Inexperience
  - Advanced age
  - Poor health/Injury
  - Physical abnormality
  - Mental illness
  - Homeliness
  - Lack of intelligence
- In each instance, the individual's condition serves as a barrier between what she might hope for in in her life and what she can actually achieve given the Limitation.

OPPOSITION/OBLIGATION

- Unlike Weaknesses, Wounds, and Limitations, which impede the character's Yearning through their *internal* influence, Opposition and Obligations are *external* factors that serve to constrain the character's dreams.
- The countering external force is normally embodied in another person or persons, which facilitates dramatic portrayal through scenes.
- Although these factors are external, they often become internalized as well and can turn into despondency or lack of confidence.
- Some of the most common Obligations or sources of Opposition include:

  - Parental influence
  - Teachers, clergy, and other authority figures
  - Peer pressure
  - Care for another
  - Class/social standing
  - Minority status

FLAWS

- Flaws are unique from other forms of Resistance in two very important ways.

  - The individual is harming not only herself but others.
  - Flaws are particularly prone to be influenced or caused by other forces of Resistance.

- One way of creating a Flaw in a character is therefore to look to one of these other areas of Resistance and examine how it might create a state of rage, fear, bitterness, resentment, or hopelessness that prompts the individual to lash out at others.
- Another way to create a Flaw in a character is to take a virtue and push it to an extreme.
- Stories that concern characters with moral failings are often premised on the need to address those failings. They typically lead

to a moment of discovery and decision where the character comes to realize the harm he is inflicting on others and is thus offered the chance to change that behavior.

THE INTERPLAY AMONG FACTORS

- The forces of Resistance typically do not act in isolation but rather often influence, enhance, or even create one another.
- They are part of a pattern of behavior that the character has developed over time given the events in her past that have most indelibly influenced her need to protect herself from the pain of life.
- Every individual exists in a state of tension between two countering impulses—the longing to fulfill the promise of life (Yearning) versus the need to protect oneself from the pain of life (Resistance).
- The action of the story, generated by the characters' internal, external, and interpersonal goals, will at every point be buffeted by these two underlying forces.

GIVING THE RESISTANCE ITS OWN *DAIMON*

- Even if you're resistant to the idea of a spirit guide or *daimon*, the use of a core symbol, image, or experience to convey the influence of Resistance on the character (just as with Yearning) can be a useful technique.
- Just as the positive *daimon* will encourage the virtues that assist the individual in the pursuit of her Yearning, so too a negative *daimon* will enhance the effects of the character's Weakness, Wound, Limitation, Flaw, and so on.
- The value of discovering or creating such an emblematic, symbolic, or individualized representation for the Resistance is that it helps both writer and reader envision the various forces that are holding the character back in one complex but unified conceptualization.
- The risk of this sort of effort lies in reducing the complexity of the character's problems with the past into an overly simplistic totem. This can diminish the character in the reader's or audience's mind.

5
Backstory as Behavior

←——————————————————————————→

> I lived a different life before I come here," Pa said. "That ain't no excuse but maybe someday you'll understand. The bad things that happened to a man can get between him and his now.
> —John Larison, *Whiskey When We're Dry*

> If you evade suffering you also evade the chance of joy. Pleasure you may get, or pleasures, but you will not be fulfilled. You will not know what it is to come home.
> —Ursula K. Le Guin, *The Dispossessed*

In the last chapter, we addressed a number of areas where characters encounter life-altering difficulties or experience personal restrictions that materially affect their capacity or willingness to pursue their dream of life.

In this chapter, we will cover how to explore the character's past—her backstory—to uncover the specific experiences that led to those problems or best exemplify them. We will also explore those key moments in the character's past that lent strength and encouragement to pursue her Yearning.

In this way, we will examine how the past has shaped the equilibrium the character has developed between pursuing the promise of life and protecting herself from the pain of life, and show how to reveal that equilibrium in *behavior* at the outset of your story. That equilibrium will lie somewhere along a spectrum from fulfilling to functional to precarious to self-destructive, but it will reveal itself most vividly in the forms of behavior we will come to recognize as Pathological Maneuvers and Persistent Virtues.

I. EXPLORING BACKSTORY FOR THE CHARACTER'S KEY SEMINAL MOMENTS

A FEW WORDS ON METHODOLOGY

I first learned this approach to exploring a character's past from the late Gill Dennis, a marvelous screenwriter who taught his "Finding the Story" workshop at the Squaw Valley Writers' Conference for many years.

Once, during an interview in the aftermath of his work on the Johnny Cash biopic, *Walk the Line*, Dennis explained how he went about questioning his subject for the script. He asked Cash what his moment of greatest sorrow was. Cash replied it was his brother's death when he was nine years old. Dennis then asked the singer what his moment of greatest shame was. Cash replied that it was when he hit his wife, June Carter, in front of their children. Dennis then asked for his moment of greatest joy, and that concerned an appearance at the Grand Ole Opry where the entire extended Cash-Carter clan performed together onstage.

Dennis explained that this approach not only suggested a story arc, from crippling sorrow to triumphant joy, but also revealed a theme connecting the various incidents together: the importance of family to Johnny Cash and the haunting effect of loneliness.

The reasoning behind these questions was that Dennis wanted to explore moments of helplessness, when emotion or action arose from within the individual but outside his conscious control, thereby revealing a deeper stratum of character.

Dennis believed such moments are the true signposts along an individual's life path. They not only reveal that deeper level of character; they also expose the superficial persona the individual assumes to get through his days, a persona that fails him in moments of sudden nakedness.

In our stories, we need to understand and depict both levels of character: the more-or-less functional, acceptable, even successful persona that has arisen through the daily struggles of life with its get-along-go-along demands, and the deeper level of subconscious emotion and response lurking beneath the surface like a submerged city.

To do this, we must first address the latter, the subsurface self. The reason for this is because much of the surface personality has been devised *in response to* the shock of what has happened at that deeper level. We will explore that deeper level by examining those moments of helplessness in the past that reveal the raw core of emotion and impulse that form the substrate of the character's personality.

This will require envisioning moments of overwhelming fear, guilt, shame, betrayal, loss, and sorrow—and also moments of courage, forgiveness, pride, trust, love, and joy. In this way we can see how the character's past has shaped the balance she has achieved between her Yearning and the forces of Resistance.

Once we've accomplished that, we can begin to imagine the various habits of behavior she has devised to create the persona or "fictitious self" she uses to minimize the pain of life and maximize the promise of life as best she can. We will cover how to explore the development of those habits in the final section of this chapter on Pathological Maneuvers and Persistent Virtues.

This tension between social self and private self, revealed versus hidden, helps create the sense of contradiction that makes a character seem vibrant, compelling, and real.

It also provides a natural narrative arc, for as the character struggles to pursue her Desire within the story—the goal around which all her actions are focused—her missteps and blunders and catastrophes will inevitably expose the maladaptive aspects of her persona that impede her success. She will realize that some of the behavior she has relied upon to protect herself also prevents or inhibits her from taking the risks necessary to achieve what she truly wants.

This is the learning curve at the heart of so many stories—the turn toward a deeper understanding of oneself created by the pursuit of something meaningful. It is in this sense that every external struggle naturally includes an internal journey.

Backstory Exploration: Moments of Helplessness

In the exercises for the previous chapter, you were asked to identify Weaknesses, Wounds, Limitations, external sources of Opposition or Obligation, as well as moral Flaws that have served as forces of Resistance, impeding your characters' pursuit of their Yearning. Here, to the extent you have not done so already, we will seek out the actual experiences in the character's past that forged that Resistance.

Following up on the methodology described above, here are ten areas of helplessness to explore with your main characters, as well as those secondary characters whose roles—and thus their motivations—are crucial to the story.

<u>Pain</u> (Resistance)	<u>Promise</u> (Yearning)
Fear/Cowardice	Courage
Guilt/Sin	Penance/Forgiveness
Shame/Failure	Pride/Success
Betrayal	Trust
Death/Loss/Sorrow	Love/Connection/Joy

Before proceeding further, a few brief points deserve emphasis:

- **BY *HELPLESSNESS* WE MEAN A REACTION BEYOND COMPLETE CONSCIOUS CONTROL**

  Though we often associate helplessness with a sense of physical or emotional peril, even moments of joy, pride, trust, and so on arouse a certain helplessness, in that the actions performed in such moments often occur spontaneously, with conscious control or even awareness coming mid-act or even after-the-fact, and the emotions that arise are largely unbidden and often overwhelming.

- **THE PAIRING OF EMOTIONS REFLECTS THE CONFLICT BETWEEN RESISTANCE AND YEARNING**

  As the heading indicates, the left-hand column refers to incidents that reflect the pain of life, or the forces of Resistance. In exploring these moments of fear, guilt, shame, betrayal, and loss, we will plumb the character's backstory for those episodes in her past

that solidified her response to the pain of life. This work will identify the character's Weaknesses, Wounds, and so on, but with much
greater specificity and thus emotional power.

In contrast, the right-hand column relates to the promise of life,
i.e., Yearning. By exploring these scenes of courage, forgiveness,
pride, trust, and joy, we will lay the groundwork for what the character realistically believes her dream of life could be. At the same
time, we will gain a greater understanding of the sources for the willfulness she will need to pursue it—i.e., where did she gain the pride,
courage, faith in others, and belief in happiness that fuel her drive?

To the extent you have had any difficulty conceiving, articulating, or specifying a character's Yearning or Resistance, this work
should make these elements far clearer, more distinct and unique,
and capable of more powerful depiction.

- **THIS LIST IS NEITHER COMPREHENSIVE NOR DEFINITIVE**

The ten areas of helplessness listed above are not sacrosanct or
written in stone. You do not need to envision individual scenes that
speak to every single one of them to create a compelling portrayal,
nor are these the only areas that can merit exploring.

For example, you may find the character's moment of greatest
rage or greatest sexual passion or worst/best date or any number
of other options just as valuable, if not more so, than any of the ten
listed above. I provide the list principally for purposes of suggestion, with the understanding that these moments of helplessness
are the ones I use in writing my own fiction.

You may find that exploring only a few such moments conjures
a sense of the character's backstory with sufficient vividness that
you feel confident you're ready to begin writing your story. On the
other hand, you may imagine scenes that do not speak to any of
the areas mentioned but nonetheless crucially shape the character's
understanding of himself and what he believes he can reasonably
expect from his life. Consider the ten categories listed as prompts,
not dictates.

You will also most likely find that one moment serves several purposes—one can easily imagine, for example, a scene of cowardice that leads to the death of a loved one, conjuring a profound sense not just of loss but shame and guilt as well—or that various moments reinforce or even enhance the impact of others, just as we learned in the previous chapter how the various forces of Resistance often interact.

The point is to seek out whatever moments of helplessness in your character's past spur insightful exploration of what created, awakened, or contributed to her Yearning on the one hand, and on the other led her to develop or succumb to her Weaknesses, Wounds, Limitations, Opposition/Obligations, or Flaws.

- **WE ARE SEEKING OUT A FEW SPECIFIC, POWERFUL MOMENTS— NOT GENERAL TRAITS**

Whereas in the previous chapter we sought to identify Weaknesses, Wounds, Limitations, and so on, here our focus becomes both more specific and more detailed. It is not general traits we are trying to identify but the moments that gave rise to them. If you already identified them in your response to the exercises in the previous chapter, here you will seek to flesh them out even further.

The focus on moments has both a psychological and dramatic purpose.

First, dramatic episodes that changed the character's life conjure a greater emotional reaction than generalized traits. They will prove far more valuable in terms of both affecting you, the writer, and providing material that will emotionally affect the reader.

Second, from a strictly practical viewpoint, moments can be visualized as scenes, and scenes are by nature more dramatic than narrative exposition. As a general rule, try to resist the temptation to think in terms of information and instead develop the habit of visualizing scenes, i.e., the dramatic rendering of moments.

The way to search for such moments is often to ask, as Gill Dennis did with Johnny Cash, what was the character's moment of greatest fear, or sorrow, or pride, or joy, and so on. It's not important to identify the exact, indisputable moment of *greatest* emotion. Rather, the point is to seek out a moment that seriously impacted the character's sense of who he is and what he might reasonably hope for in his life.

It is also important to identify *one* such moment—certainly no more than two or three—for each category, rather than a larger number. I once had a student resist the whole "single greatest incident" concept and instead argue that her character's difficulties were better described as "death by a thousand cuts." While this is often true of our characters and ourselves, it's problematic for two distinct reasons:

- *From a psychological viewpoint:* We cannot visualize or emotionally respond in a meaningful way to a thousand (or any large number) of anything. It's inherently vague due to its generality and, therefore, can be grasped at best intellectually rather than emotionally. The minute we hear the phrase "a thousand cuts," our mind's eye either produces a fuzzy image or conjures one or two especially painful examples that stand in for all the rest. In practical terms, our minds instinctively seek out the "greatest" or most emblematic moment or moments.
- *From a writing standpoint:* Similarly, writing each of those "thousand cuts" is not only impossible, it would be unwise even if it could be managed. Rather, we would have to pick at best a handful of scenes that epitomize the continuing onslaught of misfortune.

In other words, from the perspective of both practicality and evoking the most emotion possible, both for the author and for the reader, choosing one, two, or at most three scenes in any category is optimal. And I would argue that one truly, deeply affecting scene is more than enough at the outset; if the story demands more, you will likely discover them as you write.

As you imagine these moments, give yourself time to envision them in some detail, down to the colors, the smells, the time of day, the quality of the light. You do not need to render them in perfect prose—this would in fact be a waste of time—

but imagining them vividly may help you connect them through specific details to other moments you will explore with the character, facilitating the creation of a thematic thread.

- **TRY NOT TO ENVISION THE CHARACTER IN ISOLATION—AND "MAKE IT WORSE"**

Finally, as another general rule, the more you can include other individuals in the scenes you imagine, the better. This makes it more difficult for the character to deny or minimize what happened, especially when those other individuals are affected by what occurs.

Also, the rule that dictates that whatever happens, "the worse the better," applies here as well. Trying to protect your characters from severely difficult, painful, even tragic circumstances is all too often not evidence of a desire to avoid melodrama but a retreat from truly powerful emotion—and the need to deliver it capably on the page—on the part of the writer.

With all that as introduction, let's look at each of these pairings of negative and positive moments in turn.

FEAR VS. COURAGE

Nothing underlies all the forces of Resistance as powerfully as fear: fear of failure, fear of rejection, fear of mockery, fear of abandonment or being unloved, fear of betrayal, fear of injury, fear of violence, fear of death.

Thinking in such general terms, however, produces at best lackluster results. Only by focusing on a particular scene of overwhelming fear can we see how the character *behaved*—did he freeze in terror, run away, hide, make up a lie to save himself, instinctively act to save someone else, plunge ahead mindlessly right into the teeth of the danger?

The importance of visualizing that reaction is in recognizing that it is the beginning of habit formation; from that point forward, the character will likely revert to the same or similar behavior when confronted by incidents that once again elicit great fear. And since no pursuit of anything meaningful can help but arouse uncertainty and fear, this means that the character will have to recognize that behavior or reaction pattern and overcome it in order to succeed.

Where will they find what is necessary to overcome that habit pattern if it reveals an underlying cowardice? This is where discovering one or more moments of courage also proves crucial. Although dyed-in-the-wool cowards certainly exist, most people have both succumbed to their fears and, at some point or another, managed to demonstrate at least some degree of spine.

Again, visualizing the exact scene where that happens will reveal a treasure trove of information about the character: How great was the fear that was overcome? How significant was the sense of confidence that resulted? How long did that sense of confidence last?

Courage covers a spectrum of behaviors. At one end we find the spontaneous, almost unintentional leap across the chasm of fear to save ourselves or someone else from danger. The farmworker Zeke in *The Wizard of Oz*, the human counterpart to the Cowardly Lion, provides a fictional example. When Dorothy falls into the pig pen, Zeke, despite his conspicuous fear, leaps to the rescue—and afterwards sits in a cold sweat, as though waking from a bad dream.

At the opposite end of the spectrum lies the behavior found in those who face danger on a routine basis—soldiers, police officers, rescue workers, etc. The combat reporter Marie Colvin once remarked, "Bravery is not being afraid to be afraid." This is courage as it is commonly understood by those who exhibit it often. It is not the absence of fear but the management of it.

This can be a trap for a writer, however—even individuals who've grown accustomed to "not being afraid of being afraid" can point to a moment when their "habit of courage" failed them, and they stared naked terror in the face, if only for an instant. When creating such a character, *find that moment.*

GUILT VS. FORGIVENESS

By guilt I mean the feeling an individual experiences when he has violated a moral norm he himself accepts—i.e., he's done something wrong, and he knows it.

Guilt most frequently snaps into vivid relief when the wrongful act harms another person, whether through deceit, theft, psychological predation, or physical violence. It is much more difficult to sweep something under the rug when there is a flesh-and-blood victim standing there as testimony to the damage.

When exploring guilt, therefore, it's best to search out a particularly significant scene in your character's past when she did inflict harm on another person and cannot deny that fact. Picture that moment with as much specificity as you can, focusing especially on the harm done, the character's intentions for doing whatever inflicted the harm—was it deliberate or not?—and how the character behaved in that instant when it became clear something very bad had happened.

Conversely, don't neglect to search out a moment of forgiveness in the character's past. In particular, were they ever forgiven for the guilt-inducing scene just imagined? Careful: If you mitigate the guilt with forgiveness, you have to create some other emotional aftereffect or you've basically erased the import of one moment with the other.

For example, even if the character is forgiven, he may continue to have doubts about himself, his judgment, his intentions, and he may wonder if there isn't some moral or psychological defect for which he always need to be on the lookout.

In my most recent novel, *The Long-Lost Love Letters of Doc Holliday*, my main character, Lisa Balamaro, suffers a near-fatal car crash when driving home drunk from a party. Fortunately, she missed hitting an airporter van, but the awareness that she came close—and could have seriously hurt or even killed someone—haunts her long after her own wounds heal. She quits drinking but understands what every former drinker knows: Alcohol is a symptom of the problem, not its cause.

Even if your character's great sin remains unforgiven, which is typically the more poignant or dramatic option, she no doubt understands what forgiveness might mean for her, and almost certainly longs for it. If she has no hope of forgiveness, she may seek out some other form of redemption that might exonerate her. Crime fiction in particular is littered with guilty souls seeking one last chance to prove they're not the worthless, despicable miscreants everyone thinks they are, including themselves.

Alternatively, choose a moment when the character forgave some-one else. The feeling experienced when one finally lets go of his resent-ment, fear, anger, and mistrust based on a past wrong is transformative and can very much deepen the character's understanding of what he considers the promise of life.

SHAME VS. PRIDE

By shame I mean the emotion that arises when an individual does something that lowers her status in the eyes of one or more others whose respect she cherishes. Since many such actions also involve wrongdo-ing, guilt and shame are often inextricably connected.

This may sound odd, but from a writing perspective few emotions are as valuable as shame. This is because it is social—it involves not only the individual but others, linking his sense of self-worth to the regard the others have of him. This interweaves internal with interpersonal, a benefit for characterization that we will pursue in greater depth in chapter seven.

Interestingly, shame's counterpart, pride, need not involve others at all. Though it is often the case that some of our proudest moments are shared, and the resulting sense of pride is heightened accordingly, it's also true that an individual can feel a great deal of pride in something she's done without anyone else knowing about it—or without caring what others think of it. Though this can also be true of shame, a pri-vate sense of mortification implicitly suggests a dread of what might happen if others find out.

Shame can range from mere embarrassment to utter disgrace, though how intensely shame is felt is entirely an individual matter. The shy feel shame far more profoundly than the bold, and in envision-ing your character's moment of life-changing shame you should con-sider his natural disposition—how instinctively susceptible is he to the opinion of others? Someone used to taking risks openly will shrug off something a much-less public person cannot, though even a confident person can register crippling humiliation if their faux pas occurs at a significant moment—or in front of a significant someone.

As for the character's moment of greatest pride, I sometimes phrase this as, "What was the character's Golden Moment?" When did she feel best about herself and something she did? Ask who else knows about it. As with guilt that has never been forgiven, pride that has remained private has a particular poignancy.

BETRAYAL VS. TRUST

It is likely your character will need the assistance or guidance of others in solving the problem she faces at the heart of your story. Her ability to do so will depend greatly on past experiences of putting her faith in others—and what happened when she did.

As our discussion of Wounds in the preceding chapter indicated, betrayal, with its acutely intense feelings of personal violation, is one of the most shattering experiences an individual can endure. Dante famously reserved the innermost circle of Hell for betrayers.

To conjure betrayal effectively, you also have to understand and reveal how the one who is betrayed came to place his trust in the other person—specifically, how actively did the betrayer nurture a false sense of reliability? That will determine the degree to which both your character's faith in others and her confidence in her own judgment is undermined or even destroyed by the other's treachery. This eviscerating sense of self-judgment is one of the reasons betrayal is so frequently linked to depression.

Although close associates and intimate partners provide the greatest opportunity for devastating betrayal, don't overlook the damage strangers can inflict. Flannery O'Connor's "Good Country People" provides a superb example in the figure of the nineteen-year-old Bible salesman, Manley Pointer, who manages to seduce Hulga Hopewell into surrendering her wooden leg, which she cared for "as someone else would his soul."

On the flip side, when has your character's faith in someone been rewarded by faithfulness? Exploration of a moment when the character realizes someone else has kept a confidence or remained loyal at some cost usually identifies at least one of the character's truest allies.

This naturally prompts several questions: Is that faithful individual still in your character's life? If not, why not? If so, what role might he play in your story?

Discovering that someone has remained true may also turn out to be one of the character's moments of greatest joy, for few things in life prove more rewarding than knowing someone has stood by you or told the truth on your behalf, especially if that loyalty came at considerable personal cost.

DEATH OR SORROW VS. LOVE OR JOY

In the previous chapter, we identified betrayal as one of the three major sources of Wounds along with death and lost love. Here our interest turns to that moment when the full impact of the loss truly registered, when the individual realized that, whatever the cause, the loved one is not coming back, ever.

Focus on the shock of that, the sense of emptiness, the aching sorrow and loneliness. Own the moment in all its disheartening specificity the better to understand how, even if that impact has diminished, it continues to echo into the present.

How has it affected the character's sense of safety or connection? How has it undermined the sense of meaning or purpose the character once believed life possessed? In what way has it dampened the character's willingness to love again?

If the moment you imagine for the character does not possess this kind of crippling impact, ask yourself why. Are you being true to the character's life, or are you the author trying to resist entering such painful emotional territory?

At the risk of repetition, when it comes to imagining the injuries your character has suffered, the general rule holds true that "worse is better." If that is not the case with your character—and it perfectly well may not be—then something else better exist to make them fascinating.

As with all the other dichotomies we've explored, the opposite quality, joy or love, also deserves thoughtful attention. Even lives of misery typically possess at least one moment when hope flickered on the edges of possibility. Envision that clearly, specifically—the rush of love, the breathless sense of flight in a moment of utter joy.

It may well be that you have already explored the moment they came crashing back to earth when you imagined their greatest loss or sorrow—if so, revisit that scene with this one in mind so that you can better register the extreme swing in emotion.

Contrarily, as you imagine your character's scene of greatest love or joy, try to imagine the moments leading up to it. Were they characterized by a fear that something distinctly other than love or joy was likely? If so, picture that vividly, make note of it. It's an inescapable truth that the impact of one emotion intensifies when preceded by the likelihood of its opposite.

EXERCISES

- If you have not already done so, select two of the main characters from you WIP and sketch out the singular, life-altering moment each of them experienced in the following categories:

Pain (Resistance)	**Promise** (Yearning)
Fear/Cowardice	Courage
Guilt/Sin	Penance/Forgiveness
Shame/Failure	Pride/Success
Betrayal	Trust
Death/Loss/Sorrow	Love/Connection/Joy

- Return to the answers you came up with for the previous two chapters on identifying the characters' Yearning and Resistance. Identify the most important scenes in each character's past and determine how it either helped shape that character's sense of the promise of life (her Yearning), or gave rise to a force of Resistance in an attempt to protect her from the pain of life. Specifically, examine how the exploration of key moments of helplessness deepens, clarifies, or in some other way enhances your understanding of what motivates and inhibits the character's pursuit of her dream of life.

II. FINDING THE CONNECTIVE TISSUE OR THEME AMONG BACKSTORY MOMENTS

One of the most curious and mysterious aspects of the methodology that Gill Dennis devised for exploring character was his conviction that these critical moments in an individual's past shared a certain thematic quality that pointed to the core problem the person was trying to solve in his life. This can sound a bit like psychobabble—or at least wishful thinking—and yet the number of times it has borne out has made a believer of me.

One shouldn't be all that surprised by this. It echoes Freud's theory of repetition compulsion, whereby individuals continue placing themselves in certain circumstances that cause them to revisit past incidents of pain or trauma; they do this in order to better understand their psychic wounds and overcome their negative effects in an unconscious effort to heal.

From a dramatic perspective, this also points us toward the character's main problem, and thus the core of the story he has to tell.

The risk of this approach is a retreat into reductionist simplicity, i.e., condensing a character's existential crisis into a pat phrase or concept. Just as in chapter three, where we noted that the character's Yearning is ineffable and shouldn't be reduced to a trite phrase—to be free, to find love, to come home—we risk cheapening the character when we slap a tidy tag line on his life.

This aspect of characterization is more art than science, more reliant on intuition than some step-by-step method. It requires us to look at the various moments we've created and try to see how they add up to up more than a random jumble of episodes in the character's past. We need to discern how they form part of the character's unconscious journey toward fulfilling the promise of life while avoiding as much of the pain of life as possible.

As that formulation suggests, a good place to start in trying to identify the thematic core of your character is to revisit the character's Yearning and the forces of Resistance holding her back. That conflict, like a battle between two halves of her soul, will likely direct you to an imagistic understanding of the core problem of her life, the problem that you have now fleshed out in detail through individual scenes of helplessness.

If you can see this pattern upon finishing the work on key backstory moments, fine. But don't despair if you don't. You may find that a great deal of writing needs to be completed, building from this backstory foundation you've built, before that resonant theme reveals itself. You may also realize that in exploring the character's backstory, looking for moments of both positive and negative helplessness, you have missed something: a moment that helps bind the others together in a more unified, coherent pattern.

Summing up, this effort to find a unifying theme will pay several dividends:

- It will help clarify the character's Yearning and the forces of Resistance holding her back, seen as part of a lifelong struggle and a coherent whole.
- It will help you recognize the equilibrium the character has struck between pursuit of her dream of life and protection from the pain of life, which will typify her behavior at the story's outset.
- It will help lend *authenticity* to the character's quest for identity, which is a crucial aspect of her Yearning—i.e., the character's dream of life will be seen more clearly, personally, and honestly, not just in terms of what is longed for but what is realistic given the individual's unique nature and past.
- It will help you devise a symbolic representation of the Lack/Yearning, or a concrete behavior that best typifies the struggle between them.
- It will identify the character's core internal problem that she will need to address in the course of the narrative. The solution or mitigation of that problem will form her Yearning Horizon within the story. (For more on this, see chapter eight).

It is sometimes said that writers have no idea what they intended to say until well after they've said it. This paradox is very much evident in the search for the thematic thread in your character's backstory. It is probably wisest to let your unconscious guide you, at least at first. That is no guarantee against clichéd conception, but neither is trying to decide the matter before you've allowed yourself to descend into your subconscious and wander at will. Besides, when it comes to human themes, there are only so many to choose from, and what may seem clichéd at first blush—or when worded too bluntly—may reveal itself to be far more subtle given your execution on the page.

EXERCISES

- Revisit the moments of helplessness you have imagined for your characters in the previous exercises in this chapter. Can you discern a connecting thematic thread among them?
- For ideas of what to look for, revisit the character's Yearning and the forces of Resistance holding him back. Imagine that conflict as two aspects of his soul struggling for dominance, created by the scenes you have examined in the earlier exercises in this chapter. Don't worry about giving this thematic thread a name—an imagistic or symbolic impression is perfectly fine, even preferable.

III. MOVING FROM MOMENTS TO HABITUAL BEHAVIOR—PATHOLOGICAL MANEUVERS AND PERSISTENT VIRTUES

At this juncture, I'm going to suggest you take a moment to reflect on how you deal with stress or conflict.

- Do you drink or eat a bit too much when fearing judgment, ridicule, rejection—or boredom?
- Do you jabber away when you meet someone you're attracted to— or withdraw into nervous silence?
- Does loneliness prompt spending or social media binges?
- Do you lash out when you feel criticized or threatened?

The psychologist Anna Freud referred to such patterns of behavior with the technical terms *adaptations* or *defense mechanisms*.

The novelist Elizabeth George (in her exceptional fiction guide *Write Away*) refers to this type of behavior as the *Pathological Maneuver*. Personally, I love that term, not just because it's more colorful. It reveals the fundamentally maladaptive nature of the behavior in question—the person is *not dealing* with the underlying emotion prompted by their experience of stress, conflict, judgment, and so on. And the episodes of helplessness we explored earlier in this chapter, especially those linked to forces of Resistance—Weaknesses, Wounds, Limitations, etc.—are precisely moments characterized by stress, conflict, and judgment.

It is now time to put that logic to work in our characterization. We accomplish that by weaving together the moments of helplessness we have just explored with the forces of Resistance they have created—Weaknesses, Wounds, and Flaws especially—and examining the resulting habits of behavior that have consequently developed.

Forces of Resistance are not merely psychological traits, revealed solely in thoughts and feelings. They demonstrate themselves dramatically in *behavior*.

And since we now know those forces of Resistance have their genesis in moments of helplessness, we can begin to build the character's behavior from generative moment to demonstrable trait to habitual behavior:

- Because the character's moment of greatest loss involved not just a devastating breakup with the man she thought was the love of her life, but also a moment of greatest betrayal when he married her best friend, she has developed such a profound fear of rejection and sense of resentment (a Weakness), colored by a stifling sense of shame, that she no longer tries to date men she is actually attracted to. Instead she devotes herself to "projects" who most likely will never leave her. If the romance ends, it will be her decision that breaks things off.
- Because the character's moment of greatest shame was losing a position she had been told she was going to get (a Wound)—only to watch as the whole office learned it was going to a woman she herself had hired and trained—she no longer pursues what she truly wants but instead settles for what is easily achieved or simply pro-

vided, while resentfully retreating into a carping sense of victim-hood, fueled in secret by drink.

- Because the character's moment of greatest sorrow was the ago-nizing death of his mother from cancer when he was seventeen (a Wound), combined with his father's subsequent descent into al-coholism, he never allows himself to get too deeply involved with anyone. Any meaningful human connection awakens the pain of loss, a pervasive sense of guilt over being unable to help his father, and fears concerning his own mortality.
- Because the character was raised poor (a Limitation), she suffered not just deprivation but frequent incidents of mockery and sham-ing. As a result, she has become obsessed with success, works her-self to the bone, secretly takes delight in bettering her competition, feels suspicious of anyone making demands on her time (including friends and family), and basically lives in secret terror that without that constant, unrelenting focus she may slip back into poverty—and humiliation.
- Because of being bullied and even abused as a child (a Wound), he now lashes out with irrational rage at anyone who triggers his fears of being victimized—not just his enemies and competitors but also his loved ones (a Flaw).

Not all Pathological Maneuvers follow such a neat, linear, causal path. Consider the following:

- Return to the character whose mother died of cancer when he was a teenager and whose father subsequently turned to alcohol to numb the pain. The son has refrained from any deep emotional commit-ments, resulting in a loneliness so severe he, too, has developed a drinking problem, which he cynically explains away as "like father like son" (a Weakness). During one of his drinking binges, the el-derly neighbor suffers a heart attack and cries out to him for help, but he's too wasted to respond (a Flaw).
- The character's most terrifying moment came when he watched his drunken father beat his mother nearly to death (Wound). Unfortu-

nately, he learns the wrong lesson from this experience and grows into a man with a hair-trigger temper, living by the credo "The angriest person wins."

- The character's moments of greatest pride revolved around being the class clown, typically cracking jokes at the expense of others (Flaw). Unfortunately, she too learned the wrong lesson from this and now deals with uncomfortable feelings (her own and others'), through deflection, making jokes instead of actually facing the anxiety, nervousness, or discomfort in the moment.

As these examples indicate, the moments of helplessness and the forces of Resistance they created also developed into a *pattern of behavior* that often is characterized by one or more of the following:

- Avoidance, denial, settling for less.
- Acting out, self-injury, irresponsible risk taking, casual sex, substance abuse or some other form of overindulgence.
- Unconsciously modeling one's maladaptive behavior on someone else's (because that person seems to get what she wants).
- Some form of abusive behavior toward others, exemplified by a selfish regard for one's own wants over any concern for others, or a disregard for the pain one causes.

These habits and patterns of thought and behavior were developed in moments of loss, anxiety, terror, stress, etc. and continue to hold the character back, limit her confidence, her sense of hope, or otherwise force her to focus more on avoiding pain than embracing hope and promise. In other words, they have created a way of behaving that is ruining her life.

That is not melodramatic exaggeration. Remember, the character's Yearning defines the kind of life he truly wants to live, the kind of person he wants to be. The Resistance creates internal barriers that stand between where the character is now and the fulfillment of that Yearning. And as we said earlier, Yearning, if unfulfilled, creates a kind of living death.

The Pathological Maneuver is the collection of behavioral traits that reveals the false sense of safety, control, empowerment, or concealment that allows the character to ward off the depression, self-hatred, or anxiety he feels when he recognizes that he is not the person he truly wants to be, living the life he truly wants to live.

Just as there are self-damaging habits of behavior, there are also beneficial ones: Persistent Virtues. Following the same methodology we used above, we will start with the moments of courage, forgiveness, pride, trust, and love or joy we explored, and examine the resulting habits of behavior that have consequently developed.

- Because the character's moment of greatest bravery involved rescuing a driver from a burning car after an accident, he has confidence that he will not panic or freeze if called upon in the future to act decisively in the face of danger. (But he also realizes that one of the reasons he acted so boldly was because the driver was a very attractive young woman, and this admission undermines his absolute certainty in his courage.)
- The character's most significant encounter with forgiveness involved her stealing money from her grandfather when she was twelve years old, after which the old man first made her admit what she'd done and return the money, then made her sit with him silently on the porch for several hours, during which time the full impact of his forgiveness and love gradually sank in. Because of that experience, she understands not just her own Weakness—a reckless fascination with transgressing boundaries—but what it means to be loved regardless, which has given her a quiet self-confidence and mindfulness that has helped her resist, if not exactly overcome, similar temptations.
- The character's moment of greatest pride—a good deed no one else knows about—came when he was a lonely, stuttering ten-year-old boy whose parents argued constantly. He was as always walking alone to school when he spotted on the sidewalk an envelope with several hundred dollars in it, together with a deposit slip. He went to the address listed on the slip, and when no one answered the bell he simply nudged the envelope through the mail slot and once again

headed off to school. When he was reprimanded for tardiness by first the principal then his parents, he said nothing in his own defense, savoring the secret sense of vindication he experienced. This devotion to undisclosed acts of virtue has remained with him into adulthood, not just for the sake of doing good. Whenever he is badgered by bosses, loved ones, even strangers, he recalls that moment of silent victory and takes heart from the fact that absolutely no one knows the real truth about him.

I have deliberately made my examples of Persistent Virtues a bit more complex, as it has been my experience that moments of pure joy, pride, courage, etc. are rare, and they seldom filter forward in time without serious transfiguration. Life is simply that way—as most athletes will tell you, losses always register more profoundly than wins, and our moments of triumph quickly acquire a weather-worn sheen.

The foregoing analysis reveals a methodology for moving from a moment of painful helplessness to a force of Resistance to a Pathological Maneuver on the one hand, and from a moment of self-affirming helplessness to a Persistent Virtue on the other.

For Pathological Maneuvers:

- Start with the painful moment of helplessness. Recognize how it has struck a blow against the character's belief in himself or his dream of life.
- Allow that initial blow to develop into a force of Resistance—inflicting a psychic Wound, reinforcing a Weakness or a Limitation, enhancing the debilitating effect of an Obligation or some source of external Opposition, or encouraging the development of a Flaw where others are harmed as well.
- Forge from the foregoing a habit of behavior—including attitude, interpretation of events, response to difficulty, perspective on the world—by asking which of these tendencies has the character developed:

  - Avoidance, denial, settling for less.

The Compass of Character

- Acting out, irresponsible risk taking, substance abuse or some other form of overindulgence.
- Unconsciously modeling one's maladaptive behavior on someone else's (because that person seems to get what he wants).
- Some form of abusive, self-serving behavior toward others.

For Persistent Virtues:

- Start with the moment of courage, forgiveness, pride, trust, love, or joy.
- Recognize how, even if only in a small way, that moment has bolstered the character's self-confidence and belief in the promise of life—i.e., reflect on how it speaks to the character's Yearning.
- Reflect on how the natural hardships of life have worn away some but not all of the luster of that shining moment. In particular, how much of the initial sense of self-worth, hopefulness, connection to others, and happiness has the character retained?
- Again, how does that reveal itself in habits of behavior—attitude, interpretation of events, response to difficulty, perspective on the world? Imagine specific activities—volunteering, charitable giving, routine acts of kindness or self-sacrifice—that have become second nature.
- Specifically, analyze how the past continues to influence the character's capacity for commitment, perseverance, self-confidence, and faith in others.

Going through these steps will allow you to envision opening scenes for your story where the character, by exhibiting the Pathological Maneuver or the Persistent Virtue—or both—implicitly indicates her troubled or confidence-boosting past without belaboring it through detailed explication of backstory.

This manner of revealing backstory through behavior allows you to show rather than tell how the past has shaped the person the character is as your story begins. The unique, problematic, puzzling, or just plain odd nature of that behavior will create empathy, intrigue, or both, forcing the reader to wonder what in the past has produced the curious thoughts and actions exhibited by the character.

IMPORTANT: Although this methodology may seem daunting and labor-intensive at first, it soon becomes second nature as you use it more and more. Your facility with the concepts and your understanding of how the various moments of helplessness affect and amplify one another; how they give rise to Wounds, Weaknesses, Flaws, etc., which also influence each other; and how they all combine to form habits of behavior will gradually grow more natural, insightful, and compelling.

Depending on the demands of your story, revelations concerning the actual moments of helplessness underlying her behavior can be woven in at appropriate places in the narrative—usually when the character is reflecting on a certain unforeseen or unfortunate turn of events. This is the most natural place for the character to wonder what it is about her personality, her circumstances, or her past that has led her to this place, and what changes she may have to make to turn the matter more to her advantage.

However—and this is an important point—*it is by no means necessary to reveal to the reader or audience the underlying events or factors that led to your character's behavior.*

The premise of this chapter is to give you, the writer, a means of creating the revelatory behavior your character will exhibit when he first appears in your story. Sometimes not answering the question of what caused that behavior lends intrigue or poignancy to the character's portrayal, and explicit explanation would only undermine that.

It is up to you to determine how much explanation is necessary. Unless confusion is created by its omission, it's generally best to keep backstory explication to a minimum. Increasingly, the film industry in particular and the world of fiction as well agree that less is more when it comes to backstory.

Bottom line: Pathological Maneuvers reveal how our misfortunes and personal limitations have embedded themselves in our day-to-day behavior, shaping our attitude, our perspective, our responses, and our actions. In much the same way, however, Persistent Virtues also reveal themselves in our attitude, perspective, our choices, and the risks we take. They demonstrate our resilience in the face of all those misfortunes, our ability to claim not just a sense of pride and joy and self-worth but also a confidence that the promise of life is worth pursuing.

Example: *Bloodline*

For an example of how this methodology works in practice, let's consider the Netflix TV series *Bloodline*, created by Todd A. Kessler, Glenn Kessler, and Daniel Zelman. Specifically, let's focus on the two main characters driving the action, brothers Danny and John Rayburn. The story begins with the forty-fifth anniversary of the opening of the oceanside resort John and Danny's parents have operated most of their lives. After years of being away, Danny suddenly reappears, and it is clear from the response he engenders that no one is happy to see him, especially John.

The key episode in their past involves the death of their sister, Sarah, at the age of ten. She happened onto their mother while the older woman—after a vicious fight with her husband, Sarah's father—was angrily packing, intending to leave the family. Sarah became visibly upset at this, and Danny, himself only fifteen or sixteen, decided to take her for a boat ride to help her feel better. John, age fourteen, protested, quoting their parents' rule that they not go out on the boat without an adult. Danny ignored this and headed out anyway. Though Sarah asked him to join them, John remained behind.

While out on the boat, Sarah's seahorse necklace fell into the water. While trying to retrieve it from between two jagged pieces of coral, her hand got stuck, and she could not get it free. Danny dove to help her, but he could not free her hand, either, and she drowned.

Sarah was very much the apple of their father's eye. In contrast, even at this early age, Danny, the oldest, was constantly going toe to toe with the old man. When the father learns Sarah is dead and that Danny had taken her on the boat, he explodes into a violent rage so ferocious he nearly beats his oldest son to death.

Terrified of what will happen to the family if news of this near-murder gets out, the mother reconciles herself to her familial role and instructs John and his younger siblings to lie to the authorities, claiming Danny was the victim of a hit-and-run accident, not a brutal thrashing from his own father.

The incident haunts the entire family from that point forward, but Danny and John are affected in distinctly different ways.

Danny already had a Weakness at the time of his sister's death—an arrogant, anti-authority streak combined with a reckless love of testing boundaries. This contributed to the mistake that led to his sister's death, which registers first and foremost as a moment of greatest fear, greatest guilt, and greatest loss combined (a Wound). This is compounded when his siblings lie to protect their father, which creates the moment of greatest betrayal (another Wound). Any chance the incident might lead to some kind of soul-searching gets destroyed by his father's merciless violence and the rest of the family's deceitful cover-up. Danny leaves home once his wounds heal and drifts from one place to another, relying on drugs and alcohol to balm his soul and pursuing a number of criminal activities (a Flaw).

Danny's intrinsic Weakness and dark moments of helplessness combine to form the Wound and Flaw that generate his subsequent behavior—a rootless lack of attachment, careless disregard for the pain he causes others, a scheming sense of getting over on the sanctimonious hypocrites who want to claim the moral high ground, and a desire for vengeance. He is charming, manipulative, and cunning (Pathological Maneuver), but he's also resourceful, daring, and genuinely insightful, especially when it comes to seeing through hypocrisy (Persistent Virtues).

This is how he appears as the story opens—the Prodigal Son returned, cagily planning his own revenge on the family that turned him out, in particular manipulating his mother's guilt to his own advantage.

John also revealed a Weakness as a boy—the need to be in the right at all times, to earn his parents' favor, to be the good and loyal son. This leads both to his trying to stop Danny from taking Sarah out on the boat alone and his refusal to join them. Thus his moment of greatest loss is also a moment of greatest guilt, but for reasons different than Danny's. If he'd broken the rules for once and gone along, maybe he could have prevented Sarah's death.

That guilt intensifies when he conspires with the others to betray Danny, and it acquires a veneer of shame because Danny knows the truth. It also creates a lifelong fear of what might happen if that truth is ever revealed—something that becomes a distinct possibility when Danny returns.

In contrast to the aimless life of dissolution and manipulation that Danny has lived in the wake of their sister's death, John has doubled down on the role of good son, working as a detective with the sheriff's department and becoming a respectable family man. He has learned to silence his guilt, shame, sorrow, and fear by perfecting his role as the calm, responsible, reliable one. The good son has become the good father and good cop, accentuating his virtues and hiding his faults. This is an excellent example of how even Persistent Virtues—a sense of duty, honor, and responsibility, an implacable calm in the face of difficulty—can become Pathological Maneuvers when serving a dishonest purpose.

It's important to note that Sarah's death is never openly shown until late in the series' first season, and even then it is revealed in disjointed pieces. This creates suspense by delaying explanation of what generates so much animosity between Danny and the other family members, especially John, as well as what explains the distinctly different patterns of behavior the two brothers exhibit. This is what makes the series such a strong example of how to reveal backstory through behavior at the outset of the story, creating intrigue and tension by revealing the characters' Pathological Maneuvers and Persistent Virtues without explanation, forcing the audience to wonder why they're acting that way.

EXERCISES

Revisit the same two character from your WIP that you used in response to the exercises for moments of helplessness earlier in this chapter. Then address the following concerns:

For Pathological Maneuvers:

- Start with the painful moment of helplessness. Recognize how it has struck a blow against the character's belief in himself or his dream of life.
- Allow that initial blow to develop into a force of Resistance—inflicting a psychic Wound, reinforcing a Weakness or a Limitation, enhancing the debilitating effect of an Obligation or some source of external Opposition, or encouraging the development of a Flaw where others are harmed as well.
- Forge from the foregoing a habit of behavior—including attitude, interpretation of events, response to difficulty, perspective on the world—by asking which of these tendencies the character has developed in response to the moment of helplessness and the resulting force of Resistance:

  - Avoidance, denial, settling for less.
  - Acting out, irresponsible risk taking, substance abuse, or some other form of overindulgence.
  - Unconsciously modeling one's maladaptive behavior on someone else's (because that person seems to get what she wants).
  - Some form of abusive, self-serving behavior toward others.

For Persistent Virtues:

- Start with the moment of courage, forgiveness, pride, trust, love, or joy.
- Recognize how, even if only in a small way, that moment has bolstered the character's self-confidence and belief in the promise of life—i.e., reflect on how it speaks to the character's Yearning.
- Reflect on how the natural hardships of life have worn away some, but not all, of the luster of that shining moment. In particular, how much of the initial sense of self-worth, hopefulness, connection to others, and happiness has the character retained.
- Again, how does that reveal itself in habits of behavior—attitude, interpretation of events, response to difficulty, perspective on the

world. Imagine specific activities—volunteering, charitable giving, routine acts of kindness or self-sacrifice—that have become second nature.

- Specifically analyze how the past continues to influence the character's capacity for commitment, perseverance, self-confidence, and faith in others.

SUMMARY OF MAIN POINTS IN THIS CHAPTER

EXPLORING BACKSTORY FOR THE CHARACTER'S KEY SEMINAL MOMENTS

- Compelling stories demand the depiction of both levels of character—the public persona and the deeper level unconscious emotion and response lying beneath the surface.
- To explore the subsurface self, we need to identify key moments of helplessness in the character's past that reveal the balance she has achieved between her Yearning and the forces of Resistance.
- By moments of helplessness, we mean incidents when emotion or action arose from within the individual but outside his conscious control.
- Once the moments of helplessness have been identified, we can then begin to imagine the various habits of behavior she has devised to create her Pathological Maneuvers and Persistent Virtues.
- The tension between social self and private self helps create the sense of contradiction that makes a character seem compelling and real.
- Ten potential areas of helplessness to explore with your main characters, as well as those secondary characters whose roles—and thus their motivations—are crucial to the story:

Pain (Resistance)	Promise (Yearning)
Fear/Cowardice	Courage
Guilt/Sin	Penance/Forgiveness
Shame/Failure	Pride/Success
Betrayal	Trust
Death/Loss/Sorrow	Love/Connection/Joy

- These ten areas of helplessness are not written in stone. You do not need to envision individual scenes that speak to every single one of them to create a compelling portrayal, nor are these the only areas worth exploring. They are prompts, not dictates.
- Often one moment serves several purposes, or various moments reinforce or even enhance the impact of others, just as the various forces of Resistance often interact.
- It is not general traits we are trying to identify but the moments that gave rise to them.
- The more you can include other individuals in the scenes you imagine, the better.
- "The worse the better"—trying to protect your characters from severely painful circumstances all too often evidences a retreat on the part of the writer from the demands of credibly depicting truly powerful emotion.

FINDING THE CONNECTIVE TISSUE OR THEME AMONG BACKSTORY MOMENTS

- The critical moments of helplessness you've explored in your character's past share a thematic quality that points to the core problem the person is trying to solve in his life, and thus the core of the story he has to tell.
- This aspect of characterization is more art than science and requires an intuitive grasp of your character's fundamental nature. This requires imagination; no step-by-step method will get you there.
- To find this thematic thread, we need to look at the various moments we've created and try to detect how they form part of an unconscious journey, not a random jumble of episodes. That journey will lead the character closer to fulfilling the promise of life as she understands it while avoiding as much of the pain of life as possible.
- This attempt to find a unifying theme will pay several additional dividends.

- It will help clarify the character's Yearning and the forces of Resistance holding her back, seen as part of a lifelong struggle and a coherent whole.
- It will help you recognize the equilibrium the character has struck between pursuit of her dream of life and protection from the pain of life, which will typify her behavior at the story's outset.
- It will help lend *authenticity* to the character's quest for identity, which is a crucial aspect of her Yearning—i.e., the character's dream of life will be seen more clearly, personally, and honestly, not just in terms of what is longed for but what is realistic given the individual's unique nature and past.
- It will help you devise a symbolic representation of the Lack/Yearning, or a concrete behavior that best typifies the struggle between them.
- It will identify the character's core internal problem that she will need to address in the course of the narrative. The solution or mitigation of that problem will form her Yearning Horizon for that story. (For more on this, see chapter eight).

- A good place to start that process is to revisit the character's Yearning and the forces of Resistance holding him back. That conflict will likely direct you to the core problem of his life.
- Don't be discouraged if such a theme does not suggest itself at the outset. It may not reveal itself until you are well into your story—or even at its end.

MOVING FROM MOMENTS TO HABITUAL BEHAVIOR—PATHOLOGICAL MANEUVERS AND PERSISTENT VIRTUES

- Pathological Maneuvers and Persistent Virtues are patterns of habitual behavior that develop from moments of helplessness.
- They take the form of a prevailing attitude, perspective, sense of the world, connection to others, self-worth, and an assessment of the value of taking risks.

- Pathological Maneuvers have their genesis in moments of painful helplessness that create or reinforce some aspect of Resistance—Wounds, Weaknesses, Limitations, etc.—and often take the form of one or more of the following:
  - Avoidance, denial, settling for less.
  - Acting out, self-injury, irresponsible risk taking, casual sex, substance abuse or some other form of overindulgence.
  - Unconsciously modeling one's maladaptive behavior on someone else's (because that person seems to get what he wants).
  - Some form of abusive behavior toward others, exemplified by a selfish regard for one's own wants over any concern for others, or a disregard for the pain one causes.

- Pathological Maneuvers reveal how our misfortunes and personal limitations have embedded themselves in our day-to-day behavior, shaping our attitude, our perspective, our responses, and our actions.
- Persistent Virtues speak to the character's Yearning in that, having their genesis in moments of courage, pride, forgiveness, trust, joy, or love, they reinforce the character's faith in the promise of life and lend her at least some of the self-confidence and resilience necessary to pursue it.
- From a writing perspective, the great advantage of Pathological Maneuvers and Persistent Virtues is that they permit us to reveal the character's past through behavior rather than exposition, showing rather than telling how the past has influenced the present when it comes to how the character acts and thinks. The unique, problematic, puzzling, or just plain odd nature of that behavior will create empathy, intrigue, or both, forcing the reader to wonder what in the past has produced the curious thoughts and actions exhibited by the character.
- It is by no means necessary to reveal the underlying events or factors that led to your character's behavior. Unless confusion is created by its omission, it's generally best to keep backstory explication to a minimum.

6

Prime Mover, Desire—Not Conflict—Drives Story

I wake to sleep, and take my waking slow.
I feel my fate in what I cannot fear.
I learn by going where I have to go.
—Theodore Roethke, *The Waking*

I. DESIRE DRIVES STORY

To recap our development from the previous chapters:

- The character begins in a state of **Lack**: Something is missing from his life.
- This Lack speaks to an unfulfilled **Yearning**, or dream of life: the kind of person the character longs to be, the way of life he hopes to live.
- The reason this Yearning remains unfulfilled is due to various forms of **Resistance** holding him back, internally and externally.
- The Resistance and Yearning are embodied in habitual behaviors referred to as **Pathological Maneuvers** and **Persistent Virtues**.

Then *something happens*—the character makes a decision, goes on a journey, confronts an adversary, helps a stranger, discovers something, conceals something. Or the world around the character shifts, yields, convulses. The market crashes. At long last: rain.

That occurrence triggers the **Desire** to respond or to act.

It is the *desire to act* that is often easiest and simplest to identify and define—to win the loved one, repel the invaders, complete the expedition, or simply to "clean up one's act." Gatsby pursues Daisy, Ahab hunts the whale, Katniss Everdeen strives to win the Hunger Games.

It rightfully can be said that the story truly begins once the character is propelled into action. The decision to act is typically prompted by some disturbance in the status quo, some change however slight—or monumental—in the life of one or more of the main characters.

Remember also that the status quo is defined at least in part by the balance your characters have achieved between Yearning and Resistance—their need to protect themselves from the pain of life and their hopes for pursuing the promise of life. The disturbance or change that disrupts this balance typically takes one of the following forms:

- An opportunity arises: a new school year begins, money needed for the expedition arrives, the storm passes, the loved one appears "across a crowded room." This is sometimes referred to as *showing the character what he wants and making him pursue it.*
- A misfortune occurs: a loved one falls ill, the levee breaks, the money is stolen, a body is found. This is sometimes referred to as *giving the character what he wants and then taking it away*; or *inflicting on the character what he dreads and making him escape or defeat it.*

There is no law forbidding multiple prompts to action of different kinds over the course of the story. The character may begin by pursuing something she wants only to possess it momentarily before having it snatched away, or her pursuit may lead her to something she dreads, forcing her to defeat or escape it.

Similarly, the character's Desire may change in the course of the story as events or his own ambitions dictate; those changes may also result in an awakening, transformation, or evolution of his underlying Yearning.

For example, in the film *A Prophet*, nominated for the 2010 Oscar for Best Foreign Language Film of the Year, Franco-Arab Malik El Djebena enters Brécourt prison in Normandy at the age of nineteen after a history of juvenile offenses. His first goal as a young, isolated inmate goes no further than simply to survive. The prison, however, is strictly controlled by two factions: the Muslims and the Corsicans. Malik feels no affinity for either group; the latter despise him, and he feels no connection to Islam despite being half Arab. César Luciani, the brutal head of the Corsicans, forces Malik to kill a Muslim inmate who had approached Malik for sex. With that crime, Malik gains favor with Luciani. Little by little, Malik finds a way to improve his status, learning to read and secretly figuring out Luciani's various criminal enterprises as he performs more and more favors for the aging gangster. At each step of the way, as Malik's competence and understanding increase, not only do his goals grow more ambitious, his sense of self and what the future holds transforms. In the end, he rises to lead his own gang within the prison—a goal, identity, and mission that were unforeseen at the start.

The initial disturbance or change in status quo that creates the Desire also generates tension by asking a question and withholding the answer. Something is going to happen next—or fail to happen. *What will it be? When will it occur? How? Why?*

A great many writing guides place conflict at the center of story, arguing that it is the source of the narrative's forward movement,[1] but this leads to many unfortunate confusions. Conflict, instead of creating movement, actually impedes it. The dramatic effect of that arrested movement is tension or suspense.

Now, tension is crucial to storytelling—it's what makes readers and audiences remain engaged—but tension does not account for the story's forward movement or narrative drive. That is created by Desire. Even if the Desire creates only *expectation*, the sense that something will or should happen creates tension between what's hoped for and what might instead occur.[2] In other words, tension is the effect produced by *impeded* desire.

It's in this sense, and this sense alone, that conflict generates story. *Conflict is Desire meeting some source of opposition.* And any genuinely meaningful desire always encounters opposition. Otherwise, there would be nothing to want. Something in easy reach may as well be in hand.

Gin up as much conflict as you want, you will still need Desire to create movement and Yearning to render meaning.

---

1 See for example, Spark, Debra, *Curious Attractions: Essays on Writing.*
2 This reflects what is commonly known as the Reader's Paradox: Readers always want to be able to predict where a story is going, but they also always want to be wrong.

EXERCISES

- Identify the "something" that happens that obliges your protagonist to act at the outset of your story. Specifically, which one of the following options best describes what occurs?
- The character sees what he wants and decides to pursue it.
- The character has what he wants but it is snatched away.
- What the character dreads is forced upon him and he must defeat or escape it.

  - Having identified what prompts the character to act, now identify his Desire, i.e., his overarching goal in the story, or at least at the story's outset.
  - Once you've identified the character's Desire, identify the obstacles, the sources of opposition, that stand in the way of his achieving his goal. How might you make them more formidable and, thus, make the Desire harder to achieve? Given the increased difficulty of achieving his overarching goal, what motivates him to continue regardless?
  - Answer the preceding two questions for another main character—in particular, the protagonist's opponent if there is one.

II. DESIRE AND CHANGE

To say "something happens" is to say that things change. This is what Aristotle meant when he said that the opening of the story concludes and the middle of the story begins when something happens to alter the fortunes of the protagonist.

Taking it one step further, we need to keep in mind that stories are about problems, and problems pose questions: *What's going on? Why?* The movement from an unanswered question to an answered one implicitly suggests a change—in circumstances if not the characters. It is likely, but not inevitable, that a change in circumstances should effect a change in your characters, if only in their understanding.

WHAT PRECISELY DO WE MEAN BY A CHARACTER CHANGING?

One of the reasons the issue of character change elicits so many varied answers is because different people harbor different notions of what they mean by the term. In truth, the concept covers a considerable range of ground, from a Saul-on-the-Road-to-Damascus transformation to a "new normal" that differs from the old in nothing more profoundly earthshaking than the character's awareness.

To learn is to grow and to grow is to change—and it is to this extent that all stories offer at least the opportunity for the character to alter course. The character may ignore that opportunity, misunderstand it, fumble it away, run from it screaming—or embrace it and forge ahead. But by saying "something happens" we implicitly present the characters with a question and an opportunity to answer it. Whether they rise to the challenge or not frames the core of the story.

THE ISSUE OF CHANGE WHEN THE CHARACTER'S STRUGGLE IS LARGELY EXTERNAL

As noted in our discussion in chapter two on "traveling angels," a great many of the protagonists that validate the claim that not all characters must change reside in genres where the principal action is external: mysteries, for example, and adventure or action stories.

Heroes such as Hercule Poirot, James Bond, and Jack Reacher exemplify such protagonists and arguably are loved by readers in no small part precisely because they do *not* change. These stories typically reveal a change in circumstances or the situation rather than the hero.

This kind of protagonist typically has a unique skill set that elevates him above the common man. This quality inspires awe rather than empathy. We do not necessarily want to feel what Bond or Reacher feels; we simply want to watch them overcome the incredible odds they face and save the day.

What of protagonists whose struggle is largely external, but do not have a Bond-like skill set, i.e., they need to acquire those skills during the course of the story?

Again, to learn is to grow and to grow is to change. Obtaining a skill typically makes a person more confident, if only in the performance of that skill. She feels differently about herself and her capability—less uncertain and doubtful. That may not be a huge change—though your story will be more engaging if it is—but it's still a change.

WHEN CHANGE REFLECTS AN INNER TRANSFORMATION

The preceding section raises a crucial point: When the protagonist changes, it's usually because the struggles he has faced have forged a different *understanding* of himself, his abilities, and/or his world, including the people in it.

Even in instances where the "action" of the story would seem to be chiefly, if not entirely, internal—recovery/reform narratives, spiritual awakenings/religious conversions, stories of philosophical or scientific discovery—the characters and their struggle to achieve their goals do not exist in an immaterial vacuum. Only by testing internal change against the external world and one's relationships with others can any such transformation be considered manifest.

A criminal in prison may undergo a profound "crucible moment," where she sees the error in her ways and discovers a new path. But that new path will lead nowhere unless it effects a change in behavior that convinces not just her but others of her transformation—not to mention the test the outer world and all of its triggers, temptations, boredom, and infuriating, demeaning disappointments will place on that reformed state of mind once she gains release.

The acolyte may achieve enlightenment through sitting in mindful repose or contemplation of the divine—but what happens when he rises from the prayer mat and opens the door to the outer world?

What we often refer to as change in a character normally points toward such internal issues being tested by the external world: Will the character address the forces of Resistance holding him back? Will he resolve his concerns about his own merits, self-worth, purpose, authenticity? If so, such a change, if anchored in real conviction, will reveal itself in *external behavior*, i.e., by resolving his internal issues, the individual is more capable of achieving his goals in the world, including building and maintaining better relationships with others, and facing the challenges of his life honestly, bravely, and compassionately.

However, in tragedy, this new awareness, whether of self or circumstances, often comes too late to change the misfortune that's been lurking in the shadows. Nevertheless, that shocking new awareness is itself a change, which the reader feels along with the character. Even if the character is paralyzed by what she now understands, it is also clear that she is profoundly different than before that shock of insight.

There are also cases where the change in understanding is not reflected in a change in *behavior*, and it's characters of that sort who are often (mis)identified as not having changed.

An example is Brick in *Cat on a Hot Tin Roof.* At the end of the play he is still resisting Maggie's attempts to resume their lovemaking, and when she begins putting away his liquor with the intention of conceiving a child with him, he responds with a phrase he used at the outset of the play: "Wouldn't it be funny if that was true?" But though his words are the same, their meaning is not, for we have witnessed him forced to confront the truth about himself, his lies, his best friend's homosexuality—and the real reason for that friend's suicide. Bitter cynicism has been replaced by a deeper, more honest awareness, prompted in no small part by a newfound awareness of his wife's indomitable strength.

THE SO-CALLED STEADFAST CHARACTER

This leads to discussion of a character type sometimes referred to as the Steadfast Character, whose dramatic arc is premised precisely on his *refusal* to change, usually for one of two reasons.

- He refuses to sacrifice an ideal or give up on a goal he believes he cannot live without.
- He clings to the "pathological maneuvers" he uses to protect himself from the pain of life.

Examples of the first type of character include Antigone, Romeo, Jake Barnes in *The Sun Also Rises*, and Dr. Richard Kimble in *The Fugi-*

tive. In each case, it would seem that the character in question is defined precisely by a refusal to surrender his or her core goal, moral stance, or personal commitment.

This notion of "steadfast," however, glances past a key point. Though it might be said that the motives or behavior of such characters don't appreciably change, their emotions, insight, or attitude toward life does. They have gained a new understanding of the cost of standing firm.

For example, one might say that Romeo's *love* is steadfast, but as the stakes change, so does his appreciation and acceptance of what that love requires of him.

As for the second type of steadfast character mentioned above, it is exemplified by Blanche Dubois, who refuses to give up the misty illusions that blur the hard reality of growing older and the loss of her sexual allure. Her psychotic break at the end, after Stanley rapes her, testifies to a continued, pathological preference for delusion over truth, but also an awareness, however dim, that those delusions did not and cannot protect her.

For other examples, turn to James Joyce's story collection *Dubliners*, which he described as a study in paralysis—a fatalistic state of mind inflicted by the two insidious, overwhelming powers controlling and stagnating Irish life: Great Britain and the Roman Catholic Church.

THE ROLE OF FAILURE IN CHANGE—AND REVEALING THE CHARACTER'S YEARNING

Nothing prompts profound reassessment of oneself or one's situation like disaster. Even minor failures and setbacks normally cause us to rethink what we're doing, how we're going about it, or why. This learning process is what is meant by the phrase "success through failure."

All stories in one way or another concern one thing: trouble. Even if stories begin by the sudden appearance of a golden opportunity, optimizing that opportunity must quickly present problems or the story is over. Those problems are caused by something going wrong and, more times than not, that "something" gets progressively worse before there is any hope of it getting better.

It is in *how* the character responds to this gauntlet of challenge and failure that distinguishes him from the one who does not. If your protagonist never appreciably doubts his capabilities or sense of purpose—as Poirot, Bond, and Reacher do not—then feel no need to jerry-rig some sort of change. It's one reason we admire such characters—they lack the doubt, confusion, weakness, and fear of mere mortals, like us.

For the vast majority of other characters, the problem solving that the novel requires will engender doubt, confusion, anxiety, even dread. In such cases, it is not just the external situation that needs to be better apprehended; the character must also address whatever personal shortcomings and misconceptions are hindering solution of the problem. He may also need to reevaluate his relationships with others to the extent they are helping or hindering his progress. Moving through such emotional evaluations cannot help but alter the character's sense of competence, capability, judgment, and worth. And how he conducts that process of ongoing evaluation and reevaluation—courageously or not, honestly or not—will determine the extent to which he indeed proves capable of solving the story's core problem, or whether, despite his best efforts, a solution simply lies beyond him.

If the failure to solve the problem has particularly severe consequences, or the setbacks encountered are especially painful, the character will be forced to ask: Why go on? Why not go back, give in, strike a bargain, accept defeat? He may also ask, What's wrong with me? Why can't I do this? What is it about me that needs to change before I can get this right?

As we noted in chapter three in discussing how Yearning defines the stakes, the answers to such questions expose who the character truly wants to be and the way of life he hopes to live. It also exposes the forces of Resistance—the Weaknesses, Wounds, Limitations, external Opposition or Obligations, the Flaws—that are holding him back.

TO LOVE IS TO CHANGE

In the modern love story, the core question is, What's keeping the lovers apart? A difference in class, status, or religion typically no longer serves as an insurmountable impediment as it once did. Similarly the availability of divorce no longer makes it impossible for married lovers to cut the nuptial knot and move on.

What's keeping modern lovers apart is each other. There is some combination of traits on the part of one character or the other—or both—that is preventing the couple from resolving their differences, coming to terms, and committing to each other.

This means one or both characters at some point are obliged to ask themselves the question: *What do I need to change about myself, my life, or what I'm doing to get that person to say yes?*

The setup implicitly dictates change. This is equally true if the love connection takes the form of a family tie, a friendship, a student-teacher relationship, or any other significant bond, or if it is simply a subplot. The lone wolf who realizes he needs to be more of a team player is observing an identical logic.

CAN THE OPPONENT AND SECONDARY CHARACTERS CHANGE?

The "rule" that the opponent never changes basically reflects the routine use of this character as the embodiment of evil—a villain. And all too often villains are conceived as psychopaths or other types of individuals with rigid personality disorders that by their nature resist change.

But the opponent can and often does change, especially in dramas where the conflict is motivated meaningfully on both sides, as when good is pitted against good: the Kansas father who fears losing the farm versus the artistic son who desperately needs to leave.

There are also stories that use a plot technique known as the *double reveal*. In such stories, both the protagonist and the opponent experience a crucial insight into themselves—they each learn something from the other, and that insight changes their sense of self.

It's perhaps ironic that this technique is not only common in love stories but appears in tales of war and sports as well, where the adversaries gain a grudging respect for each other through their combat.

As for secondary characters, there again is no hard-and-fast rule. If they endure a similar gauntlet of trials and struggles as the main characters, how can they not change in some way? And yet their dramatic function—mentor, ally, betrayer—suggests a certain fixedness, though more in role than understanding. Their distinct personalities will determine the degree to which they do or don't evolve or even transform.

EXERCISES

- Pick two of the main characters from your WIP. What do they learn in the process of the struggles they face in the course of the story? How does that learning curve affect their understanding of themselves, the world, and their relationships with other key characters?
- If this learning curve does not appreciably change the character's behavior or attitude toward life, explain why.
- Does the character's new awareness come too late to change the course of events, as in tragedy? If so, explain.
- Can either of the two main characters you've selected be described as a Steadfast Character, i.e., his dramatic arc is premised precisely on his *refusal* to change, either because he won't sacrifice an ideal or give up on a goal he believes he cannot live without, or he clings to the "pathological maneuvers" he uses to protect himself from the pain of life? If so, do that character's emotions, insight, or attitude toward life change? If so, how? If not, why not?
- Do either of your characters remain unchanged because they have refused an opportunity to change that's presented? If so, how did the opportunity to change present itself? Why did the character fail to take that opportunity?
- How do your characters fail through the course of your story? How do they then answer the following questions?
    - Why go on? Why not go back, give in, strike a bargain, accept defeat?
    - What's wrong with me? Why can't I do this? What is it about me that needs to change before I can get this right?

- If you're writing a love story, what is keeping the lovers apart? If something about one or the other character's nature is causing the problem, how does she answer: *What do I need to change about myself, my life, or what I'm doing to get that person to say yes?*
- If your story has an opponent, does he change? How does that happen—for example, is it failure that prompts the change, or is it something about the conflict with the protagonist that forces him to reflect on himself, his behavior, or his life?
- Select two secondary characters from your WIP. How does the action of the story prompt them to change their behavior, their self-understanding, or their attitude toward the world? How does this effect their dramatic function—mentor, ally, loved one, betrayer—within the story?

III. LINKING DESIRE TO YEARNING

As noted in the introduction of this book, simply knowing what the character wants is seldom enough. The reader also wants to know why she wants it, how badly she wants it, what she will risk to get it, what will be lost if she fails, who else will be affected—all of which connects the Desire to deeper needs and longings, i.e., her Yearning.

We have already discussed how different individuals become aware of their Yearning in different ways and at different times. Some experience a "calling" at an early age that speaks to a fundamental sense of self, purpose, or mission. Others don't sense their Yearning clearly until it crystalizes into a sense of personal vocation. Still others need an encounter with death or some other profound loss or figurative "gun to the head" before they recognize that the inescapable fact of their mortality demands some sort of answer to the questions of who are they, why are they here, and how should they live.

Desire, by forcing the character to act, typically also forces the character to adjust to a sudden disequilibrium in the balance he has devised between Yearning and Resistance. Since the old equilibrium suited different circumstances, it can no longer perform adequately—otherwise your story is over. And the longer it takes for the character to realize his old ways will not serve the new situation, the greater the chance his reckoning will come at great cost.

HOW PURSUIT OF THE DESIRE CLARIFIES THE CHARACTER'S YEARNING

The range of ways a character may be aware of her Yearning and Resistance at the story's outset also suggests a range of ways the story can develop once she is obliged to act. The following list, which is by no means exhaustive, offers suggestions on how that might occur:

- **Yearning clearly apprehended and fully embraced:** This is the narrative terrain of the traveling angels—Poirot, Bond, Reacher, Mary Poppins—and of characters blessed with a firm sense of personal mission or an unwavering moral compass. Not that this setup always turns out well; black comedy heroes such as John Yossarian in *Catch-22* also fall into this category. They know who they are and what is demanded of them. The only question is, Will they succeed? The action of the story will test the character's capabilities and luck but not his sense of purpose, unless it results in shattering failure.
- **Yearning clearly apprehended but uncertainly embraced:** Here lie a great many of literature's heroes. The forces of Resistance, especially in the form of self-doubt, still hold at least a bit of the upper hand. The character, though aware of her dream, mission, or ambition—either at the story's outset or at some later point in the narrative—has not yet mustered the clarity, certainty, or resolve to pursue it with all her heart and soul. The story's action will need to reveal the inadequacy of those half measures and make it quite clear that if she does not grasp her dream now, move past her uncertainty or fear or past regrets, she might lose this chance forever, to her own detriment or that of others. Great leaders who nonetheless suffered their own Gethsemane moments, from Jesus to Dr. Martin Luther King Jr., reside here, as do such classic literary heroes from Sydney Carton in *A Tale of Two Cities* to Katniss Everdeen. Another variation is the character who is content, but new

circumstances arise that demand much more of him, the iconic example being Frodo in *The Lord of the Rings*. Not all such stories end in triumph, of course; disillusion narratives fit this template as well. In David Hare's *Plenty*, Susan Traherne's career as a Special Operations courier in Nazi-occupied France creates in her a fierce sense of promise, moral clarity, and ambition, which gets crushed against the rocks of postwar British hardship and fecklessness. She struggles but fails to find some meaningful direction, only to become increasingly bitter, bored, and self-destructive.

- **Yearning clearly apprehended but shunned:** Here the Resistance is clearly in control, with the character profoundly devoted to protecting himself from the pain of life. Fear of failure, paralyzing self-doubt, stifling cynicism, or obsession with his own inadequacies seal the character within a protective shell. In this case, the action of the story will need to present a clear, undeniable, and inescapable "gun to the head" to force the character out of his posture of self-defense, which blinds him to the better if more difficult path available. Brick in *Cat on a Hot Tin Roof*, by preferring alcohol to honest but harsh acceptance, is an example. Indeed, many addiction, revenge, and noir narratives portray this logic.

- **Yearning vaguely apprehended but clarity sought:** Here the character is aware something is missing from her life but does not know exactly what it is or how to find out. Here the learning process of the plot is most crucial. The story first needs to offer clarity concerning the character's main objective, giving her a concrete goal or ambition. The struggle to achieve that goal or ambition will present a way for the character to address the forces of Resistance that have been holding her back. As she tackles those forces a greater sense of promise, confidence, and even self-worth might emerge. Example: Because Patrick Sumner in Ian McGuire's *The North Water* is betrayed by superiors in the British Army in India and forced from the service in disgrace, he takes last-chance employment as a ship's surgeon on an ill-fated whaling voyage to the Arctic Sea. When a variety of disasters strike, he first must struggle simply to survive, but as he does he also finds increasing purpose in exposing those responsible, from a child killer crewman to the corrupt financiers of the expedition, and a new sense of personal identity, worth, and ambition emerges.

- **Yearning vaguely apprehended and clarity pursued haphazardly:** Here the character feels lost, but lacks the will or the ability to turn things around. To prevent the story from becoming a meandering episodic mess, it will once again be necessary to produce either a "gun to the head" or a clear-cut opportunity within reasonable reach for the character to pursue—and more times than not, the sooner the better. His lack of clarity and haphazard methods will create a gauntlet of missteps and failures—but that's the story. Example: Holden Caulfield in *Catcher in the Rye*.

- **Yearning vaguely apprehended and clarity avoided:** We are once again in "refusal of the call" territory, except the character's defensive posture is even more absolute—it isn't that she's shunning pursuit of the promise of life, but that she doesn't know what that might be and feels no ambition to find out. Reform and recovery narratives fit this mold. The opportunity that spurs her to act must be even more conspicuously golden to shake her out of her defensive crouch or lethargy—or the gun to her head needs to be of howitzer proportion. In the film *Shame*, written by Abi Morgan and Steve McQueen (who also directed), it takes the attempted suicide of his younger sister—with whom he once had an incestuous affair—to finally convince the protagonist, Brandon, that he might have a problem with sex addiction.

- **Yearning misapprehended or mistaken:** This is often described as a story where what the character wants differs from what he needs. Here the Resistance not only has the upper hand, it has fashioned through some sort of denial or self-delusion a mistaken goal or even a false dream of life. That false dream seems to offer the promise of fulfillment, but in the end it results in the same, a similar, or even worse state of Lack. In *Les Misérables*, Javert's obsession with the letter of the law, his ironclad conviction that evil deeds are proof of evil character, ultimately crumbles when, at the novel's end, he realizes that Valjean, despite a criminal past, is a truly honorable man. The epiphany is so devastating he commits suicide.

- **Yearning unidentified and unpursued:** Welcome to the Land of Fools. Nothing short of a thunderbolt from God—or a pot of gold dropped on her head—will kickstart this character's engine. And given her entrenched oblivion, it is far more likely she will end up where she began, if not worse off, due to the story's action. Folktales abound with such characters, reminding us that for the better part of human history the average person has held a jaundiced view of ambition.

I don't mean to suggest in the foregoing examples that the character's Yearning, if inadequately apprehended by the character, nonetheless exists in some ideal form just waiting to be recognized, like a shipwreck on the ocean floor. As noted earlier, Yearning often acts more like a force directing the compass of selfhood, a sense of when we are living up to our own potential and pursuing the life we want—or not. It can take the form of a core image or innate sense of identity guiding the individual toward his greater self, but things are often not quite so clear-cut.

Sometimes when Yearning is misapprehended a life of ease or complacency is the culprit, an existence where nothing great is demanded or expected, or conformity is prized above accomplishment. In such circumstances, one can be fooled into believing all that life requires is sticking to the program. Why dream big? It can only rock the boat.

Alternatively, life's travails and setbacks can enervate the individual's sense of purpose, worth, confidence, or hope, and intensify her desire simply to protect herself. Her grasp of any real sense of promise fades into the background. It's enough simply to get by.

It is in these two senses, whether through comfort or suffering, that the character's Yearning can be said to be inadequately apprehended or recognized. Instead of the Compass of Character directing the individual forward, it points to the floor beneath his feet and nails him in place.

This is where the need to act, whether through opportunity or misfortune, proves most crucial. The character's Yearning only begins to take shape through the pursuit of the Desire. The goal represented by that Desire, even if only uncertainly embraced or desultorily pursued at first, will eventually, step-by-step, through both success and failure, increasingly come to feel not only possible but necessary—otherwise, why soldier on?

Contrariwise, it is often only by experiencing what one doesn't want, either by failing in pursuit of the goal or succeeding but with unsatisfactory consequences, that the dream of life takes shape, if only in opposition: *Whatever my dream might be, I know it isn't _this_.*

THE MIRROR EFFECT BETWEEN DESIRE AND YEARNING

The fact that pursuit of the Desire clarifies the character'sYearning suggests that some character goals—saving the miners, catching the killer, marrying the loved one, finding the way home—may speak more clearly or directly to that Yearning than others. For example, a character whose Yearning makes itself most evident in hopes of love, home, and family will make a somewhat curious choice for a protagonist in a story about space exploration, unless the story centers on a catastrophe that creates a desperate desire to return to earth, as in Alfonso Cuarón's film *Gravity*.

Note that what compels the protagonist to act in *Gravity* is a misfortune—actually a series of them—the effect of her spacecraft being pummeled by satellite debris. This is an important point, for how the character gains a firmer grasp of her Yearning typically differs in a story launched by misfortune rather than opportunity.

An opportunity typically speaks to a longing already present to some extent within the character. If she is not at some level hoping for romantic love, introducing that special someone across a crowded room will likely go nowhere.

It is therefore wise, if obliging the character to act by introducing an opportunity, to spend some time reflecting on how that opportunity reflects, knowingly or unknowingly, the character's dream of life—or distracts, deters, or disillusions her. In the first instance, the struggles

of the pursuit and the possibility of failure will help clarify why success is not just desired but important, meaningful, and necessary. In the
latter instance, the story will address how pursuing the wrong thing,
or the right thing for the wrong reasons, awakens the character to his
error, forcing him to reconsider what he truly wants and why—or get
used to the disaster he has created.

When a character's Desire leads him astray from his Yearning, it is
normally because the Desire offers some variety of fool's gold, or it offers what appears to be an easy way out.

In contrast, stories that begin with a misfortune, like *Gravity*, present a distinctly different problem. By and large, we do not choose our
misfortunes.[3]

In structuring a story that begins with a misfortune, therefore, it is
not so much a question of linking Desire to Yearning as having it echo
in some way the character's Resistance, since misfortune introduces
the threat of increasing the pain in the character's life. The action will
therefore test the character's previous strategies for minimizing that
pain and will likely fail (or your story is over).

The obvious example is the story of the character terrified of fire
who finds herself trapped in a burning building, or the many variations
thereof, including the inveterate lady killer horrified by the prospect of
marriage who meets the woman of his dreams.[4] (This latter example, by
the way, also shows how presenting the character with what he wants
is at times not dissimilar with confronting him with what he dreads.)

The suspense genre capitalizes on this format by having the villain
specifically prey on the protagonist precisely because of some innate
fear, weakness, or need, forcing the protagonist to deal with it to survive. Patricia Highsmith's *Strangers on a Train* is the classic example,

---

3 There are two notable exceptions to this rule. First, those instances where we are
unconsciously seeking ruin in order to "bottom out"—as happens in many recov-
ery/reform narratives. The second exception reflects what is known as repetition
compulsion, such as when trauma victims unconsciously revisit situations that evoke
the original trauma through an unconscious impulse to heal. Such strategies are the
exception, however. For the most part, we hope to avoid misfortune and arrange our
lives accordingly.
4 For an example, see the film *Indiscreet* starring Cary Grant and Ingrid Bergman,
based on the play *Kind Sir* by Norman Krasna.

where Bruno, learning of Guy's bitter estrangement from his wife, preys on that vulnerability to manipulate him into a murder plot.

However, a great many misfortune stories reflect the randomness of life and the fact that terrible things can come seemingly out of nowhere. War stories and disaster-survival stories fall into this category. The kind of severe circumstances that arise in such situations force the character to pursue a variety of goals, some presented by necessity rather than want. In some cases, this means the original dream of life must be abandoned for something more attainable in the new circumstances. And yet it may also be true that the character's Yearning provides the "compass" that leads him toward right action:

- In Anthony Doerr's *All the Light We Cannot See*, young Werner Pfennig possesses a knack for electronic tinkering, made evident when he repairs a short-wave radio he and his sister find. Once properly fixed, it receives broadcasts from France designed to teach young students about science, and Werner feels an expansive sense of awe about the possibilities of scientific understanding, with its inherent power to reach across borders and transcend cultural differences. But when Germany invades Poland such dreams get sidelined. His skills are recognized as useful to the war effort, and he is recruited into the Wermacht. There he is obliged to track the sources of French Resistance radio broadcasts, and when he learns that one such success results in the death of a young girl, he comes to hate his talent and what it obliges him to do. When the Allies invade Normandy, he is sent to the coastal town of St. Malo to track down broadcasts emanating from that village. He meets the story's other main character, the blind girl, Marie-Laure LeBlanc, and learns that her uncle is not only responsible for the local Resistance broadcasts, but he was the man behind the science broadcasts Werner found so inspiring before the war. That sense of scientific wonder and promise that defined his dream of life before the war now provides a moral compass for what to do in the present. The fractured Desire line that his story followed due to the exigencies of the war gains a new, steadier direction once he taps into his Yearning and recovers a sense of what he wants his life to be.

EXERCISES

- Keeping with the two main characters from your WIP employed in the previous exercises in this chapter, how do their core goals in the story reflect their Yearning? How does success or failure serve to define that Yearning or bring it into sharper focus?
- In identifying the core goal for each character, also identify why they want it, how badly they want it, what they will risk to get it, what will be lost if they fail, and who else will be affected.
- How do the answers to the first two questions further clarify each character's dream of life—the kind of person she wants to be, the way of life she hope to live?
- For each character, how does the need to act force him to adjust to a sudden disequilibrium in the balance he has devised between Yearning and Resistance, his Pathological Maneuvers and his Persistent Virtues. How does that old equilibrium fail to solve the new problem(s) created by the opportunity or misfortune that obliges him to act?
- Which of the following alternatives best describes the situation for your characters at the story's outset:
  - Yearning clearly apprehended and fully embraced.
  - Yearning clearly apprehended but uncertainly embraced.
  - Yearning clearly apprehended but shunned.
  - Yearning vaguely apprehended but clarity sought.
  - Yearning vaguely apprehended and clarity pursued haphazardly.
  - Yearning vaguely apprehended and clarity avoided.
  - Yearning misapprehended or mistaken.
  - Yearning unidentified and unpursued.
- Does either character gain a better understanding of her Yearning by succeeding but with disappointing results? (Hint: What prompts the character to keep struggling despite her disillusioning success?)

- If the character is compelled to act because of an opportunity, how does that opportunity speak to a longing already present to some extent within the character, i.e., the character's dream of life?
- Does the opportunity speak to a mistaken or misunderstood longing? In what way? What happens?
- If the character is compelled to act because of a misfortune, how does the character's action mirror her Resistance—i.e., how does the misfortune threaten to increase the pain in the character's life, and thus test the character's previous strategies for minimizing that pain?
- If the misfortune that prompts the character to act is particularly cataclysmic or reflects the randomness of life, such as in war or disaster-survival stories, is a new horizon of hope and promise forged through the struggles in the story? If so, how is that new Yearning different from the one she harbored before? If not, how is it the same? Has she been able to hold on to the same dream of life despite the devastating misfortune and ensuing struggles? How? Why?

IV. MOTIVATING THE CHARACTER WHO IS RELUCTANT TO ACT

The preceding discussion has centered around what happens near the outset of a story that compels the character to act. But what if he feels no such compulsion?

The entire point of motivating a character tacitly assumes that, absent that motivation, he might well do nothing. This problem occurs not just at the story's outset, of course, but all along the way, especially as difficulties multiply, failures mount, doubts intensify, and disaster looms.

Our solution to this problem so far has been to find a way for the character to tap into her Yearning. And the way the character "taps into her Yearning" is simply to recognize it for what it is—her dream of life. Her reason for being.

But it's seldom that simple.

Given our discussion in chapters four and five concerning the forces of Resistance and the Pathological Maneuvers that result, it should come as little surprise that, when some characters are faced with genuine hardship or when confronted with something they know they want but feel inadequate or unprepared to pursue, they are likely to get stuck. They may have even made a practice of compromise, turning away or backing down, and have a drawer full of justifications for doing just that.[5]

Such is the general picture, but what you're facing right now is a particular character in a specific scene who feels reluctant to do anything meaningful to solve the unique problem he faces.

First, make sure it's the character's reluctance at issue, not the author's. Writing problems are personal problems, and a great many reluctant protagonists can be traced back to overly timid or risk-averse writers.

Second, analyze how the reluctance to act echoes in some way the character's history of avoidance, denial, cowardice, heartbreak, betrayal, illness, prejudice—the forces of Resistance you have identified and the Pathological Maneuvers she has created. Gain a good, firm understanding of why she has every reason not to act given who she has been and how she has lived her life up to that point.

Then give the character a good, hard shove—or, as we put it in chapter three, put a gun to her head or place a bagful of money just out of reach, figuratively or literally.

To jolt her out of her paralysis, you have to entice her to act or terrify her by what will likely happen if she doesn't. Open a door onto someplace so conspicuously better than where she now stands that the gravitational pull forward is irresistible. Either that, or show her that failing to act will cause such significant and undeniable harm—to her, to loved ones, to innocent strangers—that her horror at the foreseeable consequences of inaction serves like an inner convulsion propelling her into motion.

In other words, make the stakes apparent enough that non-action is no longer an option. What will be lost is so devastating, or what will be gained so invaluable, that the character feels she will not be able to live with herself if she doesn't do *something*.

---

5 A quote from Camus previously cited in chapter four is apropos here: "There is always a philosophy for a lack of courage."

Obviously, the likely consequences of any action are seldom that crystal clear, and the character will need to some degree to fly blind. But if the character remains reluctant to act, *bring the peril or the reward closer*—reduce the time available to make a decision, place the danger or reward nearer in physical space or within the realm of possibility, or make it matter more to the character or someone she cares about. The more a specific action speaks to identity—the kind of person the individual wants to be—or the welfare of those she loves, the more devastating the consequences of not doing it.

To make that decisive move, the character will need to call upon those Persistent Virtues you also explored, and which up to this point have existed in a state of relative equilibrium with her Pathological Maneuvers. Now, however, whatever crisis or sudden chance the character faces acts like a surge of adrenalin for those virtues.

"ANSWERING THE CALL" VS. "RISING TO THE OCCASION"

A character who has felt a sense of calling at an early age or even in adolescence (or one who has come to possess a reasonably firm sense of personal identity)—and whose Yearning will involve maintaining or serving that strong sense of self—will likely also have a relatively clear sense of purpose and some sort of moral code. The need to act in this sense very much resembles "answering the call." A reluctance to act on the part of such a character will not merely speak to fear or uncertainty of what he must do; he likely will also suffer doubts about what his sense of identity actually demands and whether he is indeed up to it. This can be profoundly affecting and dramatic, since it cuts to the core of the character's sense of self. The action doesn't just determine what will happen; it confirms or undermines who he is.

In contrast, a character with a more fluid, go-along-get-along identity, especially one faced with a random, out of-the-blue misfortune, will not necessarily suffer an identity crisis in the middle of all her other difficulties. Success or failure may ultimately affect the character's sense of self-worth or change how others view her, and knowing that may motivate her all the more, but any reluctance to act is likely based less on defining herself than fear of what she must do and the likely consequences. That's not a hard-and-fast rule, of course, and drama is always intensified when it incorporates issues of identity. But if the character overcomes a reluctance to act under these circumstances, where selfhood takes a back seat to circumstances, that decision will more closely resemble "rising to the occasion" than "answering the call."

The difference between "answering the call" and "rising to the occasion" lies principally in the direction from which the "gun to the head" is pointed. In the case of rising to the occasion, it comes primarily from the outside world. In the case of answering the call, it ultimately comes from within the character herself.

EXERCISES

- Take one of the main characters from your WIP, the protagonist would be best, and place her in a scene where she is reluctant to act.
- How is that reluctance anchored in self-doubt or even outright fear?
- Can she find a way to act by tapping into her Yearning—the kind of person she wants to be, the way of life she hopes to live? If not, why not?
- How does his reluctance to act echo the forces of Resistance that have impeded his pursuit of his Yearning in the past?
- How might you "put a gun to her head," figuratively or literally? (How can you appall her, scare her, even terrify her by what will happen if she doesn't act?)
- Alternatively, how might you open a door onto an opportunity he can't ignore?
- What are the stakes? How might you make them apparent enough that non-action is no longer an option? (Hint: Make what will be lost so devastating, or what will be gained so invaluable, that the character feels she will not be able to live with herself if she doesn't do *something*.)
- If the character remains reluctant to act, how might you *bring the peril or the reward closer*? For example, can you reduce the time

to make a decision, place the danger or reward nearer in physical space or within the realm of possibility, or make it matter more to the character or someone he cares about?

- How does the specific action in question speak to the character's sense of identity—the kind of person she wants to be—or the welfare of those she loves?
- Does the character's overcoming his reluctance to act more resemble "answering the call" or "rising to the occasion?" Why?

SUMMARY OF MAIN POINTS IN THIS CHAPTER

DESIRE DRIVES STORY

- Desire is created when *something happens* to disturb the status quo of the story world.
- That triggering occurrence typically takes one of two forms:
  - An opportunity arises: *Show the character what he wants and make him pursue it.*
  - A misfortune occurs: *Give the character what he wants then take it away*; or *Inflict on the character what he dreads and make him escape or defeat it.*
- Desire, by putting the characters into motion in pursuit of some objective, drives story.
- Conflict is Desire meeting some form of opposition.
- Conflict is central to story solely because it creates *tension*—i.e., will the character get what she wants or not?

DESIRE AND CHANGE

- To say "something happens" is to say that things change.
- It is likely, but not inevitable, that a change in circumstances should effect a change in your characters, if only in their understanding.
- To learn is to grow, and to grow is to change—and it is to this extent that all stories offer at least the opportunity for the character to change.

- Characters in genres where the principal action is external—mysteries, adventure stories, and action stories, for example—have no implicit need to change. Rather, these stories typically reveal a change in circumstances rather than the hero.
- When the protagonist changes, it's usually because the struggles he has faced have forged a different *understanding* of himself, his abilities, and/or his world, including the people in it.
- What we often refer to as change in a character normally points toward internal questions.
- However, in tragedy, this new self-awareness often comes too late to change the course of events.
- There are also cases where the change in understanding is not reflected in a change in *behavior*, and it's characters of that sort who are often (mis)identified as not having changed.
- The Steadfast Character's dramatic arc is premised precisely on his *refusal* to change, usually for one of two reasons.

  - He refuses to sacrifice an ideal or give up on a goal he believes he cannot live without.
  - He clings to the Pathological Maneuvers he uses to protect himself from the pain of life.

- This notion of "steadfast" glances past a key point, however. Though it might be said that the motives or behavior of such characters don't appreciably change, their emotions, insight, or attitude toward life does.
- Even in cases where characters seem to remain unchanged, often they have in fact refused the opportunity to change. Change isn't impossible, it's forsaken.
- Failure is a great motivator of change. If the failure has particularly severe consequences, or the setbacks encountered are especially painful, the character will be forced to ask: Why go on? Why not go back, give in, strike a bargain, accept defeat? He may ask, What's wrong with me? Why can't I do this? What is it about me that needs to change before I can get this right? The answers to such questions

expose who the character truly wants to be and the way of life he hopes to live, i.e., his Yearning.

- In the modern love story, what's keeping the lovers apart is each other. This means one or both characters at some point are obliged to ask themselves, *What do I need to change about myself, my life, or what I'm doing to get that person to say yes?* The setup implicitly dictates change.

- The "rule" that the opponent never changes basically reflects the fact this character is often conceived as an individual with a rigid personality disorder that by its nature resists change.

- However, the opponent can and often does change, especially in dramas where good is pitted against good.

- There are also stories that possess a plot technique known as the *double reveal*, where both the protagonist and the opponent learn something crucial from the other, and that insight changes their sense of self. This technique is not only common in love or other relationship stories but sometimes appears in tales of war and sports as well, where the adversaries gain a grudging respect for each other through their combat.

- Secondary characters can also change if they undergo a gauntlet of trials and struggles similar to the one suffered by the main characters. Though their dramatic function—mentor, ally, betrayer—suggests a certain fixedness, it's more in role than understanding. Their distinct personalities will determine the degree to which they do or don't change.

LINKING DESIRE TO YEARNING

- To create depth and complexity in the character, as well as enhance the stakes, her core goal in the story must somehow reflect her Yearning, so that success or failure serves to define her deepest longing and core identity—the person she longs to be, the way of life she hopes to live—and the ways in which this affects her connection to others.

- Simply knowing what the character wants is not enough. The reader also wants to know why she wants it, how badly she wants it, what she will risk to get it, what will be lost if she fails—all of which connects Desire to Yearning.

- It is through struggle and especially failure that the character learns, adapts, changes. The key element that guides her as she moves through her failures is a sense of direction she may barely recognize but which points her toward the kind of person she wants to be, the way of life she hopes to live: It is her Yearning.
- Desire, by forcing the character to act, also forces the character to adjust to a sudden disequilibrium in the balance he has devised between Yearning and Resistance, as revealed in the equilibrium between Pathological Maneuvers and Persistent Virtues.
- Since the old equilibrium suited different circumstances, it cannot help but perform inadequately in the new ones—otherwise your story is over.
- It is in recognizing the poor match between old behavior and new challenges that the character, step-by-step, becomes aware of what she genuinely hopes for as well as what is holding her back.
- The range of ways a character may be aware of his Yearning and Resistance at the story's outset also suggests a range of ways the story can develop once he is obliged to act.

  - Yearning clearly apprehended and fully embraced.
  - Yearning clearly apprehended but uncertainly embraced.
  - Yearning clearly apprehended but shunned.
  - Yearning vaguely apprehended but clarity sought.
  - Yearning vaguely apprehended and clarity pursued haphazardly.
  - Yearning vaguely apprehended and clarity avoided.
  - Yearning misapprehended or mistaken.
  - Yearning unidentified and unpursued.

- Yearning, if inadequately apprehended by the character, does not exist in some ideal form waiting to be recognized, like a shipwreck on the ocean floor. When her Yearning is not yet clear to the character, the story, by forcing her to act in pursuit of some objective, will also step-by-step clarify for her what it means to live in accordance with some sense of promise and hope. Yearning in this sense is created through struggle, not discovered.

- It is often only by experiencing what one doesn't want, either by failing in pursuit of the goal or succeeding but with unsatisfactory results, that the dream of life takes shape if only in opposition: *Whatever that dream might be, I know it isn't this.*
- An opportunity that compels the character to act speaks to a longing already present to some extent within the character.
- It is therefore wise, if obliging the character to act by introducing an opportunity, to spend some time reflecting on how that opportunity speaks to his dream of life—or distracts him from it.
- In contrast, stories that start with a misfortune present a distinctly different problem. It is not so much a question of linking the Desire to Yearning as having it echo the Resistance, since misfortune introduces the threat of increasing the pain in the character's life. The action will therefore test the character's previous strategies for minimizing that pain.
- However, a great many misfortune stories reflect the randomness of life, and the fact that terrible things can come seemingly out of nowhere, like war stories and disaster-survival stories. Here especially the character's Yearning is forged through the struggles of the story toward some freshly imagined horizon of hope and promise, especially when the misfortune is cataclysmic in nature.

MOTIVATING THE CHARACTER WHO IS RELUCTANT TO ACT

- When a character is reluctant to act, that reluctance is typically anchored in self-doubt or even outright fear; the character sees the challenge ahead as overwhelming, beyond her real powers, a recipe for disaster—for herself or others, or possibly both.
- One solution to this problem is to find a way for the character to tap into his Yearning—the kind of person he wants to be, the way of life he hopes to live.

- Given the forces of Resistance that have impeded her pursuit of her Yearning in the past, it will come as little surprise if she becomes paralyzed.
- To solve the problem in a particular scene, first make sure the aversion to act is actually the character's and not yours (the writer's). Next, analyze how the problem echoes in some way his history of avoidance, denial, cowardice, etc. After analyzing how the present echoes the past, put a gun to his head, figuratively or literally— appall him, scare him, even terrify him by what will happen if he doesn't act—or open a door onto a golden opportunity he simply cannot ignore. Make the stakes apparent enough that non-action is no longer an option. What will be lost is so devastating, or what will be gained so invaluable, that the character feels he will not be able to live with himself if he doesn't do *something*.
- If the character remains reluctant to act, *bring the peril or the reward closer*—reduce the time to make a decision, place the danger or reward nearer in physical space or within the realm of possibility, or make it matter more to the character or someone she cares about.
- The more a specific action speaks to identity—the kind of person the individual wants to be—or the welfare of those he loves, the more devastating the consequences of not doing it.
- A character with a firm sense of identity will likely also have a relatively clear sense of purpose and some sort of moral code. A reluctance to act on the part of such a character will not merely speak to fear of what she must do; she likely will also suffer doubts about what her sense of identity actually demands, and whether she is indeed up to it. The need to act in this sense very much resembles "answering the call."
- In contrast, a character with a more fluid, go-along-get-along identity will likely not suffer an identity crisis in the middle of all his other difficulties. If such a character overcomes a reluctance to act, that decision will more closely resemble "rising to the occasion" than "answering the call."

7

Weaving a Life

←————————————————————————————————→

The Three Levels of Dramatic Action

The cause doesn't have to be righteous and the battle doesn't have to be winnable; but over and over throughout history, men have chosen to die in battle with their friends rather than to flee on their own and survive.

—Sebastian Junger, *War*

I. STORY'S THREE-TIER STRUCTURE

Characters experience Lack, Yearning, Resistance, and Desire on three distinct levels:

Internal Questions: These involve how the character views himself, addressing questions of integrity, dignity, purpose, worth.

External Challenges: These reveal the character's capabilities and involve tasks in pursuit of a specific goal, often in the face of great odds—catch the killer, rescue the child, escape the disaster, find the way home.

Interpersonal Relationships: These involve connections with others, whether positive or negative, and address whether those connections are growing stronger or weaker. They possess elements of both the internal (because they often reflect how the character views himself) and external (because they involve other people).

Interpersonal relationships in particular also provide an excellent means for:

- Raising the stakes (making success matter to more than just the protagonist or opponent);
- Creating competition for the same goal;
- Eliciting empathy—we care about those who care about others.

At some point as you're planning or reworking your story, you should take a moment to analyze which level of dramatic action you intend to emphasize: External, Internal, or Interpersonal. This is because the various levels of dramatic action reveal different aspects of character, and they elicit different responses from readers and audiences:

- External challenges typically reflect the character's Desire. They create curiosity—i.e., about the limits of the character's prowess and willfulness. They ask the question, Is the character capable of achieving his goal? They can also inspire admiration because of his skill, determination, persistence, etc.
- Internal and interpersonal struggles typically reflect the character's Yearning. They create empathy, i.e., concern for the character, and elicit an emotional response from readers and audiences.

IMPORTANT POINT: As the rest of this chapter will demonstrate, *none* of these levels of dramatic action act independently of the others in truly compelling fiction.

EXERCISE

- Return to the WIP you have used in preceding chapters. Identify the three levels of struggle that at least two of the main characters face:

  - What is the character's external goal? What does the pursuit of that external goal reveal about the character's prowess or willfulness?
  - What internal questions regarding meaning, worth, identity, integrity, authenticity, or purpose does that outer goal address— i.e., how does the Desire speak to the character's Yearning?
  - What interpersonal relationship(s) influence or affect the other two struggle threads?
  - How do the internal and interpersonal struggles elicit empathy for your main character(s)?

II. STORIES THAT CONTAIN ONLY ONE OR TWO STRUGGLE LEVELS

Stories can proceed along merely one or two levels of struggle, and many do.

TRAVELING ANGEL STORIES

As mentioned previously, here the protagonist travels from place to place (or merely situation to situation in a single locale), solving problems.

What change occurs does not affect the traveling angel so much as the others he encounters and the circumstances that need to be rectified:

- The grieving family that needs to learn how to live and love again.
- The persnickety scold who needs to rediscover the ability to forgive.
- The town run by gangsters that needs to get "cleaned up."

One often finds such characters in mysteries, Westerns, and crime or action stories, where the external action drives the plot. If internal or interpersonal questions arise, they tend to affect the other characters more profoundly than the protagonist, who is there primarily to solve the problem afflicting those other characters.

In the sentimental subcategory of this genre—Mary Poppins, Amélie, Toro-san—interpersonal struggles drive the plot, but in a unique way. It's the protagonist's concern *for others* that moves the story forward. Whatever relationships she forms will often only be temporary, for the traveling angel is fated to fix others' problems, then move on, not enjoy a deep abiding connection of her own. That kind of relationship is typically reserved for characters in the next genre we will discuss.

LOVE STORIES

This category includes all stories of profound personal connection, not just between romantic partners but friends ("buddy stories"), siblings, children and parents, students and teachers, and so on. Here the external challenge and the interpersonal relationship are typically one and the same—the external goal is to connect with the loved one—except where the following occurs:

- The suitor has a rival.
- The suitor needs (or believes he needs) to meet some external test to win the loved one's affection.
- Some other external source of conflict or opposition presents itself, such as:
  - Racial, religious, or class anomie.
  - Family disapproval of the relationship.
  - Money troubles, professional demands, official duties, etc.

Absent this sort of external difficulty, the main characters' struggles are chiefly internal and interpersonal.

Specifically, one or both characters must recognize and rectify whatever inner Weakness, Wound, Limitation, or Flaw is ruining their chances at winning the affection of the other character. The inner and interpersonal are intrinsically linked, and the story concerns only these two levels of dramatic action.

There are also interesting hybrids, such as the French film *The Intouchables*, which combines the traveling angel trope with the love story, in this instance a story of friendship. The angel character, an African working-class caretaker, is himself a flawed human being, and he and his foil, the stuffy Gallic bourgeois in his care, end up changing each other.

Important Point: There is nothing obliging a traveling angel story or a love story from possessing all three levels of struggle. The instances where love stories also contain an external struggle were just mentioned. And the traveling angel may form deep, emotional, interpersonal connections to those she decides to help or protect, and this may in turn affect and even transform her internal sense of identity, purpose, or worth. The choice is yours, not obliged by the form.

EXERCISES

- Is your WIP a Traveling Angel story—e.g., a detective story, a Western, or a story where an itinerant stranger comes to town and solves others' problems?
  - If so, is it more action-oriented, e.g., a Western, mystery, or crime story? Is more than an external struggle thread in play— e.g., does the character have a meaningful relationship with another character? How does that affect or influence his pursuit of his external goal? Does the external action in some way affect the character's sense of identity, integrity, purpose, or worth?
  - If it is more the sentimental variety, where the protagonist heals wounds and mends interpersonal bonds, is there some external goal or internal question that is also addressed? Specifically, do the interpersonal connections in some way affect the protagonist's sense of identity, integrity, purpose, or worth? If so, how?
- Is your WIP a love story?
  - If so, how do the internal and interpersonal struggles affect and influence each other—i.e., how does solving the internal problem help solve the interpersonal difficulty?
  - Is there also an external struggle? How does it affect or influence the other two struggle threads?

III. INTERWEAVING STRUGGLE LEVELS

Whenever more than one struggle level exists, you need to weave them together so that solving a problem on one level has material repercussions on the other. A satisfying conclusion to the story requires the integrated resolution of all three levels of dramatic action.

For example, as noted above with love stories, solving the internal problem is necessary to mastering the interpersonal one; and the interpersonal relationship is the impetus for the character to face and resolve his internal issues.

If the struggle threads merely run parallel—going along at the same time but not affecting or influencing one another—they will likely feel disconnected and possibly undermine one another. Worse, they may come to feel gratuitous, and test the reader's or audience's patience.

A classic example is the attempt to "humanize" a detective by giving him family problems that have no impact whatsoever on the crime he's trying to solve, or dragooning a wife or daughter into the role of hostage to raise the stakes in a way that feels contrived.

Question No. 1: *If it's necessary to interweave the three lines of struggle for a character, why separate them in the first place? Why not just meld them all together from the start and keep it that way?*

As stated in chapter one, simplicity is an asset. By distinguishing three clear-cut struggle threads, we make it easier to see the distinct areas of longing and conflict that the character will face.

We can also make clearer decisions about which struggle threads to include and emphasize. Yes, we could simply mash this all together, but doing so all too often leads to muddled thinking about both motivation and action, and tends to confuse more than it clarifies.

That said, if in conceiving your character you can see the wholeness of her pursuit in a glance, and understand the interconnecting and often competing threads of her inner life, outer goals, and interpersonal connections and disconnections, by all means proceed. This is a skill eventually acquired by most accomplished writers.

Question No. 2: *It's all well and good to say one should interweave struggle threads, but how exactly does that happen?*

Typically, the character's pursuit of his external goal engenders a deeper understanding of who he is, what he is capable of, and what matters to him. By pointing him toward a desired end, it also implicitly defines the kind of future he wants, or at least can accept—including the type of person he needs to be to merit that future. This also deepens his understanding of who he loves and with whom he wants to share that future.

EXERCISES

- Pick two characters from your WIP. For each, identify their external goal. How will achieving that goal affect the character's sense of self? How will it change how others feel about him, or how he feels about someone else?

- How do each of these interwoven levels of concern actually influence and change the other two? For example, how does the character's changing sense of self affect how he feels about the other character, and how does that affect his motivation in his pursuit of the external goal?

IV. USING INTRINSIC LONGINGS TO INTERWEAVE STRUGGLE LEVELS

The natural interweave among levels of dramatic action can be seen more clearly by gaining a better understanding of the underlying motivations typical of each kind of longing.

Each level of dramatic action speaks to a specific set of inner needs, which represent partial representations or reflections of the character's Yearning. The following list is hardly exhaustive, but it should point out the kinds of internal longings that tend to motivate each particular type of struggle.

1. Internal Questions
    a. A need for a sense of truth, meaning, value, significance, purpose.
    b. A need for identity, authenticity, integrity, dignity, honor.
    c. A need for self-confidence, success, self-realization, fulfillment.

2. External challenges
    a. A need for safety, security, survival.
    b. A need for justice, peace.
    c. A need for adventure, challenge, freedom, power.

3. Interpersonal relationships
    a. A need to love and be loved.
    b. A need for belonging, respect, acceptance.
    c. A need for revenge or retribution.
    d. A need to be forgiven and given a second chance.

Notice how, in the second and third categories, the *internal* needs motivating the character's actions can only be gratified through success on the *external* or *interpersonal* level, respectively.

This is the simplest and most direct way of weaving the internal together with the external or interpersonal—realizing that even external goals and interpersonal connections reflect to underlying needs that speak to the individual's sense of self.

Secondly, the items in these categories are not mutually exclusive. Quite the contrary.

The person who craves adventure may do so purely for the adrenalin rush. Far more likely, she needs to define, test, and surpass her limits, to constantly challenge what is supposedly possible. This latter set of needs intrinsically speaks to issues of confidence, success, self-realization, and identity. The alpine climber isn't testing the mountain; she's testing herself.

Throw in the need for the climber to prove herself to someone else—her father, her coach, a lover, a competitor, an outright enemy—and you add an interpersonal struggle into the weave.

As noted earlier in this chapter, almost all love stories—whether they concern romantic partners, family, or friends—naturally involve internal questions.

- Am I worthy of the other person's love?
- How will earning the loved one's affection affect my understanding of my own value, even my purpose?
- How will it influence my self-confidence?
- Will it gratify my need for fulfillment—if not completely, at least significantly?

For a more detailed example, consider the following storyline:

A rural fire chief accused of incompetence for his mismanagement of a house fire in which three children died faces a second crisis when an out-of-control wildfire threatens his small community. Notice how the story interweaves deep-seated needs on three distinct levels:

- **External:** He must meet the challenge of the fire, and make sure the townspeople remain safe.
- **Internal:** The battle against the fire has the potential to redefine his sense of worth, competence, and purpose. Perhaps he was accused of cowardice in the earlier tragic incident; this challenge might allow him to prove his courage not just to others but to himself.
- **Interpersonal:** If he succeeds, he may finally earn (or at least deserve) the right to be forgiven by those who have blamed him for his previous failure, especially the parents of the children who died.

Take a moment to imagine how such a story might proceed. Can you see how, with every external action he takes to organize resources and fight the fire, the issues of forgiveness and self-worth are equally present, influencing his ability to function? As his sense of self wavers or solidifies, so does his confidence and capability to do his job. And as he succeeds or fails, others in the community will either stand with him in support or turn against him in condemnation, further affecting not just his sense of identity but his ability to protect them all.

In truly memorable portrayals, this is how the three struggle levels act in concert, influencing and reinforcing each other—*and that is how you weave the various levels of dramatic action together.*

This is also how you can begin to formulate the character's Yearning Horizon for the story as discussed in chapter three. We noted there the amorphous nature of the character's Yearning, since it is never really fulfilled in life but continues calling the individual to be greater, to do more. For the purposes of storytelling, however, this obliges us to identify a Yearning Horizon, a partial fulfillment of the greater Yearning that the character strives to achieve within the confines of the plot.

From the various needs identified at the beginning of this section, a complex, interrelated set of needs, woven together, creates this Horizon, which may take symbolic form—like Ahab's white whale or Gatsby's green light—always with the understanding that beyond this Horizon lies the greater Yearning beckoning the individual to continue in his quest to become a better person, to lead a more fulfilling life.

EXERCISES

- Return to your responses for the exercises at the end of the previous section. How might you change those responses given a deeper understanding of how external, interpersonal, and internal longings naturally interweave, influencing each other in every scene in the story?
- How would you define the character's Yearning Horizon given your preceding answer? Go back to your answers to the exercise in Chapter 3, the section titled "Bringing Yearning Down to Story Size." Compare your answers here to the ones you submitted there. How has your understanding of the Yearning Horizon changed in light of this chapter's discussion?

V. INTERWEAVING STRUGGLE LEVELS— TWO EXAMPLES

Let's now consider two specific examples, one from literature and film, the other from television:

"THE DEAD"

James Joyce's "The Dead" is not only a great short story but was brilliantly adapted for film by the iconic director John Huston and his son, Tony Huston, who wrote the script.

The setting is the annual Christmas party thrown by Kate and Julia Morkan, the spinster aunts of Gabriel Conroy. Though the story embraces not just family but community, its focus lies primarily on Gabriel and his wife, Gretta, an outwardly happy and affectionate couple.

Tensions lie beneath the surface, however. Gabriel's mother opposed the marriage, because she saw Gretta, who comes from the rural and largely impoverished west of Ireland, as inferior to her son in social standing and education. And though Gretta profoundly misses the west country and hopes to visit there soon, Gabriel harbors no such desire. An anglicized Irishman, he is content to remain in Dublin, teaching literature and writing book reviews for a conservative newspaper.

But Gabriel's alienation extends beyond his sense of what it means to be Irish. He is riddled with self-doubt and worries endlessly about how the speech he has prepared, to be given near the end of dinner, will be received.

As it turns out, his speech is a grand success, and he glows with pride as the evening comes to a close. However, as he goes to collect Gretta so they can leave, he finds her transfixed on the stair, listening to a young man singing "The Lass of Aughrim." He notices that her cheeks are colored and her eyes are shining, and he interprets this as a sign that tonight, at their hotel, they might at last rekindle the warmth of their marriage.

But when they get to their room, Gabriel finds Gretta remote and cold. When he inquires why, she mentions the song and begins to cry, then tells him the story: When she lived in Galway, a boy she knew named Michael Furey used to sing that song. Gabriel is at first jealous, thinking Gretta longs to reunite with the young man, but she tells him Michael is dead. The night before she was to go away to the convent school where her parents had enrolled her, he stood outside her window in the freezing rain despite his tuberculosis. She begged him to go home, but he refused, saying he preferred to die, which he did within a week.

News of such a passionate love makes Gabriel feel ridiculous and petty, and he shrinks before the knowledge of how meager a part he has played in Gretta's life. And yet, as he lies awake with Gretta sleeping beside him, he moves from despair to a state of "generous tears," and he hopes for a love like Michael Furey's. "Better to pass boldly into that other world, than fade and wither dismally with age. … The time had come for him to set out on his journey westward."

Gabriel's *external challenge*—to deliver his speech impressively—is part of the larger overall goal on the part of Kate and Julia to ensure the party is a success. Thus already we see an interweaving of external and interpersonal—Gabriel's successful achievement of his external goal will also serve to please his aunts, whom he loves dearly.

The speech is also meant to bolster his self-confidence. That need for self-confidence forms his *internal question*—and notice how it influences the other two struggle threads. It infects the whole of his fretting over his speech and his worries over the increasing emotional distance in his and Gretta's marriage, which is the *interpersonal relationship* most at issue in the story.

But his internal struggle also involves issues of authenticity—his love and loyalty for Ireland are not only questioned by one of the guests, but his ambivalence goes to the core of his difficulties with Gretta, who loves and longs for the west country where England's influence is felt the least, and the old ways maintain.

His external struggle ends in success, but that only provides Gabriel with false confidence. That confidence is dashed in the story's climax when he learns the real reason Gretta was so moved by the song she heard. His lack of self-worth deepens, forcing him into a dark night of the soul in which he resolves to live his life with a greater sense of purpose and passion, with the hope, however tenuous, of this rekindling the warmth between him and Gretta.

BREAKING BAD

For our second example, let's consider the five-season TV series *Breaking Bad*.

Walter White is a brilliant chemist who once had sterling prospects, but when his girlfriend left him for his business partner, he sold his interest in their venture, which was based largely on Walt's research, for a paltry $5,000. The company went on to make billions, but his former friend and lover never credited him. Walt moved to Albuquerque, married, and began raising a family while working as a high school chemistry teacher, supplementing his meager pay with part-time work at a local carwash.

At age fifty, Walt is diagnosed with inoperable Stage III lung cancer. Desperate to provide for his family given his impending death, he makes the bold, reckless decision to manufacture crystal meth, enlisting a former student, Jesse Pinkman, to help make and market the product.

Walt's external struggle is to sell enough methamphetamine to ensure his family's financial security. By definition, it weaves together the external and interpersonal struggle threads. But the fact he must keep what he is doing secret, combined with the danger it invites into his life, alters those interpersonal relationships in significant ways.

Even with all the external challenges and disasters and the interpersonal chaos his decision entails, it's Walt's internal struggle that drives the story. As he grows in expertise, he not only becomes more self-confident, his very identity changes. He transforms from a mild-mannered man who accepts his fate into a ruthless kingpin who demands that everyone—including the friends who sold him out for $5,000 and the family that supposedly motivates his criminal turn—acknowledge that he is the very best at what he does, a man deserving of not just respect but fear.

As each of the preceding examples indicates, the external struggle is often the easiest to identify and the simplest to outline; it drives the outer action of the story. It is often influenced if not motivated by interpersonal considerations, which alone or combined with internal questions often deliver the most meaningful and profoundly affecting aspects of the story. If the three levels of the story do not work in concert, however, the impact of each is undermined.

Step-by-step through the story, each distinct aspect of the overall struggle—inner, interpersonal, and external—affects and influences the other. Regardless of what form the outer object of desire might take, whether it's a cherished loved one or a murderer brought to justice, overcoming the resistance required in its pursuit presents the character with a transformative opportunity: to face herself, her decisions, and her life more honestly. This is typically how the internal and external struggles weave together. The character does not exist in a universe of one, however. Her outer actions and inner transformation cannot help but affect her relationships to others, just as those relationships will motivate her actions and influence her sense of self.

EXERCISE

- Take a favorite novel, story, film, or TV series and perform the same kind of analysis just conducted with "The Dead" and *Breaking Bad*. Pay particular attention to how the various struggle levels crucially influence each other and how they resolve at the end.

SUMMARY OF MAIN POINTS IN THIS CHAPTER

- All stories potentially possess three levels of dramatic action: Internal, External, and Interpersonal.

  - External challenges elicit curiosity regarding the character's abilities and willfulness, and can inspire admiration for the character's skills and virtues.
  - Internal questions address the character's sense of identity, purpose, and worth.
  - Interpersonal relationships concern the character's connection or disconnection with others.

- Internal and interpersonal struggles inspire empathy.
- Not all stories include all three struggle threads. Two notable examples are: traveling angel stories and love stories. These story types in no way exclude all three struggle threads, but they don't require them either.
- Distinguishing among the three distinct story threads allows us to identify the distinct areas of longing and conflict each level requires, and thus see more clearly how each affects and influences the others.
- To interweave struggle threads, think of how accomplishing the external goal speaks to the character's sense of self—his identity, integrity, sense of worth or purpose—and how achieving the goal will affect a specific relationship or how another person or persons view him.
- Each level of struggle speaks to a specific set of inner needs. However, these unique inner needs do not act in isolation, but rather influence and affect each other in every action the character takes throughout the story. Interwoven in this way, they form the Yearning Horizon, i.e., the partial reflection of the greater Yearning that the character strives to fulfill within the context of the story.
- The simplest and most direct way of weaving the internal together with external or interpersonal is to recognize that external goals speak to underlying questions regarding the individual's sense of self and naturally affect the character's relationships with others.

Part Two

Developing a Deeper Understanding

If I try to seize this self of which I feel sure, if I try to define
and to summarize it, it is nothing but water slipping through
my fingers. I can sketch one by one all the aspects it is able to
assume, all those likewise that have been attributed to it, this
upbringing, this origin, this ardor or these silences, this nobility
or this vileness. But aspects cannot be added up.

—Albert Camus, *An Absurd Reasoning*

8

Folly's Footsteps

←——————————————————————————→

Misguided Desires and Misbegotten Yearnings

> I know I am not a seeker after anything, and ambition in this world never stirred my heart once. Yet it seemed as if I was caught up by what came over the others, and they were the same. There was a great tug at the whole world, to go down over the edge, and one and all we were changed into pioneers, and our hearts and our lonely wills may have had nothing to do with it … it may have been the stars.
>
> —Eudora Welty, *The Robber Bridegroom*

> Be careful what you set your heart upon, for it will surely be yours.
> — James Baldwin, "Nobody Knows My Name"

I. INTRODUCTION

In the preceding chapters, we have explored how Yearning and Resistance interact to both define the character's dream of life and impede its fulfillment due to two deep-seated but antagonistic drives: the pursuit of the promise of life and protection from the pain of life.

Implicit in this exploration has been an understanding that at some point in the individual's life, his Yearning, his dream of life—the kind of person he wishes to be and the way of life he hopes to enjoy—becomes clear, recognizable, and worth pursuing.

No doubt some of you have harbored questions as to whether that is always or even often the case. Rather, in your own experiences, both as a sentient being and as an avid reader, the exact opposite more frequently seems to be true. As noted in this book's introduction, people not only often have no idea what they want, the ones who appear most confident on the matter are often the most misguided. And our examination in chapter six of the frequent disconnect between Yearning and Desire revealed similar instances of want and longing gone astray.

A great many stories are premised exactly on this kind of confusion or uncertainty—the character wants the right thing for the wrong reasons, the wrong thing for the right reasons, the right thing for noble reasons that lose their luster in the cold harsh light of day, the wrong thing for justifiable reasons that prove threadbare when the bill comes due, et cetera.

This confusion or uncertainty typically results either in the individual stumbling blindly toward something/anything that promises an improvement in his circumstances, or latching on first to some false idea of what he wants only to recognize, in suffering the consequences obliged by its pursuit, how badly he was mistaken. The revelation of that mistake, the learning curve that it defines, may lead the individual to a deeper, wiser understanding of his needs and wants, and what he must do to fulfill them. It also may lead to a new, equally misguided pursuit of something else deemed valuable, or it may instead create such a profound sense of misgiving and self-reckoning that he no longer trusts his instincts concerning what he wants or why he wants it. In this last instance, he may even, like Oedipus, feel compelled to tear out his lying eyes.

In a great many cases, it is precisely the forces of Resistance, by intensifying the need to minimize the pain of life—both physical wounds and those that result from shame, hatred, rejection, betrayal—that have undermined her belief in what she truly longs for and who she wants to be. That longing now seems like a mere pipe dream, something childish to be put aside. In the name of a more realistic outlook, she limits her ambitions; whether that limiting impulse reveals maturity or cowardice depends on the individual and the circumstances she has faced and continues to face. And the possibilities there, especially from the perspective of story, are virtually limitless.

It is precisely the innumerable ways that an individual can veer off-course in his pursuit of his deepest longings that makes any attempt at an exhaustive list of possibilities fruitless. In the third section of this chapter, we will present a number of examples from fiction, film, television, and the stage to show how the character's misbegotten Yearning or mistaken Desire creates the story, with the hope that these examples will help you understand the possibilities for your own stories.

Before presenting those examples, however, we are going to analyze a common understanding of character arc in fiction, and assess its strengths and weaknesses, the better to comprehend how what we've explored so far—the ongoing struggle between Yearning and Resistance once the character begins to pursue her Desire—tracks with this fundamental writing concept.

EXERCISES

- Focusing now primarily on your protagonist, or a second main character if you wish, identify at what point in the story the character clearly recognizes her Yearning: the kind of person she wants to be, the way of life she hopes to live. (If it happens before the story's outset, note as much.) What happened to clarify this Yearning?
- Has your character made a mistake as to what he wants, or why he wants it? Has he pursued the right thing for the wrong reasons? The wrong thing for the right reasons? As best you can, identify why he pursued something (Desire) that proved mistaken, or why he did so for motives (Yearning) he misconceived.

II. A COMMON VIEW OF CHARACTER ARC—ANALYSIS AND CRITIQUE

Some writing guides[1] use the mistaken understanding of Yearning and/or Desire described above to chart out a standard character arc. Generally speaking, that arc observes the following format:

- The Protagonist enters the story in a state of Lack, which combines both her ambitions and frustrations, her joys and heartbreaks, into a way of viewing the world and her life. (In our terminology, it is the ultimate effect of the conflict between Yearning and Resistance.)

---

1 See in particular *The Hero's 2 Journeys* by Michael Hauge and Christopher Vogler; and *Creating Character Arcs* by K.M. Weiland.

- Something happens that prompts the Protagonist to act—specifically, it creates a problem he needs to solve.
- The Protagonist's state of Lack creates a mistaken understanding of the problem, what's needed to solve it, or both.[2] This misunderstanding is rooted in the character's "backstory wound" or fundamental resistance to change.
- By pursuing this mistaken understanding, the Protagonist takes many false steps, wanders down blind alleys, suffers many setbacks, and otherwise endures a series of failures, near misses, or half successes that leave the core problem of the story unsolved.
- This series of missteps and setbacks ultimately leads to a moment of such drastic failure, often including the death of a loved one or an ally or the prospect of death for the Protagonist herself, that it seems like total defeat is at hand. In the resulting "dark night of the soul," in which the Protagonist searches her heart and mind for one last solution to the story's core problem, she experiences an insight that reveals the nature of her original mistaken understanding. This may include a greater awareness of her own personal investment in that misunderstanding, i.e., why it seemed so true and convincing and why she embraced it so wholeheartedly.[3]
- This new awareness will prompt a decision by the Protagonist to change methods, change allies, and/or change himself in order to get one last chance to solve the problem. From that point forward, the question at the heart of the story will no longer be, What must be done? That is settled, at least as far as the Protagonist can determine at that point. The core question from that point forward becomes, Will the Protagonist succeed? That question will be answered in the climax.

---

2 This mistaken understanding of the story's core problem or how to go about solving it is sometimes referred to as the "Misperception" or the "Lie." It is also often what is implicitly referred to when writers are advised to make what the character needs different from what he wants, i.e., what she wants is based on a misunderstanding of what she truly needs—or in our terminology, yearns for.
3 This revealing moment of self-awareness is often called, not surprisingly, the "change-or-die moment."

The Protagonist may of course have more than one moment of transformative insight in the course of her numerous missteps and failures and partial successes. The key such insight, the one that prompts the greatest change, technically can appear anywhere in the story, though it usually appears two-thirds or three-quarters of the way through the plot; otherwise the reader or audience may begin to wonder, if the Protagonist possesses sufficient insight to make a decision as to what should be done, why it is taking her so long to do it? A reluctant hero's dallying—or inept hero's bungling—can be endured only so long.

The answer in such situations usually lies not in the difficulty of knowing what to do or lacking confidence in oneself but rather the number or severity of the obstacles in the character's path, i.e., the difficulty of the task or the ferocity of the opposition he faces from other characters. That said, one needs to be wary of merely stacking up dragons before the castle. Repetition undermines tension, and the reader or audience will sit through only so many struggles of similar type before growing restless.

This is why, normally, the greater amount of narrative time and space is spent depicting the Protagonist's struggle to understand the problem, overcome her doubts as to what should be done, with whom, and whether she is capable of doing it; subdue the internal forces holding her back from the challenge of positive change; and devise a plan for going forward that stands a decent chance of success. That effort offers the prospect of greater variety in action, emotion, and reflection, thus providing broader opportunity for variation in scene and thus surprise.

The preceding outline of a generic character arc enjoys the advantage of both sufficient clarity and flexibility to prove adaptable to most story types.

However, by focusing on *misunderstanding* as the factor leading the character astray in his attempt to solve the core story problem, this methodology suggests that his error is fundamentally conceptual, i.e., one of belief or perception.

As we saw in chapter five, however, where we explored Pathological Maneuvers and Persistent Virtues, the character's problem at the story's outset goes beyond what she thinks; it is embedded in her *behavior.* Certainly how the character interprets her problem is part of that behavior, but it also encompasses how she treats others, how she acts under duress, how she responds to frustration, anxiety, uncertainty, confrontation, terror—as well as how she handles kindness, assistance, trust, and support from others.

Furthermore, as we saw in chapter four when examining the forces of Resistance, we saw how it is seldom the case that a single factor accounts for the character's problem with his past. Rather, whatever Weaknesses, Wounds, Limitations, Opposition/Obligations, or Flaws he possesses often interact, influencing and enhancing one another. Amplifying that point, as we observed at several junctures, pinning a character's behavior to a single factor tends to diminish him in the audience's or reader's eyes. Rather, whatever problem he faces has to be seen to emerge from the whole of his personality.

Finally, returning once again to chapter five, we saw how the character's various moments of helplessness typically reveal a thematic thread that helps to identify his core problem. This is perhaps the best, most complete, and most organic way of identifying the "misperception," and doing so in a fashion that goes beyond merely how the character thinks or feels. Instead, it incorporates life-changing moments and the habitual behavior that resulted from them, cohering into a way of life that melds Pathological Maneuvers and Persistent Virtues into a coherent (if maladaptive) way of being in the world.

As long as by *misperception* we include this broader concern not just with interpretation but behavior, the interweaving of influences, and the full complexity of her nature, incorporating not just her thoughts or feelings but her physical reactions and habitual behaviors and moral worldview, the standard character arc outlined above can serve our purposes.

Incorporation of behavior into our understanding of what constitutes the character's Lack—understanding that the sense of emptiness, incompleteness, malaise, boredom, etc., is rooted not just in attitude but grounded in behavior created by the conflict between pursuit of the promise of life and protection from the pain of life—also permits a greater range of dramatic depiction, i.e., a clearer, more compelling, and more concise means of showing the character engaged with the world at every stage of the story. Rather than have the character think through his problems or reflect on how he has changed, we can demonstrably *show* that change in the way he acts—the resentful introvert reaches out to another outcast with understanding kindness; the embittered lone wolf at last submits himself to the discipline of the group; the arrogant, hyper-competitive hotshot steps out of the limelight, surrendering it to someone more deserving.

When conceiving of the narrative arcs of your story's main characters, don't limit yourself to how they think or feel about themselves and their world. Imagine as fully and concretely as possible, using the techniques outlined in chapters three through five, how they behave at the story's outset and how that behavior has changed, if at all, at the end. If it hasn't changed, why not? Has the character rejected the opportunity to change? Is her behavior outwardly the same but inwardly reflective of a deeper understanding of her situation and herself?

The more you can ground the character's predicament in behavior, not merely thought or feeling, the greater the opportunity to dramatize his struggle and transformation. This is not to denigrate inner life—it is one of the novel's preeminent advantages as a storytelling medium. For those writing plays or scripts, however, focusing on behavior should be embraced not just because it is unavoidable but because of its unique advantages, as it is for novelists who intend to rely more on drama than voice or narrative exposition to tell their tales.

EXERCISES

- Analyze your story in terms of the standard character arc outlined above. How does your story fit? How does it not fit? In the latter case, analyze just how it doesn't conform and why.
- Given your previous work on Yearning, Resistance, Persistent Virtues, and Pathological Maneuvers, how would you define your Protagonist's "misconception" as the need to act becomes inescapable—i.e., which habits of behavior will assist and which

will impede her ability to solve the core problem she faces? If the core problem remains unclear, start with the initial problem and work your way forward to successive ones as she "succeeds through failure."

- Can you see a way to show whatever change the protagonist experiences—or rejects, or bungles—in a depiction of his behavior at the outset juxtaposed against his behavior at the end? If his behavior remains the same despite the gauntlet of conflicts and challenges he has faced, has his understanding of himself, his world, or his behavior changed? If not, why?

III. ILLUMINATIVE EXAMPLES

As noted at the end of Section I of this chapter, there are countless ways that an individual can err in his pursuit of what she believes she needs or wants. Accordingly, rather than make a futile attempt at a comprehensive list of possibilities, we'll instead explore a number of examples from fiction, film, television, and the stage that reveal how such missteps generate story, with the hope they will provide guidance on how to create similar difficulties in your own work.

BURIED YEARNING AND MISGUIDED DESIRE LEADING TO TRANSFORMATION

Michael Clayton

This story tracks well with the common character arc outlined above, which is why we will spend so much time analyzing it. The main character has buried his true Yearning beneath a cynical dismissal of what he truly believes and the kind of man he hopes to be, and accordingly pursues mistaken methods to pursue an illicit objective until circumstances force him to face himself, his actions, and his situation honestly.

In the film—written and directed by Tony Gilroy—Michael Clayton, the protagonist, possesses a moral failing that lies at the center of his narrative arc. Once a key litigator with the Queens District Attorney's Office, he is now a "fixer" at KBL, one of the world's largest, most well-respected law firms. He is the go-to guy for helping both his fellow lawyers at the firm and their wealthy clients shirk responsibility for any scandalous harm they've caused. Thus he not only shares in but enables their moral failings (Flaw). He also has a gambling problem, which he is trying to get under control (Weakness). This adds an ironic element to his backstory issues since luck lies beyond responsibility—it is one thing a fixer can't fix—but it also reflects an obsession with "being in the game." His core longing, which he only vaguely recognizes at the outset of the story, is to put aside forever the role of moral "janitor" and reclaim, by finally accepting responsibility for who he is and what he does, some semblance of self-respect (Yearning).

In three brief scenes, we observe the core concerns of Michael's world at the outset of the story:

- He collects his son, Henry, from his ex-wife's house, and drives him to school.
- He meets with a loan shark to whom he owes $75,000 for a hard-money loan he used to finance a restaurant with his brother, Tim, who through drink and drugs drove the business into ruin. He asks the loan shark for time and learns that's not an option.
- At his office, Michael puts out fires—an associate being shaken down by a "motivated" stripper ex-girlfriend; a corporate client facing a damning exposé. Meanwhile, rumors swirl—KBL is about to be acquired by a British firm, and he doesn't know if he will still have a job if the merger goes through.

Karen Crowder, general counsel for U/North (Opponent), is giving an interview when interrupted by an emergency. Arthur Edens, the lead counsel in KBL's defense of U/North in a multi-billion-dollar wrongful death litigation, stripped down naked in the middle of a deposition in Milwaukee.

Michael gets on a plane to meet with Arthur and put out the fire (Desire/Objective). The U/North case has created a crisis of conscience for Arthur. Michael responds that the "crisis" is Arthur's falling off his meds—he's bipolar. Arthur refuses to renounce his newfound clarity;

Michael is equally resolute. This impasse poses the fundamental story question: *Will Michael recognize the legitimacy of Arthur's crisis of conscience and allow it to change his own life?*

Karen learns Arthur was in possession of a highly damning internal memo, one that clearly implicates U/North in manufacturing an herbicide they knew could kill people, but the retooling of their manufacturing process would be prohibitively expensive. Fearing what other damage might lie in wait, she calls her own "janitors," a pair of security contractors who make Michael look like a lightweight. Meanwhile, Arthur vanishes from the Milwaukee hotel room.

Karen discusses the curious appearance in Arthur's possession of the damning memo with KBL lead partner Marty Bach, Michael's boss and in-house protector. With a merger looming, Marty cannot risk damaging the firm's standing further—Arthur's recklessness needs to be controlled.

Michael tells Marty Bach and Barry, another KBL partner, that Arthur is back in New York but won't answer calls. Barry curtly tells Michael to get the situation "under control." Meanwhile, Arthur wanders Times Square, ecstatic in his mania, while one of Karen Crowder's security ops, known simply as Verne, follows along in the crowd. The other, Ikers, plants surveillance devices in Arthur's Tribeca loft and reviews his medications. Later, Verne and Ikers listen in as Arthur calls one of the plaintiffs in the U/North case, a young Wisconsin woman named Anna with whom he has fallen in love and who helped crystallize his moral awakening.

In the midst of this disaster, Michael asks Marty for a loan to pay his restaurant debt. Marty is his meal ticket—if the merger goes through and Marty leaves, Michael is at the mercy of Barry and others who feel uncomfortable with what he does. He's forty-five and broke, having wasted his walkaway money on the restaurant. He wants to return to litigation. Marty responds that anyone can go to trial, what Michael does is a unique "niche" and he's brilliant at it. If he does his job, controls Arthur, in a week everyone at the firm "will be reminded of his infinite value"—because what Arthur has done is cancer, and everything and everyone is vulnerable. *Here, Michael's "protector," whom we've already* seen conspiring with Karen Crowder to contain the damage Arthur has created, continues in the role of betrayer, undermining Michael's desire to leave his morally corrosive work and do something honorable.

Michael finally finds Arthur, clearly still manic, outside his loft. Michael tries to explain that if he continues undermining U/North they'll "cut him off at the knees." He lets it slip that he knows Arthur has spoken with Anna, and Arthur assumes rightly his phone is bugged but wrongly that Michael is involved. Arthur accuses Michael of being "a bag man not a lawyer." Wounded by Arthur's remark, Michael says, "I'm not the enemy." Arthur responds, "Then who are you?" *This scene, midway through the story, defines Michael's key identity issue, forcing him to reflect on who he is and what he's doing.*

Aware his phone is tapped, Arthur reads over the phone the contents of the smoking gun document Karen Crowder was stunned to find in his possession—a reckless dare. Verne confers with Karen on how to proceed. In clumsy code they attempt to reach agreement, both not wanting to state the obvious openly: Arthur must be killed with nothing implicating U/North.

At a birthday party for their father, Michael speaks to his older brother, Gene, a detective in Queens. Michael can barely contain his rage over the bar. Gene intimates their brother Tim's not the only one with a problem. Michael fires back that he hasn't placed a sports bet in a year, hasn't been at the tables in ten months. He says his gamble was the bar, and Tim wiped him out.

As Arthur is leaving his loft, he's intercepted by Verne and Ikers who with cold efficiency drug him, kill him, and meticulously arrange it to look like a suicide.

As Michael is leaving his father's house with his son, Henry, Tim shambles up. Tim knows how badly he ruined things and tries to apologize, but Michael is still furious. In the car, he sees that Henry is upset. He tells him he will never be like his uncle Tim, wondering what's going to fall next from the sky. The unspoken message, however, given Michael's own gambling problems and moral failings, is that it's not just Tim's example that is poisonous. Michael is failing his son. Then his cell phone rings, and he learns of Arthur's death.

Michael meets with the detective on Arthur's case. The downstairs neighbors reported overflowing water. The cops found pills everywhere. The apartment is now sealed; no one but police can enter until the toxicology report comes back, which could take weeks.

At an impromptu wake, Michael meets with Marty. They can't believe it's suicide—no note, and Arthur "couldn't take a piss without leaving a memo"—and yet an accident also makes no sense: Why stuff down pills when only hours before he was blissed out from *not* being medicated? Barry interrupts, says Karen Crowder sees "a window" and U/North wants to settle.

Remembering Arthur's fondness for Anna, the Wisconsin farmgirl plaintiff, Michael calls to notify her of Arthur's death. Instead, he learns Arthur invited her to New York and then stranded her at La Guardia. At Anna's motel, Michael intuits from what Anna tells him that Arthur was right, his phone was bugged. Alarmed by what he's learned, Michael goes to his brother Gene to get a replacement seal so he can visit Arthur's loft. Michael enters the loft, unaware that Verne and Ikers are watching. Michael finds a receipt from a copy center and is putting it in his pocket when police, called by Verne, arrive and arrest him.

Gene collects Michael from jail. Michael asks who called 9-1-1. He was quiet, the apartment below was empty. Gene is furious. He's had to pull some serious strings, his pension is at risk if he's found out. He tells Michael to drop it. It never happened. Michael keeps arguing and the two brothers go toe-to-toe. Gene says, "All these cops think you're a lawyer. Then you got all these lawyers thinking you're some kind of cop. You've got everybody fooled, right? Everybody but you. You know exactly what you are." *This is the second time Michael's identity, his moral center, is challenged by someone close to him.*

Michael goes to the copy shop listed on the receipt he found at Arthur's. He finds that Arthur ordered three thousand copies of the smoking gun memo. He takes one box of one hundred, pays the clerk $50 to hold onto the rest and leaves. Ikers is standing in line behind him.

Karen Crowder and the rest of their legal team are approaching the KBL offices to go over the settlement. Karen gets a call from Verne, who is standing across the street. He shows her one of the copies Arthur had made, asks if she knows a Michael Clayton, and then says, "We have a situation."

Michael goes to see Marty with a copy of the memo and asks, "What would U/North do if they thought Arthur was going public?" Marty responds, "They're doing it." If the settlement falls apart, U/North is withholding $9 million in fees and suing KBL for malpractice, effectively destroying the firm. Marty has an $80,000 check for Michael that is dependent on that not happening. Barry makes an even uglier point: Given what Michael knows about everyone in the firm, his asking for $80,000 feels like a shakedown. He demands a confidentiality agreement that's bulletproof and retroactive. Marty and Barry head off to meet Karen Crowder. Michael is left behind, holding his check in one hand, Arthur's memo in the other. He has a choice to make.

In many stories, this is where the character has his dark night of the soul, reflecting deeply on what he has done, who he has become, and why it seems to get him no closer to what he wants most from his life. This is where the character often turns from the darkness toward the light. Michael chooses a different path. He decides to abandon his pursuit of the truth and avenge Arthur; instead, he reverts to form and takes the money. Once again, he helps the guilty slide. He goes to the loan shark with a check for the $75,000 he owes—the man is stunned to receive the whole amount and wonders what Michael did to get it— then heads to a Chinatown gambling den, completing his reversion to the Pathological Maneuvers that defined him at his worst.

Michael suffers mockery from one of the other gamblers who remembers him from a previous night when he lost his shirt. Meanwhile, outside, Ikers is planting a bomb in Michael's car. In the middle of the card game, Michael gets a call from KBL to help a client in Westchester—a wealthy individual who fled the scene of a possibly fatal accident. Outside, Ikers is having difficulty placing the bomb and has to wrap up quickly as Michael suddenly appears from the gambling den. The rush job proves critical—the connection with the trigger is so inconsistent Verne and Ikers have to stay in visual range and wait for the right moment to set off the bomb.

Michael drives north with Verne and Ikers following, the signal with the trigger so erratic they can't trust it will work. After dealing with the Westchester client, who expected a "miracle worker" and insults Michael for not being able to make his problem vanish, Michael speeds away along winding country roads. Verne and Ikers lose him and are outside visual range when, having suffered two demeaning, insult-ridden encounters, and recognizing the moral depravity to which he has returned, Michael stops. He sees three horses atop a fog-laced hill at dawn and approaches the animals like "a pilgrim stumbling into a cathedral." Verne and Ikers, seeing from the signal the car has stopped, decide to trigger the bomb even though they can't see where Michael is. It explodes, scaring off the horses—and Michael realizes he's supposed to be dead. He also knows who is responsible. He flees, finds a phone booth, and makes a call. Before long, Tim pulls up, saying "Thank you," as Michael gets in. Lucky to be alive, Michael has decided to try forgiveness.

Here is the first indication (through behavior) that Michael has elected to change. Having forsaken his earlier chance, deciding instead to take the money and let U/North get away with murder while reverting to his own worst impulses, he now realizes that U/North won't stop until he, too, is dead. This shakes him out of his cynical self-cratering and obliges a new path.

Karen Crowder presents the settlement offer to the U/North board. Given tax advantages, the settlement will essentially pay for itself. Once finished, she goes out into the lobby while the board discusses the offer. Michael appears. She's shocked to see him alive. He shows her the memo; she says that it's now irrelevant. He tells her he knows she killed Arthur. When she continues to protest, he tells her, "I'm not the person you kill, I'm the person you buy. Are you so blind you can't see that? … I sold out Arthur for eighty grand and you're going to blow me up?"

She asks what he wants. He demands $10 million, offshore, bank of his choosing. After haggling, she agrees. He makes her say it out loud. He's been recording the entire exchange for the benefit of NYPD. While officers and detectives rush in, Karen crumbles to her knees as the realization of what has happened hits.

Michael walks out onto Sixth Avenue and hails a cab. For the first time in years, he's a free man. He can face himself, face his son, and he's avenged Arthur's murder. But he's breached his agreement with KBL—he'll have to return the $80,000, he'll lose his job, and his debt with the loan shark is back on the books. There's no telling yet how high the cost of his conscience will be, or whether he'll prove strong enough in the long run to make his transformation stick.

WHEN CRISIS FORGES A NEW DREAM OF LIFE

The Doctor and *Regarding Henry*

Sometimes illness or injury, though seemingly a crushing, hope-destroying blow at first, actually offers a chance at a new, wiser, healthier life overall once the healing process begins.

The most obvious examples of this approach are those instances where illness or injury actually prompts a determined, heroic effort to overcome the limiting influence of the disease or trauma—such as with athletes overcoming the effects of amputation, partial paralysis, or childhood illness. One of the most inspirational of such stories is that of Wilma Rudolph, the African-American track star who overcame not just racial animus but scarlet fever, pneumonia, and infantile paralysis caused by the polio virus to win three gold medals at the Olympics.

In fiction and film, this approach often uses the illness or injury not as a preexisting condition but instead allows it to provide the inciting incident within the story itself.

In *The Doctor*, a film based loosely on the memoir of Dr. Edward Rosenbaum, *A Taste of My Own Medicine*, a prominent surgeon's elegant, high-flying life gets seriously derailed when he discovers he has cancer of the vocal cords. This begins a journey of reckoning, wherein he learns life as a patient at the hands of arrogant, indifferent men like himself, and his transformation into a far more caring and compassionate man and doctor begins.

In the film *Regarding Henry*, it is not illness but injury that causes the health issue. As in *The Doctor*, the protagonist is a prominent professional (a lawyer this time) prone to arrogant indifference to the havoc he creates in others' lives. It is a life he embraces with absolute gusto, until the night he interrupts a robbery at a convenience store near his home and is shot twice. His wounds result in both cardiac arrest and serious brain damage, and a long, slow process of physical rehab begins, during which he also reconsiders his values, his relationships, and his reason for living.

In both of these examples, where the illness or injury occurs at the outset of the story itself, the character embodies the Pathological Maneuvers that have come to define his life, which include Weaknesses such as arrogance and cynicism, which in turn create moral Flaws such as selfishness and a callous indifference to the pain suffered by others. The injury, acting as "a gun to the head," provides a shock to the system that forces the character to see more clearly his dependence on others, his own fallibility, and his selfishness. The recovery process enhances that newfound understanding and extends beyond the character's body to his conscience, his spirit, his way of life.

It is not just illness or injury that can create this sudden shock to the system—as we noted in our earlier discussion in chapter four of the film *Fearless*, based on the novel by Rafael Yglesias. There, it is actually *the escape* from devastating injury that provides the crisis that forces two survivors of a horrific plane crash to reexamine their lives.

Crisis doesn't always lead to productive insight and positive change, of course, and there is nothing to prevent you from revealing a character whose life-altering injury, illness, or other debacle poisons her outlook for good, and the story concerns her inability or unwillingness to accept healing as a means of transforming their life.

Good Morning, Midnight by Jean Rhys provides an example of this sort of story. Granted a stipend from an inheritance, Sasha, the narrator, has no need to work as long as she lives modestly. The idleness is a mixed blessing, for she finds it increasingly difficult to fend off recollections of the man she loved who abandoned her in the final stages of her pregnancy with his child, and the infant's death a mere five weeks later. She wanders from café to café, drinking away her grief. Her backstory Wound and her Weakness overwhelm her, making any real pursuit of love or happiness impossible. There is just wreckage, and waiting at last for the ship to go down.

THE TRUE YEARNING BURIED, REPLACED BY A FALSE, SELF-CREATED ONE

Midnight Cowboy

In this novel by James Leo Herlihy, adapted to film by screenwriter Waldo Salt and director John Schlesinger, Joe Buck first becomes aware of the people in his life as a boy living in Albuquerque with three attractive young women, one of whom is his mother, though he doesn't know which one; he thinks of the women as "The Three Sisters." One day they drop him off at the home of a hairdresser named Sally Buck, whom they call his grandmother, then leave and never come back (Wound).

Joe grows up with Sally Buck, who as a hairdresser emphasizes appearance and teaches Joe a superficial understanding of what attracts men to women and vice versa. She enlists him into giving her after-work back rubs, coos and calls him "Lover" when he pleases her, then leaves him alone with the television and a warmed-over dinner while she goes off and spends the night with her current fling. One of those flings is a cowhand who actually pays attention to young Joe and refers to him as "Cowboy," a nickname Joe relishes. But the man soon disappears the same way all of Sally's suitors do. Joe learns that love is a come-and-go affair, and appearance is what matters most.

By the time he reaches high school, Joe has grown into a handsome if shy young man of polite disposition and below-average aptitude in school. Many of his fellow students, boys and girls alike, take pleasure in his body, though they express little interest in the fact that Joe is inside. He develops a crush on a mentally handicapped young woman known as "Crazy Sally," whom the local boys use for sex. Joe is unaware that Crazy Sally isn't the kind of girl you fall in love with.

We see the general outline of how the past has shaped his behavior: He has deep issues with abandonment (Wound) that reveal themselves in a sense of loneliness and doubt about his worth (Weakness), as well as questionable intelligence (Limitation). He feels so desperate for affection and recognition that he pursues even futile connections in the hope of being liked (Pathological Maneuver).

He joins the army, does an uneventful tour, and returns to find that Sally Buck has passed away. She never bothered to write while he was gone so her death comes as an utter shock. This last in a string of abuses and abandonments pushes him over a psychological edge. He realizes that no one ever really loved him, no matter how much they claimed to, though the old cowhand who called him "Cowboy" came the closest. The only thing Joe has ever been good at is sex, and he decides to take revenge against all those who have used him by becoming a hustler— from this point forward, he will be the one using them, not the reverse (Pathological Maneuver). This reimagination of himself and his life is so total he likens it to a Native American rite of passage, and just as Indian adolescents receive a new name based on their spirit vision, he decides to choose a new name for himself—from that point forward, he will be the Midnight Cowboy (Mistaken Identity/Yearning).

Notice how Joe's misperception here is not merely conceptual. It is the natural culmination of his Pathological Maneuvers up to this moment. They crystallize the pain and loneliness he has felt into a mask of vengeance that from that point forward will make him the aggressor not the victim (Flaw).

He travels to New York, where he thinks the predominance of homosexuals will work in his favor as a gigolo; he will make money hand over fist giving women the good time they want and deserve (Misguided Desire). He promptly learns he is out of his depth when he gets used by an older woman prostitute who makes him pay for their sexual interlude instead of the other way around. Next, a street hustler named Enrico "Ratso" Rizzo promises to introduce Joe to a pimp but instead takes him to the apartment of a psychotic holy roller and abandons him there.

Time passes, winter arrives, Joe goes broke, and he haunts the porno theaters on 42nd street hoping for paying pickups. By accident he reconnects with Ratso there, and after his initial anger subsides he accepts Ratso's invitation to share his waterless, heatless squat in a condemned high-rise.

The two make an unlikely pair: Joe is handsome but none too bright (Limitation), and Ratso prizes street smarts above all other qualities, with no qualms about victimizing the gullible (Flaw). He calls Joe stupid and mocks his hokey cowboy attire. Ratso is disfigured and thus ugly (Limitation), a major sin in Joe's book, and suffers from tuberculosis (Limitation). Nevertheless, the two team up, suffering hardship through the winter together, and develop a grudging camaraderie. Ratso ultimately agrees to try to get Joe real work as a hustler so the two can go to Florida, where Ratso hopes his health will turn around.

At a Warhol-esque happening, Joe ends up meeting a wealthy woman named Shirley willing to pay him for sex—better still, she's willing to refer him to her friends. It seems his dream to be the Midnight Cowboy is finally coming true. At the same time, however, Ratso's TB has become so severe that he needs to leave New York immediately or die. The money Joe received from Shirley is not enough to pay for their bus fare, so Joe is obliged to turn one more trick. He discovers a closeted Midwesterner who backs out at the last minute. Joe, desperate for the money, robs him and beats him savagely out of self-disgust (Weakness transformed into Flaw).

On the bus ride to Florida, Joe confesses to Ratso that he isn't cut out for hustling, and once they get settled he hopes to find a job working outside, maybe in landscaping (Realistic Desire). He has at last surrendered his false dream, created out of resentment and a refusal ever to be abandoned, betrayed, or lied to again, and has accepted instead what he truly wants—a genuine connection with another person who can accept him for who he is (True Yearning). No sooner has he admitted this, however, than he discovers Ratso has died in the seat beside him. Joe is once again alone—only now he stands beyond the point where the Midnight Cowboy's protective persona can shield him from the inescapable pain of loss. He must bear this most painful abandonment of all with nothing to protect him but the truth.

YEARNING RECOGNIZED, BUT IT EVOLVES THROUGH THE CHARACTER'S STRUGGLES

The Hunger Games Trilogy

In chapter six, we discussed the film *A Prophet* in terms of how the sequence of events and the challenges it presented created not just an evolving Desire line, whereby the character's goals adapted to changing circumstances, but an evolving understanding of his Yearning as well, since both his sense of identity and his understanding of what the future might hold were developing as his confidence grew and capabilities multiplied.

This is a common technique, one whose chief benefit is its grounding of the character's Yearning and Desire in the emerging truth of the story rather than trying to force the character's sense of identity and purpose, as well as her goals, into conformance with some preconceived understanding.

Another example, and one more widely known, especially by English-speaking readers and viewers, is The Hunger Games Trilogy by Suzanne Collins. Although the three connected dystopian novels seem at first to conform to the "Everyman rises to great hero" format, the actual story is more complex and reveals not just shifting goals but a shifting sense of identity, purpose, and meaning on the part of the story's protagonist, Katniss Everdeen.

Katniss, age sixteen at the story's start, lives in an impoverished region known as District 12 (based on Appalachia) in a repressive autocracy called Panem. Ever since the central government brutally crushed a rebellion, it has conducted a yearly competition pitting two random recruits—one male, one female, both between the ages of twelve and eighteen—from each district in a fight to the death until only one contestant survives. This lone winner is crowned victor and his district is rewarded with food, supplies, and other benefits.

When Primrose, Katniss's younger sister, is selected by lottery for the games, Katniss volunteers to take her place. Though Katniss worries about surviving, she is an expert archer who has hunted to supply her family with food from a young age and knows she stands a much better chance of coming home than her younger sister would. (Notice how a Limitation—poverty—enhances a strength instead of enhancing a Weakness or Flaw, and that her skill provides a well-founded sense of pride, prowess, and worth.)

It is in fact Katniss's identification with hunting that defines her identity and seemingly her destiny at the story's outset—she reflects the goddess Diana, the virginal huntress owing allegiance to no man—not even Peeta, the other recruit from her district. The local baker's son, Peeta secretly provided Katniss with bread when her family was starving. He did this not only out of kindness but because he is secretly in love with Katniss.

As the game progresses, Katniss relies on her skill and resourcefulness as a hunter and also on her compassion and decency (Persistent Virtues), forming temporary alliances with other competitors. These alliances are contrary to the spirit of the games, however, and the government sees them as acts of defiance. As the competition proceeds, the rules are arbitrarily changed as the rich place bets or provide infusions of capital on behalf of one participant or another. Katniss realizes how much luck and her ability to inspire "sponsors" to invest in her (and thus provide needed supplies) will determine her survival, above and beyond her prowess. When Peeta's affection for Katniss is revealed, the government issues a sudden rule change that partners from the same district can win as a couple if they are the last two to survive. The game ends with only Katniss and a badly wounded Peeta as the sole survivors.

Then the government decrees another sudden rule change: Only one of the recruits can win. One has to kill the other. Katniss, again in an act of defiance, collects a handful of poison berries so that she and Peeta can die together. The government, sensing that this could inspire outbreaks of rebellious violence, if not a total uprising, retracts the last rule change and declares Peeta and Katniss joint winners.

Though unaware of the effect her actions had on those watching the games, Katniss soon learns that her example has inspired exactly the acts of rebellion the government feared. The head of the government, President Snow, threatens to harm Katniss's family and other loved ones if she does not profess that her questionable acts were motivated by her love of Peeta, not defiance of the government. Having developed fond but not romantic feelings for Peeta, she agrees, and they travel the provinces as a betrothed couple to counteract stirrings of revolution that her behavior in the games inspired.

To be brief, complications ensue—the uprising grows, and ultimately Katniss is rescued by rebel forces, who see her as their figurehead, a role she reluctantly accepts after the government destroys her home district. President Snow, facing defeat, barricades himself inside his remote mansion. As rebel forces approach the mansion, Katniss sneaks away in the hope of killing Snow herself. She discovers that the mansion is surrounded by children from the Capitol being used as human shields. A hovercraft appears, dropping parcels by parachute that the children rush to, believing them to be food. Some of the parcels explode, creating carnage. The rebel forces send in medics, including Katniss's sister, Prim. Once the medics arrive, the remaining parcels explode, killing Prim before Katniss's eyes.

The rebel forces complete their overthrow of the government, and Snow is taken prisoner with plans for Katniss to kill him. But before this happens, Snow informs her that it was the leader of the rebels, Alma Coin, who planned the bombing attack on his mansion—it was a false flag operation designed to eliminate all remaining support for Snow's regime. When it comes time for Katniss to kill Snow with her bow and arrow, she instead kills Coin in retaliation for the death of the children hostages, Prim, and the other medics. Observing this, Snow breaks into laughter, and Katniss slays him as well.

Katniss is tried for the leader's murder but is deemed to have been under extreme mental duress. She is returned to her home district where she reunites with Peeta. Given the ordeals they have shared, a profound respect and love has grown between them, and though the rebellion continues, they no longer believe fighting will achieve the change they consider most valuable. After several years together, they have two children, one boy and one girl.

The preceding synopsis does not do justice to the whole of the story, of course, and in particular fails to account for the numerous turns and complications in Katniss's interpersonal struggles with friends, allies, family members, and enemies, all of which profoundly affect her sense of allegiance and duty. This is significant, because given the ending of her story, where she renounces the role of rebel icon, it is tempting to view her Yearning as always having been limited to a sense of personal loyalty to those closest to her rather than identification with a greater cause.

Such an interpretation, however, fails to take into account the ongoing interplay between the larger rebellion and its devastating effect on the people and district she loves. She embraces the uprising until the true nature of its leader is revealed to be a mirror image of the corrupt President Snow. Without that embrace of the rebellion, her subsequent disillusion would lack emotional power, especially as it now includes shedding her identification with the huntress and the assumption of a more domestic, though by no means submissive, role. Just as her outer goals evolve from saving her sister to surviving the games to accommodating Snow to aiding the rebellion to becoming its figurehead to avenging her district and her sister to returning home, so her Yearning first expands then retracts to accommodate the humbler dream she feels justified in embracing. But there is no "misperception" in her story. She never pursues a false idea of what she should do out of fear of what the right thing would oblige of her, nor does she have to rectify some maladaptive form of behavior. Her choices are consistently based on her best understanding of what is right. Her decisive struggle is not internal but external, due to the powerful, arrogant, vicious, and deceitful forces arrayed against her on every side. But that external struggle redefines her sense of self in profound ways.

YEARNING APPREHENDED, BUT WITH NO CLEAR IDEA HOW TO FULFILL IT

The Man Who Gave Up His Name

This is a common template for characters who awaken to their Yearning early in the story. The dream of life or call of destiny seems apparent—but how to get there from here? What must be done, what obstacles stand in the way and how many are there, how difficult will they prove to be, what are the chances of success, and will success even be recognizable if it's achieved?

In this novella by Jim Harrison, the Protagonist, a former corporate hatchet man named Nordstrom ("North Storm"), realizes early on in the story, after an encounter with his teenage daughter in which she calls him a "cold fish," that he wants to change his life. He soon realizes how puzzlingly difficult this can be, no matter how profound the longing to do so. The greater share of the story follows Nordstrom as he tries, step-by-step, to change both the circumstances of his life and his inner response to its enigmas, doing so with an honesty of introspection and stoic wit that serve him admirably (Persistent Virtues). He and his wife divorce, he gives up his job, his father dies, all of which force him to look inward. He analyzes how he became the man he was and what needs to be done to move beyond that past. Ultimately, after a series of adventures and misadventures, he winds up as a short-order cook in the Florida Keys, dancing to the jukebox after hours with two of the waitresses, and when they leave he continues on his own for several more hours. He has decided the key to selfhood is not ambition but acceptance—and having the courage to be happy, even if that means dancing alone.

THE DREAM UNREALIZED, FOLLOWED BY A DESCENT INTO NIGHTMARE

Plenty

In David Hare's play *Plenty* and the film based on it, for which he also wrote the script, we once again meet a character at the story's outset with a distinct sense of beckoning promise but an ill-defined sense of how to fulfill it. Her name is Susan Traherne; she is British, age seventeen, working as a courier behind enemy lines for the French Resistance. Unlike Nordstrom, her dream of life is not premised on a need to change; quite the contrary, she virtually burns with confidence in who she is.

When the war ends, Susan brims with hope for the future, certain that the victory of the Allied forces will usher in a new era of confidence, courage, and promise. She virtually stands at the doorstep of her dream of life (Yearning). However, she also possesses a sense of entitlement to that promise, given her work during the war, which conjures a bristling superiority with no sense of personal responsibility for creating that better world (Weakness). It is far easier to find fault—and mock, undermine, betray—those others who seem so lackluster in the gray, boring aftermath of glorious victory (Flaw).

As she wanders from meaningless job to meaningless job and one man to the next, her boredom curdles into depression. She marries a diplomat for whom she feels no real affection because his obsession with her guarantees that he won't stray, and his career offers at least some promise of travel and prestige. But the drifting sense of pointlessness keeps returning, and she responds with medication and bitter vindictiveness. She tries to recapture a flicker of her past enthusiasm through a random liaison with a former colleague in the clandestine services, but he proves as listless, aimless, and disappointing as everyone else. The promise she felt so clearly in the fields of France in spring of 1945 has faded away, never to return. All she's left with is her vain sense of entitlement and vast disillusion that ferments into a bitterness so profound it ends up destroying not just those she blames for her malaise but herself.

INCOMPATIBLE YEARNINGS

Homeland

This formulation, where a character realizes she holds two distinct and incompatible ideas of who she should be and how she should live, has particular dramatic power. It is especially relevant for women characters, who are often torn between an individual Yearning and one more in line with what family or society would expect of them, which they have internalized. That said, men are hardly immune to the problem, as we shall see in the next section on moral dilemmas. Being torn between two equally valid but incompatible imperatives—familial obligation vs. personal ambition, official duty vs. romantic love, loyalty vs. morality—makes for great drama.

In this Showtime TV series, CIA case officer Carrie Mathison is a "born spy." As a child she was fearless and her father called her his

"Little Daredevil." As an adult she actively pursues a career as a CIA case officer and demonstrates remarkable talent, skill, and courage in her work (Persistent Virtues/Yearning). At times, however, her self-assurance can redline into arrogance, recklessness, and defiance of authority (Weakness and Flaw).

At age twenty-two, she begins to suffer from bipolar personality disorder (Limitation), and thereafter tries as best she can to maintain control over her illness. Unfortunately, her demanding, important, and dangerous work routinely creates such intense pressure, anxiety, and stress that it exacerbates her symptoms. During manic episodes, especially, she becomes increasingly obsessive, overwrought, and reckless; she also begins to see connections and intuits secrets others fail to see. Her certainty in herself becomes not just abrasive but uncooperative (Limitation, Weakness, and Flaw influencing each other). This both enhances her value when she's right and also diminishes her credibility when she is discovered to be wrong, which only creates an even greater obsession to prove herself correct.

Her supervisor and mentor, Saul Berenson, both relies on her and feels profound concern for her emotional well-being. Her family fears the job is actually worsening her illness, despite the fact they understand espionage is her natural calling. It is unclear what would become of her if she were denied the opportunity to do the work she loves so much.

Despite health setbacks and the bureaucratic and political betrayals so intrinsic to her profession, she continues her work until the death of a loved one and pregnancy with his child leads her to decide to give up the spy trade and focus on being a parent, which brings an unexpected sense of love, meaning, and purpose to her life (Newfound Yearning). She takes work with an nongovernmental organization in Berlin and lives there for two years, only to be drawn back into the shadow world by Saul.

This divided sense of identity and purpose—espionage versus parenthood—becomes an ongoing battle for her soul. Her intelligence work increasingly enhances her obsessive preoccupations to the point she often neglects Frannie, her daughter—forgetting to pick her up at school, abandoning her to the care of her Aunt Maggie, Carrie's older sister. The neglect becomes so routine and dangerous that Maggie files for sole custody of the child. Carrie is forced to choose between being a parent or being a spy. In so doing, she is forced to honestly soul search: She comes to realize that despite her profound and genuine love for Frannie, she is inflicting very real damage on her. She also comes to appreciate the degree to which vanity and guilt motivate her insistence on caring for the little girl, not just maternal instinct. Finally, Maggie tells her to do what she was born to do, saying, "I will make sure Frannie is safe and cared for."

This constant conflict between two equally valid Yearnings creates a constant thread of tension in the series, though many critics and audience members complained that it interfered with what made Carrie truly fascinating: her work as a spy complicated by her illness. Part of this is a repetition problem—only so many scenes of bad parenting can be truly revelatory without beginning to feel like more of the same. Why not have Maggie step in sooner? To their credit, the show's writers did indeed push the situation to a credible crisis, forcing Carrie's sister to act and Carrie to honestly reflect on her divided moral Obligations.

THE DREAM OF VENGEANCE

The Limey

Apparently Confucius never actually said that one who embarks on a journey of revenge should begin by digging two graves, but it's still a worthy aphorism. It points to the fact that the burning fire of vengeance is often all-consuming—ask Ahab—or that dreams of vengeance all too often disguise a longing to punish someone else in order to expurgate one's own feelings of guilt, shame, or despair. What happened is so intolerable that only by making the perpetrator pay can life be worth living again; except post-vengeance life is never what one expects, because it's impossible to return to the way things used to be.

In the film *The Limey* (directed by Steven Soderbergh, screenplay by Lem Dobbs), an ex-con named Wilson arrives in LA from England after learning his daughter, Jenny, has died. The official cause of death is automobile accident, but Wilson suspects something much more insidious. After speaking with two of Jenny's closest friends (and clearing them in his own mind of involvement in Jenny's death), his focus turns to Jenny's boyfriend, Terry Valentine, a one-time music producer now involved in drug trafficking.

His inquiries gain the attention of Valentine's head of security, Avery, and a violent game of cat and mouse begins as Wilson gets closer to Valentine and the truth. In the midst of these efforts, he confides to Elaine, Jenny's closest female friend, that his criminal activities created discord between him and Jenny as she was growing up. She would often threaten to call the police if she discovered indications that he was about to commit a crime, because she loved him and didn't want him to go away to prison. He ultimately did get caught due to an accomplice's turning on him, and his connection to Jenny slipped away.

Wilson ultimately learns that Avery has a home in Big Sur, and guesses rightly that Avery will try to hide him there. When Wilson finally corners Valentine alone, Valentine confesses to murdering Jenny, but by accident. She threatened to go to the police if he didn't give up his involvement in the drug trade, resulting in a violent argument that led to the head injury that actually killed her. Avery staged the car accident to cover up Valentine's involvement in her death.

Hearing this story, Wilson not only recognizes the echoes of his own past with Jenny, but he understands as well that this means she loved Valentine and would not have blown the whistle on him. His need for vengeance dissipates. He understands that he is not guiltless in Jenny's death, for she was acting out the very same scenario she used to conduct with him. He lets Valentine live, and returns to England.

In a story of this kind, the phrase "dream of life" can seem wildly off point. The "dream" died with his daughter's murder; now there is just the settling of scores (Desire). But that goal speaks to a way of life and a sense of identity, in the form of a moral code, that Wilson clearly feels a need to live by (Yearning). A man like him does not let his daughter's murder go unavenged. And that identity reveals the balance he has struck between his Persistent Virtues, such as loyalty, courage, resourcefulness, and determination, and his Pathological Maneuvers, which include criminality in general and deceit, violence, and indifference to the pain he causes others. His recognition of the self-serving lie in his dream of vengeance offers a chance at self-reckoning, but his chance at redemption is gone. Instead, there is just a painfully self-aware regret. As in many crime stories, the pursuit of the villain is in fact a journey of self-discovery.

FORSAKING A DREAM IMPOSED BY ANOTHER FOR ONE'S OWN

The Fighter

This novel by Craig Davidson features mirrored stories of two young men whose ambitions have been directed by their fathers with all the best intentions in the world, only to lead each son to destroy himself in the hope of creating an authentic life.

Paul Harris is the son of former farmers who turned to viniculture and became rich. They now live as landed gentry, and Paul has a token job with the wine company to justify his generous income and support his aimless lifestyle. His parents have worked hard so he doesn't have to, unaware that this would cast him adrift (Weakness).

One night, on an arranged date with the daughter of a potential business associate, Paul mocks a young man trying to horn in on his date. The would-be flirt is of a lower socio-economic station, and Paul verbally spars with him for a bit before finding himself alone with the young tough outside where he suffers a vicious beating.

The thrashing proves epiphanic. Paul first shuns his cushy indoor job to work with the immigrant field hands out among the vines. His parents believe it's just a phase, but then Paul finds a small gym where he begins to learn how to box. He lacks talent but can take a punch and discovers an inner fire, a determination he did not know he had. He also discovers in physical pain and suffering the promise of purification, redemption, transformation.

His trainer informs him of a tradition of itinerant fighters who used to go town to town, challenging the local toughs to a fistfight until either he was down for good or there were no more challengers. This wandering belligerence wasn't to make a living so much as to honor a calling. They were sluggers—it was all they knew, all they were good for, their reason for being. The story awakens in Paul a newfound sense of identity. He will be that rambling pugilist. Not a boxer. A fighter (Yearning).

Rob Tully is the teenage son of Reuben Tully, a former boxer of middling reputation who now works the graveyard shift at a bakery to make ends meet. Reuben's brother Tommy lives with them. Also once a boxer of decent reputation, Tommy is now a human punching bag, renting himself out to spar with up-and-coming boxers, allowing himself to get hit without inflicting damage on the rising star.

Both Reuben and Tommy have great dreams for Rob, who has revealed a natural boxer's talent. He's not just gifted, he has the stuff of stardom. His father and uncle are grooming him for the Olympics and a pro career beyond that, with the hope that his success will lift them all out of the squalid neighborhood and hand-to-mouth existence they now endure.

The only problem is that despite Rob's speed, power, and skill in the ring, he lacks killer instinct. He pursues boxing for the sake of his father and uncle, and embraces their dream as his own for their sake (Misguided Yearning/Mistaken Desire). He wants to do the right thing for the men he loves and who have loved him.

For the sake of the purse available, Tommy routinely shows up to fight at a weekly underground match out in farm country, where gamblers bet on roughnecks ready to fight without the usual restrictions of formal boxing.

Paul learns of these barn fights and sees them as the first step to fulfilling his newfound ambition of modeling himself after the roaming brawlers of old. He ends up drawing Tommy as his opponent and is in the midst of getting his head handed to him by the older, more experienced fighter when he suddenly lands a savagely lucky punch. The knockout shatters Tommy's jaw and sends him into a coma, from which he never recovers.

Rob, bent on revenge for his uncle, travels to the barn and insists on fighting Paul. His skill is so superior and his intention to inflict damage so absolute that everyone there is simply waiting for Paul to go down. But Paul refuses. He senses the rightness of his punishment and refuses to concede. Rob removes the tape from his hands to do even greater damage, thinking Paul wants to die, and he'll be the one to kill him. Even the crowd of hardened, cynical gamblers is sickened by the damage Rob inflicts, until Paul at last collapses unconscious, bloody, and broken.

Rob, horrified by what he has done and by the killer awakened within him, goes into the pasture beyond the barn, finds a fence post sturdy enough to withstand what he intends to do, and begins hammering it relentlessly until the bones in both hands are crushed to slivers and bits. He will never enter the ring again. When Reuben discovers what Rob has done, sees the unrecoverable damage to his hands, he feels profound remorse for having forced his son to fulfill his own dream. Rob's future is now uncertain, except he will no longer be living a lie.

Paul, after he recovers in the hospital, travels to Thailand, where underground matches are held, even more savage than the ones in the barn. He has found his calling. He will die in pain, broken, fighting.

Both Paul and Rob crave authenticity (Yearning)—a sense of identity and purpose that they have created themselves. Both have lived by the Pathological Maneuvers that have served them up until now: For Paul that has meant drifting through life, skating across its surface, accepting pleasure as promise and not thinking too deeply about the emptiness he feels. For Rob it has been accepting the role that has been devotedly fashioned for him, keeping his head down and his mouth shut, returning misguided love with dutiful obedience and a silencing of his own nascent dreams for something else, something solely his.

Both find that only through extreme physical damage to themselves can they break the chains of habitual self-deceit and bad faith, hoping to rise from the ashes into a newfound selfhood—a more honest if uncertain one for Rob, a darkly self-sacrificial but gratifying one for Paul.

THE ECSTATIC YEARNING GIVING WAY TO MADNESS

Equus and *Through a Glass Darkly*

In the Middle Ages, as Church investigators tried to determine whether an individual's reports of experiencing a vision or hearing voices was divine or demonic in nature, they often relied on inquiring into the nature of the vision or voice—was it serene, benevolent, joyful? Or was it in contrast terrifying, hostile, malevolent?[4]

It is difficult to imagine that any encounter with the divine would not conjure at least momentary terror. The testimonies of St. John of the Cross, St. Teresa of Ávila, St. Bernadette of Lourdes, and Joan of Arc all confirm as much. But in each of those cases (and many more that have received the sanction of the Church) the ecstatic moment was followed soon thereafter by a clear and concrete sense of mission. Even if that mission creates immeasurable hardships and doubts—or worse, ends in martyrdom, as it did for Joan—the divine nature of the vision remains largely unquestioned and creates the certainty with which the character's Yearning is pursued.

But what if that is not the case? What if the moment of terror expands and dominates? What if the character's Yearning for an encounter with God turns hellish?

Peter Shaffer in his play *Equus* has his therapist character, Martin Dysart, wonder if he is actually helping his patients by returning them to "normal." The particular patient prompting his doubts is Alan Strang, who has a religio-erotic fascination with horses. Alan's condition reaches an untenable point after an unsuccessful sexual liaison with Jill, a girl who works at the same stables where he is employed. Things go wrong when they attempt a tryst in the loft above the stables, and the horses become restless. Alan thinks they are objecting, and he angrily sends Jill away. Still naked, he asks the horses for forgiveness, imagining them as godlike beings. But then the horses seem to speak;

---

4 Such an approach is not confined to the Middle Ages. See Watkins, J., *Unshrinking Psychosis: Understanding and Healing the Human Soul* (2010), Michelle Anderson Publishing.

they tell Alan they can see him, see his very soul. In terror, Alan uses a metal spike to blind all six horses in the stable.

In the film *Through a Glass Darkly* by Ingmar Bergman, Karin has suffered several psychotic episodes attributed to a diagnosis of schizophrenia, but that is not how she sees it. She is trying to choose between two different realties: the one others will accept and the one only she understands.

At one point in the story, she wakes in the night to the sound of a foghorn, which terrifies her. She believes it is beckoning her to the attic, where she hears a voice whispering beyond the peeling wallpaper. The voices tell her to:

- search her father's desk, where she finds his descriptions of her illness, which he considers incurable, and she realizes he is trying to cure his own affliction—writer's block (he's a novelist)—by using her as a source for material;
- reject her husband's attempts at sexual intimacy;
- seduce her seventeen-year-old brother, Minus, which she does when he tries to comfort her after she hides inside a wrecked boat on the beach to escape a thunderstorm.

Minus tells the other men about what happened on the beach, and her father calls for an ambulance to take her to the hospital. (Since they are on a remote island, the paramedics will arrive by helicopter.) Karin admits to each of the questionable things she has done and agrees to return to the hospital, deciding the constant back-and-forth between her reality and what others expect of her is too difficult to bear.

As they are packing, she suddenly runs upstairs to once again behold the voices. She sees a spider crawl out of a crack in the wall and fixates on it. Suddenly the helicopter flies low over the house with a thunderous noise, shaking the walls. Karin runs to the closet door, expecting to see God.

> The door opened, but God was a spider. He came up to me and I saw his face. It was a terrible stony face. He scrambled up and tried to penetrate me, but I defended myself. All along I saw his eyes. They were cold and

calm. When he couldn't penetrate me he continued up my chest, up into my face and onto the wall.

In both Alan's and Karin's case, the profound longing for connection with a transcendent power disguises a deeper anxiety—in both instances, connected with sexuality—and thus serves a false dream. Small wonder it turns nightmarish. But this is actually just an extreme example of situations where a mistaken Desire, driven by a misbegotten Yearning, allows the character to pursue something less terrifying than what he or she truly longs for. In Joe Buck's case, his fear and anger over repeated betrayals and abandonment created the need to create a new identity and mission, to become the Midnight Cowboy. As the false promise of that strategy reveals itself, he has the ability to admit what he truly wants. Karin and Alan, however, lack Joe's strength, and the nightmare swallows them whole.

As noted at the outset of this chapter, the examples provided, which are presented in the hope of illustrating a variety of ways in which characters can be misled by what they want, or the deeper longing it speaks to, are hardly exhaustive. Hopefully, their variety will give some insight into the many ways you can stage your own stories in which characters suffer a "misperception" of what they want or need, and how that misperception does not express itself merely in thought or feeling but in concrete behavior.

EXERCISES

- Examine your own WIP and compare it to the various examples provided above. Which, if any, best resembles your own work? You will most likely find your story is both a match and a mismatch of whatever example you choose—and analyzing the differences will prove as illuminating as noticing the similarities.
- If your story does not resemble any of the examples provided, try nonetheless to see how the war between Yearning and Resistance creates the protagonist's Lack, how that is revealed in behavior at the story's outset, and how pursuit of the Desire obliges action that

challenges the character's understanding of herself, her relationships, and her situation—and how that challenge affects her understanding of the kind of person she wants to be, the way of life
she hopes to live.

IV. MORAL DILEMMAS AND DREAM-KILLING CHOICES

> An unhappy alternative is before you, Elizabeth. From this day you
> must be a stranger to one of your parents. Your mother will never
> see you again if you do *not* marry Mr. Collins, and I will never see
> you again if you *do*.
>
> —Jane Austen, *Pride and Prejudice*

Of all the situations that oblige a character to reexamine or abandon
a previously held conviction as to the best way to pursue her dream of
life, few are as daunting as those that obligate a choice that means giving
up forever something one wants. This is especially true when the need
to choose is not between desirable options but devastating ones, each
of which will undermine if not shatter her faith in the promise of life.

Forcing a character to make a difficult if not outright brutal choice
also instantly engages readers. Consider just these three examples, from
ancient times to the modern day:

- A ship's commander must choose between two grave perils, each
  of which will cause men to die; turning back is not an option. (*The
  Odyssey*)
- A young nobleman, whose father has been gravely insulted by his
  loved one's father, must choose between his heart and family honor.
  (*Le Cid*)
- A young mother must choose which of her two children will go to
  the death camp, which the labor camp. If she fails to choose, both
  will die. (*Sophie's Choice*)

In each of these instances and others we'll explore, the character finds
herself in a state of desperation—a choice must be made, but each avail-

able option has abhorrent, even disastrous consequences. The ultimate choice cannot help but reveal previously untapped aspects of character.

This provides an excellent device for exploring complexity similar to that provided by the tug-of-war between Yearning and Resistance— conflicting moral prerogatives, incompatible goals, contradictory demands from loved ones. Such a choice also hews down to the character's core, exposing his heart and soul in its rawest, most unguarded state.

The dramatic problem is how to force the character out of the paralysis inflicted by the conflicting directives to make a decision—or how to show why the character cannot move beyond her paralysis. Either way, choose or not, the situation is life defining.

THE LOGIC OF INTOLERABLE CHOICES

Each dilemma your character faces has four basic steps, each with its own dramatic demands:

- Presentation of the Options
- Deliberation
- The Choice
- Consequences

Each character faces these various steps in a unique way, based on his own nature and the particular demands of his situation.

The most startling moment often comes when the options are revealed, especially if they're unforeseen. Even if the character has time to watch the situation crystalize, the sudden realization there is no escape should always come as a shock—to the reader if not the character.

The deliberation phase, where the character weighs the options, can add agonizing tension, even if there is little time to figure out the best course, as is often true when danger suddenly arises. Given more time, the character may proceed through various levels of denial, bargaining, and other types of evasion before actually grappling with the true weight of the decision, which becomes more oppressive as its necessity clarifies and time grows short. She may try to protest, find a way out, or explore other options, only to see them foreclosed one by one.

Although making the decision itself is often the simplest step to stage dramatically, this needn't be the case. Often, the more you can incorporate resistance to the decision into its actual execution, the better. This creates great tension, as we wonder whether the character will retain the willfulness needed to make the difficult choice.

Finally, once the decision is made, the character still has to grapple with what he has done. This can be particularly grueling when the decision has to be made hastily or with imperfect understanding, as in the fog of war or other situations when there simply is no way to predict how events may play out. Hoping for the best may prove to have terribly bitter consequences. Or it may be that foreseeing those consequences pales before living with them.

LEVELS OF IMPACT

To adequately portray what the character faces at every stage of this process, we have to realize her decision affects the same three distinct but interconnected aspects of her life that we explored in chapter seven:

Internal: The effects the decision will have on the character's identity—his idea of himself as a moral person, his honor or dignity, his sense of his own worth or purpose.

Interpersonal: The consequences the decision will have on others, especially those dearest to her. How will those bonds change given her choice? Where will she stand in their eyes afterwards?

External: The ramifications the decision will inflict on the situation he faces—how will the circumstances of his world change for better or worse?

The character may have to weigh the potential consequences on only one level, or some combination of all three. She may have to weigh harms or benefits of one kind against those of another.

Regardless, the most important consideration is to *make the potential consequences as devastating as possible.* The stakes must be ultimate. Whatever the character is obliged to give up by choosing one option over another must feel like a kind of death—spiritual, psychological, emotional, or even physical—to himself or someone else.

TYPES OF DILEMMAS

The Lesser of Two Evils

At first glance, this might not seem a dilemma at all, since the existence of a "lesser" evil should make the choice obvious, if distasteful.

But though the decision may be clear, it may create aftereffects, both foreseen and unforeseen, that the character finds both life-changing and unbearable.

Odysseus must sail through the Strait of Messina, with the deadly whirlpool Charybdis on one side, the man-eating monster Scylla the other.[5] He's spared the agony of deliberation when Circe advises him which peril to risk—the monster will take only six men, the whirlpool will kill them all, a clear case of the lesser of two evils. That doesn't spare Odysseus the horrible sight of his men screaming and reaching out to him in agony as Scylla devours them.

A variation on this type of dilemma is the Hobson's Choice— "damned if you do, damned if you don't."

The Necessary Evil

This differs from the previous dilemma only in degree. The options presented are not just horrible to contemplate; they indelibly stain the character's soul.

Examples abound in crime and war stories, where circumstances often not only demand killing but also arouse hatred and viciousness. Handled badly, such moments can devolve into self-righteous justifications of torture and other acts of sadism. When handled well, however, they test our understanding of innocence, justice, and decency.

Albert Einstein, a devoted pacifist, had to face the reality of what would happen if the Nazis built an atomic bomb. He agonized over what to do, for he knew firsthand how the war machine corrupts science. Though spared actual involvement in the Manhattan Project—he was deemed a Communist—Einstein was horrified when, as he feared, the

---

5 Interestingly, the term "Scylla and Charybdis" is typically used to describe a situation with two equally bad alternatives. As the actual text and our discussion reveals, this is not the case.

bomb was used on civilians. From a deep sense of personal responsibility he spent his remaining days advocating for universal disarmament.

As we saw above with the example of *Sophie's Choice*, Sophie Zawistowska is forced to surrender one child to death to spare the other. The choice shatters her, for despite the fact the choice is forced on her, she can't help feeling complicit.

Caught Between a Rock and a Hard Place[6]

The term comes from the "choice" given to immigrant miners hoping to unionize during World War I: They could either work in miserable conditions at inhuman wages or go penniless and starve.

Again, what differentiates this example from the preceding one is largely a matter of emphasis. The sense of complicity is absent, but the choice between two equally devastating options is both harsh and inescapable.

Sometimes, however, the true nature of the choice is unclear at the start, if only to the character. A teenager who discovers she's pregnant may never have thought much about what it means to choose abortion or motherhood. But as the window of opportunity closes, she examines her beliefs more carefully, weighs how loved ones will respond, and ultimately chooses on the basis of her newfound sense of who she is and what is right.

The Cornelian Dilemma

Here the stakes involve personal honor or integrity. The term comes from Pierre Corneille, the author of *Le Cid*.

Rodrigue is engaged to Chimène, but her father, Comte de Gormas, viciously insults Rodrigue's father. The young nobleman can avenge the family honor by challenging Comte de Gormas to a duel, but this would mean losing Chimène. Or he can marry Chimène and accept his family's disgrace. He decides on the duel, during which he kills Chimène's father, and then spends the ensuing years trying to redeem himself in her eyes.

Anyone tempted to ignore or cross moral lines faces a similar set of questions: *Who am I? What do I stand for? How far will I go to defend that?*

6 Sometimes the term "Caught between Scylla and Charybdis" is used in this instance, but as noted above, that's a misnomer.

The Double Bind

This is a no-win situation that continues over time, in which a dominant person, often a parent, repeatedly gives mixed messages, such as professing love but behaving in a cold, judgmental manner. Often one conflicting message is spoken while the other remains unstated and must be inferred. This creates an ongoing atmosphere of uncertainty and paralysis.

Consider the stammering Billy Bibbit in *One Flew Over the Cuckoo's Nest*. His puritanical mother's "love" is echoed in the punitive "care" of Nurse Ratched. They insist their concern for his welfare is genuine even as they emasculate him, intending to ensure that he remain a docile, frightened boy. McMurphy tries to break Billy out of this paralysis but underestimates the crippling extent of Billy's shame and the ruthlessness of those who like things that way.

MAXIMIZING THE DILEMMA'S EFFECT

With all the foregoing in mind, it is time for a few concluding observations:

- As much as possible, present options that are equally demanding, horrifying, or dangerous, and make a choice inescapable.
- As much as possible, make the options few and clear-cut—and terrible. Where ambiguity works best is in creating tension by clouding the character's judgment or in sapping his will—but this only works if the need to decide continues to barrel down relentlessly.
- If the best option seems relatively clear, as in choosing the lesser of two evils, make the consequences devastating so even the clear-cut choice haunts the conscience.
- If the character's convictions are firmly held, make them irreconcilable.
- If the character's convictions are uncertain, clarify and intensify them through the deliberation, decision, and consequences.
- Amplify tension by shortening the time to decide. Find ways to shorten it even further as the action proceeds.

- Don't drag out the deliberation needlessly, but make sure the character discards every possible option other than the one she ultimately takes.
- Intensify consequences by having the choice harm, devastate, or even destroy people the character cherishes.
  - If the decision is rushed, make that hurry create terrible repercussions—for example, have the character learn there was a better option available she failed to see.
  - Make the consequences change the character's sense of worth, integrity, morality. Feed her conscience and regret.

EXERCISES

- For two of your main characters, search for a place or places within your story where they might face an agonizing choice—one that obliges them to give up something they cherish or that forces them to choose between two or more terrible alternatives.
- Break down how your characters face their dilemmas in each of the following stages:
  - Presentation of the Options
  - Deliberation
  - The Choice
  - Consequences
- What are the Internal, Interpersonal, and External challenges the characters face at each stage of the process? How do the various levels of struggle influence and affect one another?
- How have you made the potential consequences as devastating as possible?
- Which of the following types of dilemmas do your characters' situations most closely resemble?
  - The Lesser of Two Evils
  - The Necessary Evil
  - Caught Between a Rock and a Hard Place
  - The Cornelian Dilemma
  - The Double Bind

- How have you maximized the effect of your characters' dilemmas by employing these techniques?

  - Present options that are equally unimaginable and make a choice inescapable.
  - Make the options few and clear-cut.
  - Make the consequences devastating.
  - Make the character's convictions irreconcilable.
  - If the character's convictions are uncertain, clarify and intensify them through the deliberation, decision, and consequences.
  - Amplify tension by shortening the time to decide.
  - Make sure the character discards every possible option other than the one he ultimately takes—or suffers the consequences for not doing so.
  - Intensify consequences by having the choice harm someone the character cherishes.
  - If the decision is rushed, make that hurry create terrible repercussions.
  - Make the consequences change the character's sense of worth, integrity, morality.
  - At every stage of the process, *make it worse.*

SUMMARY OF MAIN POINTS IN THIS CHAPTER

INTRODUCTION

- In many stories, the character's Yearning at some point becomes clear, recognizable, and worth pursuing. But that is by no means true of all stories.
- In fact, a great many stories are premised exactly on confusion or uncertainty as to what the character wants and why she wants it.
- This confusion or uncertainty typically results in the character doing one of the following:
  - stumbling blindly toward something that promises an improvement in circumstances; or

- latching on first to some false idea of what he wants only to recognize, in suffering the consequences obliged by its pursuit, that he was mistaken.
- The revelation of that mistake may lead to one of the following:
  - a deeper, wiser understanding of her needs and wants, and what she must do to fulfill them;
  - a new, equally misguided pursuit of something else deemed valuable; or
  - such a profound sense of misgiving that he no longer trusts his instincts as to what he wants or why he wants it.
- In a great many cases, it is precisely the forces of Resistance, by intensifying the need to minimize the pain of life, that have malformed the individual's confidence that what once seemed like a promising life remains possible.

A COMMON VIEW OF CHARACTER ARC—ANALYSIS AND CRITIQUE

- Some writing guides employ the following standard character arc:
  - The Protagonist enters the story in a state of Lack, which combines both her ambitions and frustrations into a certain way of viewing the world and her life.
  - Something happens that prompts the Protagonist to act—specifically, it creates a problem he needs to solve.
  - The Protagonist's state of Lack creates a mistaken understanding of the problem.
  - By pursuing this mistaken understanding, the Protagonist takes many false steps that leave the core problem of the story unsolved.
  - This series of missteps and setbacks ultimately leads to a moment of such drastic failure that total defeat is at hand.
  - In the resulting "dark night of the soul," the Protagonist searches her heart and mind for one last solution to the story's core problem. In the course of that soul-searching, she experiences an insight that reveals the nature of her original mistaken understanding.

- This new awareness will prompt a decision by the Protagonist to change methods, change allies, and/or change himself in order to get one last chance to solve the problem. From that point forward, the question at the heart of the story will be, Will the Protagonist succeed? That question will be answered in the climax.

- By focusing on *misunderstanding* as the factor leading the character astray in her attempt to solve the core story problem, however, this methodology suggests that her error is fundamentally conceptual.
- In truth, the character's problem at the story's outset goes beyond what she thinks; it is embedded in her *behavior.*
- Furthermore, it is seldom the case that a single factor accounts for the character's problem with his past. Rather, the various forces of Resistance he faces interact, influencing and enhancing one another. And whatever problem he faces emerges not from one aspect but the whole of his personality.
- One of the best places to look for the character's problem with his past is to return to the moments of helplessness that formed his Persistent Virtues and Pathological Maneuvers and find the thematic thread linking them together. This will go beyond a mere "misperception" and reveal itself instead in a complex, organic pattern of behavior.
- Behavior also permits both greater range and clarity in dramatic depiction. One can show the character's change in how differently she acts.
- If the character's behavior hasn't changed, ask why not? Has he rejected the opportunity to change? Is his behavior outwardly the same but inwardly reflective of a deeper understanding of his situation and himself?

MORAL DILEMMAS AND DREAM-KILLING CHOICES

- Few situations a character can face are as dramatic as those demanding a choice that requires she give up something she wants forever.

- This is especially true when the need to choose is not between desirable options but devastating ones.
- Forcing a character to make an agonizing choice also instantly engages readers.
- Each dilemma your character faces has four basic steps, each with its own dramatic demands:
    - Presentation of the Options
    - Deliberation
    - The Choice
    - Consequences
- Each character faces these various steps in a unique way, based on his own nature and the particular demands of his situation.
- The most startling moment often comes when the options are revealed, especially if they're unforeseen.
- In the deliberation phase, the character grapples with the true weight of the decision, which becomes more oppressive as its necessity clarifies and time grows short.
- Finally, once the decision is made, the character still has to grapple with what she has done.
- The character faces challenges at every stage of this process, on three distinct but potentially interconnected plains: Internal, Interpersonal, and External.
- The character may have to weigh the potential consequences on only one level, or some combination of all three. The most important consideration is to *make the potential consequences as devastating as possible.*
- The types of dilemmas a character can face include:
    - The Lesser of Two Evils
    - The Necessary Evil
    - Caught Between a Rock and a Hard Place
    - The Cornelian Dilemma
    - The Double Bind

- To maximize the effect of the dilemma:
  - Present options that are equally demanding, horrifying, or dangerous, and make a choice inescapable.
  - Make the options few and clear-cut.
  - If the best option seems relatively clear, make the consequences devastating.
  - If the character's convictions are firmly held, make them irreconcilable.
  - If the character's convictions are uncertain, clarify and intensify them through the deliberation, decision, and consequences.
  - Amplify tension by shortening the time to decide.
  - Make sure the character discards every possible option other than the one he ultimately takes—or suffers the consequences for not doing so.
  - Intensify consequences by having the choice harm, devastate, or even destroy people the character cherishes.
  - If the decision is rushed, make that hurry create terrible repercussions—for example, have the character learn there was a better option available she failed to see.
  - Make the consequences change the character's sense of worth, integrity, morality.
  - At every stage of the process, *make it worse*.

9

Force of Evil

Death Wishes, Malignant Hearts, and
Summoning the Apocalypse

"The greatest temptations are not those that solicit our consent
to obvious sin, but those that offer us great evils masking as the
greatest goods."

—Thomas Merton, *No Man Is an Island*

It is sometimes easy to fall into the trap of believing that all Yearnings
involve a greater largeness of heart, generosity of spirit, or some other
enhancement of virtue: courage, honesty, compassion, forbearance.
This is a natural extension, though perhaps an oversimplification if
not misinterpretation,[1] of the psychoanalytic ideal of *individuation*,
which presupposes an instinctive drive to integration, wholeness, and
ultimate health.

As gratifying or reassuring as it might be to interpret human striving only in its most positive light, the truth is a harsh mistress. Not everyone wants to sing in the choir.

In the preceding chapter, we covered those cases where the character
misunderstands or misconceives his Yearning. That analysis addressed
instances where the character has been misled somehow as to what is
truly important, or where life has forced him off course and he no longer
feels willing or able to pursue what he might more wisely long for, but instead chooses something else. The choice of an alternative path is important. It means the character's willfulness or hope for some form of positive
outcome has not been totally destroyed or undermined, just mishandled.

---

1 The misunderstanding typically arises from failure to take into account individuation's
requirement to integrate the Shadow, i.e., the unconscious personality that contains the
repressed, negative, disavowed aspects of the Self. Absent such integration, these traits
typically get projected onto others, behavior which itself all too often results in objectifi-
cation, hatred, and evil.

Our focus here is different, or at least more extreme. We are going to discuss those characters who genuinely long for pain, destruction, dissolution, and/or chaos for themselves or others, either because that seems to be the only way to escape some profound sense of affliction or the only way to claim power that feels truly significant, right, and meaningful.

In *The Art of Character*, I noted my preference for the terms "protagonist" and "opponent" to "hero" and "villain." However, as the title of this chapter indicates and this brief introductory section makes plain, we are not about to discuss characters who merely stand in opposition to one or two others. We are about to discuss those characters who on some level understand and embrace the transgressive nature of both their ends and their means. It seems not improper, then, to give them their due and refer to them as villains.

I. ARE VILLAINS BORN OR MADE?

A common temptation in creating villains is to slap a diagnostic label onto the character, commonly from what is referred to as the Dark Triad of personality disorders[2] (ironically, the three such disorders most commonly found in successful people):

- **Narcissism** (characterized by grandiosity, pride, egotism, and a lack of empathy)
- **Machiavellianism** (characterized by manipulation and exploitation of others, a cynical disregard for morality, and a focus on self-interest and deception)
- **Psychopathy** (characterized by enduring antisocial behavior, impulsivity, risk taking, selfishness, callousness, and remorselessness)

As useful as a writer might find such diagnostic descriptions, this kind of labeling risks violating the first and most essential rule of characterization: *Justify, don't judge, the character.* Or, as frequently

---

2 Some researchers have proposed adding a fourth disorder, "everyday sadism," by which is meant the consistent embrace of cruelty, but since such a propensity readily conforms to the other three disorders listed above, for purposes of our discussion here there seems little need to include it.

remarked in writing circles these days, *The villain is the hero of his own narrative.*

Attaching a label to a character is an implicit judgment, exhibiting a need to confine her behavior within a descriptive straitjacket. This diminishes the character, and speaks more to the limitations of the author than the truth of the depiction.

Claiming a character's behavior is entirely explained by some neurological condition risks creating a "plot puppet" in scientific drag. The character becomes a mere victim or automaton, albeit of a horrific sort, draped in psychobabble.

The way to rectify this is to once again reclaim the character's dignity through imagining his Yearning. As long as he is conscious, he is more than just a robotic response to unconscious stimuli. He will possess an inner narrative that serves as justification for what he does, and the need and sense of urgency that compel it—all of which reflects the harsh freedom he embraces, the dark avenger he longs to be, the righteous nightmare he hopes to bring to life. In a word, his Yearning.

The French philosopher Simone Weil devised the term "affliction" to refer to experiences of relentless, unmitigated, and horrific violence, deprivation, and shaming—such as repeated child abuse, rape, torture, prison, combat. Children are especially vulnerable, including those who have fled drought, famine, war zones, or those confined within refugee camps.

Such experiences, especially if the sufferer feels not only that there is no escape but also succumbs to a deep and personal shame because of his suffering, can result in an utter loss of faith in human decency so profound it plunges the sufferer into the blackest despair. The doubt whether well-being will ever return or whether one's former sense of self even matters anymore destroys forever the ability to love or accept love. Such individuals live in a darkness so profound that escape no longer seems possible.

This sort of prolonged, repeated, malicious abuse finds its way into the biographies of numerous violent offenders. What might appear to be simply a "malignant heart," as the legal texts would phrase it, in fact is the consequence of unthinkable victimization, not just in childhood.

In his exceptional memoir *A Place to Stand*, Jimmy Santiago Baca recounts being told by a fellow inmate of how he once had plans for a better life, hoping to do right, but the time passed while he was still in prison. Instead there was just the continuing punishment of incarceration past any time that was justified:

> [A]nd the hurt in your heart turns to bitterness, freedom turns to vengeance, and you look forward to getting out, not to resume your life but to hurt people the way they hurt you, for punishment that made no sense, for the hurting and hurting, for the day when you couldn't take it anymore but you had to and you lost your humanity.

This can be thought of as an extreme case where experience has forged—or malformed—the individual's Yearning. Whatever innocent or benevolent "dream of life" might have once existed is lost for good. Another Yearning has risen in its place, marked by a craving for power and dominance that, in turn, echoes back to an underlying terror of weakness or bitterness at the savage destruction of any hope, even if the individual remains unaware or unconscious of that fact.

AN EXTREME TYPE: THE DYSTOPIAN VILLAIN— SUMMONING THE APOCALYPSE

Sometimes it's not just one's own life, but life itself, that seems to have suffered relentless attack, obliging the individual to do something, strike back, avenge not just the innocent but innocence itself. Burn it all down. Only by removing all the rot, the thinking goes, can goodness be reborn. And so the time has come for a purifying fire—and the perpetrator is acting not out of mere selfish compulsion but as an instrument of divine retribution. The destruction is not just desired; it's deserved.

To understand such horrific longings, one has to tap into the underlying sense of impotence, hopelessness, and extreme vulnerability fraught with terror. No one is coming to the rescue. The sense of dread is unrelenting and absolute—only by burning it all to the ground can hope once again have a ghost of a chance. Imagine what a sense of relief that purification will bring, even amid the flames.

EXERCISES

If you have a character in your WIP who genuinely craves damage and destruction, answer the following questions:

- Can she trace her destructive longings back to experiences in her youth or childhood? If so, what were those experiences, and why did the character never recover from them?
- Similarly, if the character is motivated by hatred, what experiences created the underlying terror, shame, guilt, self-loathing, or sense of degradation that created that hatred?
- If the character did not experience any such trauma, what accounts for his "malignant heart?" If he was simply "born that way," explore those incidents when he first realized he was "different from others."
- As your story begins, how does the character define and justify her identity and chosen way of life? How would she explain herself? How is she "the hero of her own narrative?" Specifically, how and why does she consider her actions heroic?

II. MORAL ARGUMENT: MORALITY—AND IMMORALITY—AS MOTIVE

Yearning implicitly suggests a moral code, some sense of how one wants to be treated and intends to treat others. Regrettably, that does not mean that the life an individual considers worth living equates with a better life for all.

This is where self-interest converges with immorality, when it goes beyond merely focusing on one's own benefit to completely dismissing the merit of anyone else's. It is one thing to think *I matter more than others*; that's bad enough. It is still another to think *others matter not at all*.

Not that wrongdoers always pursue their naked self-interest so blatantly. Some of the most compelling villains have justified their actions on the grounds that they serve a larger, benevolent purpose. Here are just a few:

- Harry Lime in *The Third Man*, screenplay by Graham Greene: He justifies his bad acts—in this case selling diluted penicillin on the black market in postwar Vienna—by invoking Nietzsche's argument to the effect that calamity and strife, not peace or virtue, forge greatness.

- Noah Cross in *Chinatown*, screenplay by Robert Towne: When asked by the hero, Jake Gittes, why he goes to such corrupt and rapacious lengths to get what he wants, Cross answers so boldly it's clear he considers the answer obvious: "The future, Mr. Gittes. The future." This is a variant on the previous theme and might be worded: Great men focus on doing great things; lesser men fret about the consequences.

- The Joker in *The Dark Knight*, screenplay by Jonathan and Christopher Nolan: This seemingly most cartoonish of all villains actually offers one of the most intricate and compelling moral arguments imaginable. The very premise of his persona echoes the sense that the universe is one vast practical joke. But he also employs two arguments to justify himself and what he does. The first is that seemingly decent people are inherently guided by their own self-interest and will turn on anyone and everyone when things "don't go according to plan." His second moral argument is a variant on the "greatness rises from ruin" argument presented above. He argues that his diabolical acts of violent cruelty have a distinct and justifiable purpose: They create chaos. "And the thing about chaos? Chaos is fair."

This sort of moral justification for one's behavior is known as *moral argument*. It should be part of a larger discussion of what is right and what is not as it is battled out between the characters in the story.

Returning to the examples just given, the moral counterargument could be worded as follows:

- Against Harry Lime in *The Third Man*: The fact that greatness often arises in times of cataclysmic upheaval first and foremost confuses correlation with causality. More importantly, there is nothing great or noble in poisoning children in need of antibiotics for the sake of money.

- Against Noah Cross in *Chinatown*: Again, the correlation vs. causality counterargument applies—there is nothing that proves the future *requires* cruelty or corruption, nor that it exonerates such things in great men. Also, the hero might ask with regards to this justifying future: *Whose future?* Blinding oneself to the pain of others objectifies them, and objectifying human life is inherently evil because no man sees himself as an object.
- Against The Joker in *The Dark Knight*: Seeing life as one enormous joke requires one to see life as meaningless. That argument withers when meaning is not viewed as an objective ideal but as something each of us creates in the course of his life. The fact many people are corrupt does not prove man is inherently corrupt—first, this is faulty induction; second, it requires belief in a distinct human nature. But what if there is no such thing? What if human beings create their identities, their "nature," as they live? Nothing in that case obliges them to be immoral any more than it requires them to be moral. Finally, the idea that chaos is fair completely overlooks the fact that anarchy implicitly favors the powerful—men with "lawyers, guns, and money."

The fact that each of the villainous moral arguments offered above has a compelling counterargument shouldn't blind us to the need to make the villain's justification for her actions not just viable but convincing. This not only makes her more credible but also makes her more frightening. Few things are as terrifying as predation that abides by estimable logic.

This battle between moral arguments expands the contest between protagonist and opponent to one of moral visions, including not just the two adversaries but the worlds they hope to maintain, create, or protect, and all those who would benefit—or suffer—by their victory.

EXERCISES

If you have a character in your WIP who qualifies as a villain, answer the following questions:

- Where does the character draw the line between his own self-interest and the interests of others? Whose interests other than his own does he consider, if anyone's? Why?
- Go back to the character's Yearning, Persistent Virtues, Resistance, and Pathological Maneuvers and develop a narrative that justifies her actions. How has her past shaped her choice of immoral means to an end?
- How would you encapsulate this character's moral argument—i.e., how does he justify his actions despite his apparent harmfulness, destructiveness, or immorality? Does he see his actions serving a larger, nobler purpose? How? Why? What do you consider right, compelling, or legitimate about your villain's moral argument? What is its flaw or weakness?
- What is your hero's counterargument? How does it exploit a flaw or weakness in the villain's argument?

III. DIABOLICAL DISTINCTIONS

We'll move on now from more general conceptual matters to distinct issues concerning approach and portrayal, with each section defined by a choice between two alternatives.

OPAQUE VS. TRANSPARENT

This distinction centers on how much if any of the villain's actual motivation to reveal. Not all come equipped with explicit biographies that explain their turn toward criminality. Shakespeare provided us with two such villains—Iago and Richard III—and their example is instructive.

The Bard was notoriously stingy in providing his characters with motivation, and this is particularly true of Iago. Though he clearly resents being passed over for promotion by Othello, he could easily have rectified that slight by merely carrying out the first part of his plan—engineering a drunken brawl involving Cassio, guaranteeing his demotion.

Iago's decision to keep going, to destroy Othello through manipulation, causing not just the Moor's fall but the murder of his innocent wife, Desdemona, speaks to a craving for more than vengeance and vindication. It speaks to an essentially malevolent nature that revels in deceit and destruction.

Richard III, as befitting royalty, is even more duplicitous, manipulative, and murderous, with a body count Iago would envy, including not just nobles but also women and children.

Though Richard's disfigurement is sometimes cited as a reason for his wickedness—the real Richard of Gloucester contracted idiopathic scoliosis in adolescence—he offers no such justification himself, nor does anyone else. He simply seems, as he himself admits, "determined to prove a villain."

Interestingly, though both characters are clearly reprehensible, they typically mesmerize audiences through the simple trick of speaking directly to them, making all who listen unwitting co-conspirators.

A similar device is used by the modern incarnation of Richard III, Frank Underwood of the American TV series *House of Cards*.[3]

We shouldn't confuse the reader's and audience's understanding with the writer's. One reason Shakespeare deprived characters of explicit motivations was to better allow the audience members to devise their own, deepening their engagement with the play. That doesn't mean he himself was unclear or unaware of what drove the character to act.

Remaining silent about the cause of the monster's passion for carnage and cruelty can intensify the terror she evokes. We are seldom so frightened as when we not only don't understand what is happening but why.

In contrast to the "opaque" villains just discussed, what of the "transparent" ones whose backstories strive to explain the sources of the character's turn toward criminality?

Francis Dolarhyde in *Red Dragon* by Thomas Harris provides an iconic example. From the outside, Francis conforms to the usual

---

3 This technique has been used for other criminal characters. Freddy Clegg in *The Collector* by John Fowles addresses the reader in first person. Patricia Highsmith in *The Talented Mr. Ripley* uses close third person. Unlike the supremely devious Iago, Richard, and Frank Underwood, however, Freddy and Ripley, though aware of what they are doing, lack any genuine insight into the fact that it's evil—an effect that only enhances the terror they invoke, for an individual who sees no evil in his actions is capable of virtually anything.

diagnostic profile of a sexual predator—a victim of severe sexual and psychological abuse as a child, resulting in fantasies of sadistic and murderous domination.

Harris, however, does not limit his character to that biography. He also gives Francis a fascination with William Blake's painting *The Great Red Dragon and the Woman Clothed with the Sun*.

This vision informs how Francis views not just himself but his sadistic longings and murders. He is not the mere product of his painful, humiliating past. He is a monster in the truest, greatest, most transcendent meaning of the word. He exemplifies what Jung referred to as "psychopathic inflation," creating a pathological identification so extreme that he doesn't merely see the Red Dragon as an analogy—he *becomes* the Red Dragon.

But what of those predators who don't have such lofty ambitions but still are responding to childhoods of extreme deprivation? The main reason to reveal those depredations instead of keeping them "opaque" is to reveal how victims are chosen to negate the character's own suffering and his profound feelings of victimization.

In many cases, those victims will serve as symbolic surrogates for his original tormentors. In others, the victims will serve as totemic replacements for the sufferer himself, helping him to erase the memory of his own violation by inflicting it on someone else: *I'm not the victim, you are.* Or he intends to expose the false nature of innocence, having lost it himself forever: *I'll show you what the world is really like.*

There is no hard-and-fast rule as to which approach, opaque or transparent, is better. It ultimately depends on what effect you want to create, both throughout the story and especially at the end.

EVIL INCARNATE VS. FATALLY HUMAN

In trying to decide whether to reveal a villain's backstory or not, the prime consideration is to what extent you want to humanize the character. Many readers and audiences expect to be terrified by the villain, want to root against him, and crave a truly gratifying, cathartic climax where he receives the violent end he deserves. This is far easier to do with a villain that embodies pure evil than it is with one that inspires that unsettling form of awareness that borders on empathy or even self-recognition.

To create the evil incarnate villain, you need not only to amplify her cruelty, her treachery, and her willingness to inflict unspeakable harm, but you need as well to show her inflicting that harm on the most empathetic victims in your story. And to get there you will need to accentuate the extremes between the villain's savagery and her victim's merit.

Such a villain must possess a single-minded longing to destroy what others find valuable in their lives. It is not enough for him to get what he wants; others must lose what they want, and that loss must be so devastating as to crush any faith or hope in a life worth living.

Humanizing the villain, however, also has benefits, though the emotional tone of the hero's victory—assuming she does, indeed, prevail—will be significantly different.

First, humanizing the villain helps to blur the distinction between him and the hero, creating a moral no-man's-land between them. Often in stories of this type the hero will have to recognize in herself the negative qualities that give the villain his power—profound willfulness, unwavering focus, an ability to seek out and attack his adversary's weakness—and muster them within herself without succumbing to the villain's immorality.

Example: Michael Mann's *Heat* (1995). The portrayals of hero and villain in this film are so balanced it is almost unfair to call Neil McCauley (played by Robert DeNiro) a villain—rather, he and the detective hero, Lt. Vincent Hanna (Al Pacino), more resemble combatants on opposite sides of an urban war than cop and criminal, but the story's arc ultimately makes clear who is on the side of right.

McCauley is a brilliant, sophisticated thief with a well-trained and heavily armed crew whose expertise is swift, well-planned heists—of an armored car, a precious metals depository, and a bank in the course of the story. Both he and Hanna are intense, committed, smart, and fearless. The difference between them lies not just in what side of the law they've chosen, but in their approach to human relationships.

Hanna is a married man, though not a terribly successful one. Mc-Cauley believes in valuing nothing he can't leave behind in thirty seconds if he feels "the heat," i.e., the police closing in. Ironically, as Hanna struggles to keep his third marriage from crumbling, McCauley falls in love, suggesting an ironic twist on expectations given what we've learned about each man so far: Hanna's commitment to marriage will prove fruitless while McCauley will at last find someone worth sticking around for. As the battle between the two men escalates to a climax, however, their true natures reemerge. Hanna answers the bell when his wife's daughter tries to commit suicide, and he and his wife reconnect in the face of this averted tragedy; in contrast, when McCauley has to choose between going on the run or salvaging his new relationship, he reverts to form and tries to flee alone. When the two adversaries face off in the climax, Hanna ultimately prevails, then holds McCauley's hand as he dies from his wounds.

If the hero does not take this approach of mirroring the villain's ferocity but not his immorality, he will to have to find different but equally forceful elements of his own personality to counteract the traits that make the villain so formidable.

What this usually means is that the hero, by employing virtues such as honesty, integrity, authenticity, determination, courage, intelligence, clarity, and compassion, will rally others to her cause, and this will prove a crucial source of strength.

Another unique facet of humanizing the villain is the ability to raise questions such as, Does he possess insight into his evil? Is he therefore possibly capable of change?

The problem with a villain that can change is that it can diminish the Unity of Opposites[4] between hero and villain, and thus lower the dramatic tension by offering the prospect of compromise rather than outright victory or defeat.

---

4 As used by Lajos Egri in *The Art of Dramatic Writing*, the Unity of Opposites refers to a condition between adversaries that makes it impossible for either individual to remove himself from the contest; not only that, only one can prevail. The other must lose, and the more devastating the loss, the greater the dramatic effect.

However, just because a villain has insight or the capacity to change does not mean she does not embrace her position with her whole strength and will. If you can justify that unwavering position through moral argument or personal history to the extent the reader or audience recognizes its validity or even empathizes or identifies with her plight, you have the opportunity of elevating your story to a moral and emotional plain that few good-versus-evil stories achieve. The thematic takeaway of such stories is that what we consider evil in the world is by no means extraordinary; it is all too human.

DEVIL VS. MONSTER

The type of villain we might refer to as satanic predates his apotheosis in the form of Lucifer in *Paradise Lost*, but the type became iconic with Milton's portrayal.

Since then we have seen an impressive parade of avatars, all striving to equal the Dark One in cunning, cruelty, and magnificence. Both Machiavelli and the Marquis de Sade were considered real-life incarnations. He often bears a whiff of Old World decadence, as seen not only in Count Dracula but Hannibal Lecter, and seldom do we find him without considerable financial means. This points to the class element in his depiction—Satan and his imitators have aristocratic pedigrees, or at least pretend to them. Though an impoverished Lucifer is by no means inconceivable—Fagin in *Oliver Twist* is an example—that sort of conception lies outside the canonical rule, and thus invites consideration from imaginative writers.

Similarly, this breed of villain often possesses a mesmerizing sensuality that flirts with perversion or claims it outright, though this, too, is not an absolute—Fagin again provides a counterexample.

The true hallmark of the satanic villain, however, lies in his insight. He is utterly self-aware. Even in his hungers he exhibits an almost surgical cognizance. That self-awareness is anchored in a profound sense of his own superiority. He longs not so much to destroy as to dominate—all of which returns us to his hallmark pride, encapsulated in Milton's immortal line, "Better to reign in Hell than serve in heaven."

In contrast, we have the beast whose criminal impulses lie largely beyond his control. Like a wasp that has received the signal to sting, he cannot contravene that signal. This villain not only lacks the satanic villain's insight but is largely the victim of unchecked impulse. That lack of insight, however, also creates this villain's greatest strength, for his commitment to his purpose, by being impervious to conscious control, is near absolute.

Sadly, once again the class element reveals itself, for the lower classes have routinely been vilified as bestial, uncivilized, coarse, and unaware. Like all stereotypes, this one begs to be ignored, and the civilized brute is the sort of intrinsically contradictory character that virtually cries out for depiction.

A classic example of the brutish villain comes, like Fagin, from *Oliver Twist*. Bill Sykes all but epitomizes the type. A more modern example appears in Ian McGuire's *The North Water* in the form of Henry Drax, a child rapist and murderer whose appetites are "fierce and surly," who "grasps onto the world like a dog biting into a bone," and who derives neither pleasure nor relief from his violence, "which only increases its ferocity."

Bill Sykes's service as Fagin's underling is hardly unique in fiction, where satanic and brutish villains are frequently paired together as a brains-and-brawn or general-and-soldier team. Bond villains are notorious for this kind of treatment, with Auric Goldfinger enlisting the aid of Oddjob, Karl Stromberg the assistance of the giant Jaws, and Ernst Blofeld the unquestioning allegiance of Mr. Wint, Mr. Kidd, Bambi, Thumper, and a seemingly endless host of nameless SPECTRE agents.

One sees similar pairings in the fantasy genre—e.g., *The Lord of the Rings* (both Sauron and Saruman employ the Orcs as their foot soldiers), and *A Game of Thrones* (Cersei Lannister has Robert Strong, previously known as Gregor "The Mountain" Clegane).

This duality between the leader and his henchmen provides a straightforward means for the writer to employ the entire spectrum of villainy in developing the forces of evil within the story. Care should be taken, however, in avoiding cartoonish simplifications. The character consigned to play the heavy no more needs to be unintelligent than the mastermind needs to be a physical weakling.

PSYCHOPATH (PATHOLOGICAL INDIVIDUALISM) VS. SOCIOPATH (DEFIANT INDIVIDUALISM)

We have previously addressed those individuals with an organic personality disorder, and we have noted that a perversion of self-interest often lies at the heart of immoral behavior. Psychopathy is such a personality disorder. The psychopath seeks his own interest, even at its most sadistic, with a callousness and remorselessness that places his pursuit of his individual longings in the realm of what is sometimes referred to as pathological individualism. His actions and motivations are solely self-directed, and he concerns himself with no one's welfare but his own.

In contrast, there are those who identify with a certain social, ethnic, cultural, or political group who evidence some of the same sadism, callousness, and remorselessness, but who nonetheless confine their hurtful behavior to those outside the group. Members of criminal gangs, organized crime, and terrorist cells fall into this category, and their motivations are distinctly different from the lone-wolf psychopath.

The term "defiant individualism" was used to define this aspect of gang membership by sociologist Martin Sanchez-Jankowski in his book *Islands in the Street: Gangs and American Urban Society.*

A particularly noteworthy example that blends aspects of terrorism with organized crime is the *Chechenskaya bratva* or "Chechen brotherhood" in Russia. Its roots lie in the traditional figure of the *abrek*, a quasi-mythical "Caucasus Robin Hood" whose banditry is seen as a form of honorable vengeance against corrupt authority—especially in the form of the Russian regime, which has historically oppressed Chechnya. An ethos of self-sufficiency combines with an almost maniacal devotion to violence as the individual criminals form ad hoc gangs to pull off daring capers and raids against the rich and powerful for the benefit of the less advantaged, with special focus on targeting their rivals in the Russian underworld.

The defiant individualist views the world at large as hostile to her interests, but also sees membership in a group as the best means to maximize her own personal efforts at success. This group mentality typically generates a moral code for members within the group, emphasizing loyalty, obedience, courage, and a certain selflessness, with behavior toward those outside the group largely unchecked except to the extent it affects the group. The killing by gang members of police officers or "civilians," for example, is generally considered off-limits, not because of the harm it causes to those individuals but because of the enhanced scrutiny from law enforcement such predation will create. In contrast, attacks against rival gang members are not only condoned but encouraged.

In depicting such individuals in a story, neglect of this us-versus-them dynamic risks creating at best an inaccurate portrayal. In contrast to the utterly self-involved psychopath, the defiant individualist combines a sense of general injustice with group allegiance in justifying whatever harm she inflicts on others.

EXERCISES

Opaque vs. Transparent

- Assuming your story possesses a villain—do you intend to make his motivations explicit or simply suggest them through his actions? How do you intend to justify them to yourself? If you're not going to explain how your character came by his evil inclinations, do you intend to allow that character to speak directly to the reader or audience, either through breaking the fourth wall (in film or on the stage) or by using first person or close third person narrative in fiction? To what extent do you intend to allow the character insight into the genuine malevolence of his actions?
- In contrast, if you intend to reveal the villain's backstory, how are her victims chosen to negate her own suffering and her profound feelings of victimization? Are they symbolic surrogates for her original tormentors? *I'm not the victim, you are.* Or do they represent the innocence the killer has lost forever? *I'll show you what the world is really like?*

Evil Incarnate vs. Fatally Human

- Does your villain represent some form of evil incarnate? If so, how do you intend to amplify his cruelty, his treachery, and his willingness to inflict unspeakable harm, and show him inflicting that harm on the most empathetic victims in your story?

- If you intend to humanize your villain, how do you intend to blur the distinction between him and the hero? Will the hero come to recognize in herself the negative qualities that give the villain his power and muster them within herself? Or will she find different but equally forceful elements of her own personality to counteract the traits that make the villain so formidable, rallying others to her side? Will your all-too-human villain possess insight into his evil? Is he capable of change? If so, how will you preserve the Unity of Opposites between hero and villain without lowering the dramatic tension? (Hint: Despite the villain's capacity for insight or change, strengthen his commitment to his purpose through moral argument or personal history.)

Devil vs. Monster

- Does your villain fall into the satanic category? How so? Specifically, how is she utterly self-aware? What justifies her profound sense of her own superiority? In what way does she believe that it is "better to reign in Hell than serve in heaven"?

- In contrast, is your villain more a monster than a devil? How is he a victim of unchecked impulse? How does his lack of insight enhance his strength? How is he "a monster on a mission"?

- Do you intend to pair your satanic and brutish villains together? If so, how will this enhance your depiction of the entire spectrum of villainy within the story?

Psychopath (Pathological Individualism) vs. Sociopath (Defiant Individualism)

- Is your villain more readily described as a psychopath or a sociopath—or neither? Justify your answer.

- Specifically, if she is a psychopath, how are her callous, remorseless actions and motivations solely self-directed with no one's welfare but her own at issue?
- In contrast, if he is a sociopath, what binds him to the group with which he identifies? Why does he view the world at large as unjust or hostile to his interests? Why does he see membership in a group as the best means to maximize his own personal efforts at success?

IV. THE VILLAIN IN SECRET SEARCH OF PUNISHMENT

> I thought that if I were broken enough
> I would see the light
> —Robert Creeley, "The Revelation"

In each of the preceding examples we've cited, the villain has sought to succeed at his criminal plan. Although this is certainly true in the overwhelming number of cases, those instances where the villain secretly wishes to be caught and either punished or killed provide a fascinating exception.

The dramatic problem created by such a character presents itself immediately. Why not just surrender, or commit "suicide by cop"? What we have is a situation much like those addressed in the previous chapter, where an explicit and implicit Yearning are in conflict. Through most of the story the character has an intense investment in the explicit Yearning, which in this case is to continue his criminal activities, while the implicit Yearning is to be caught and brought to justice. This represents a submerged longing for authenticity.

Contrarily, as we also saw in the preceding chapter, sometimes a character—such as Paul Harris in *The Fighter*—can feel so overwhelmed by self-contempt that only a prolonged, almost sacramental journey of self-destruction can purify his soul and possibly lead to change.

Raskolnikov in Dostoyevsky's *Crime and Punishment* provides the classic example. Though initially indifferent to the suffering he causes through a kind of nihilistic idealism, gradually the guilt and horror over the real-life consequences of his act begin to eat away at him. Finally—after several hundred pages of dishonest "philosophizing" and denial—he seeks salvation in confessing fully and truthfully to his crime.

A more modern example is Frank Friedmaier in George Simenon's *Dirty Snow*. Frank is a petty criminal in occupied Belgium during World War II, living with his corrupt mother in her brothel. He murders a German soldier, robs a helpless old woman, and commits a number of other crimes, and never suffers a redemptive turn; instead, up to the very end, he spends his days "hating destiny with an almost personal hatred … wanting to defy it, wrestle with it."

Though Frank cannot bring himself to admit it, he is smitten with Sissy, the teenage girl who lives across the hall, and her quietly noble father. He thinks Sissy is obsessed with him, not the other way around, which is one more way he armors himself against any feelings of affection, which he rejects as weakness. In truth, he is blinded to the concern of others by his guilt, his self-loathing, and the arrogant cynicism he hides behind.

At the end, after Frank's arrest by the occupation authorities, Sissy and her father come to visit him where he is being held for interrogation and, ultimately, execution. Sissy admits she loves him, and her father tells the story of his own son's suicide after being caught stealing from the university where he was studying medicine. "You see," he tells Frank, "it's not an easy job, being a man." After this visit, which Frank refers to as his wedding night, he confronts his Nazi captors: "I am not a fanatic, an agitator, or a patriot. I am a piece of shit." He tells them he knows nothing about what they are investigating, and even if he did he wouldn't talk. They can torture him or promise him his life, it won't matter. "I want to die, as soon as possible, in whatever fashion you choose."

Recovery and rehabilitation narratives often follow a similar logic. The individual's escalating wrongful acts, whether related to addiction or criminal behavior, have such a crash-and-burn quality that they act as a kind of crucible to burn away her weakness, her cowardice, her self-contempt. And yet often, like Frank, the character remains largely unaware of this underlying impulse, this craving for purification, until her self-destruction is all but complete.

As with characters with a misunderstood or misbegotten Yearning, this sort of character has charted a course he believes is leading toward gratification. But that belief is based on an almost all-consuming cynicism, which may not be groundless; he may well exist in an environment of suffocating inauthenticity, hypocrisy, or outright corruption, and he considers his bad acts a legitimate form of rebellion or his addiction a fitting response to the insipidity or meaninglessness of life. But there is also an element of self-hatred, a sense of weakness and futility, often colored by a caustic defiance against anyone with the audacity to demand more from him. At some level, he believes, like the Dystopian Villain mentioned earlier, that only by burning it all to the ground—including and especially himself—can a genuinely new day commence.

EXERCISES

- Does your villain have a secret desire to be caught and either punished or killed? If so, why not simply surrender? Why does she continue on her criminal path despite wanting capture and punishment? What will she do in order to make sure she's caught?
- Does he see his criminality or addiction as a legitimate path to gratification? Does he consider his bad acts a legitimate form of rebellion? Is there also an element of self-hatred, a sense of weakness and futility, colored by defiance? Does he only become aware of his underlying impulse for purification when his self-destruction is all but complete? If so, why?

SUMMARY OF MAIN POINTS IN CHAPTER
ARE VILLAINS BORN OR MADE?

- Not all Yearnings are for integration, wholeness, and health. Some individuals genuinely crave damage and destruction.
- Some such individuals seem to have been "born to be bad," i.e., they seem to possess what legal texts refer to as a "malignant heart."
- A common temptation, when turning such individuals into characters, is to slap a diagnostic label on them, such as Narcissism,

Machiavellianism, or Psychopathy. However, this kind of labeling risks violating the first and most essential rule of characterization: *Justify, don't judge, the character.*

- Also, what might appear to be simply a "malignant heart" may in fact be the consequence of experiences in childhood or early youth of relentless, unmitigated, and horrific violence and deprivation—such as repeated child abuse, rape, or torture.

- Such experiences, especially if the sufferer feels not only that there is no escape, but also succumbs to a deep and personal shame because of his suffering, can result in such an utter loss of faith in human decency that the ability to love or accept love is forever lost.

- This can be thought of as an extreme case where experience has forged—or malformed—the individual's Yearning. Whatever innocent or benevolent "dream of life" might have once existed is lost for good. Another Yearning has risen in its place, marked by a craving for power and dominance.

- The Dystopian Villain seeks wholesale destruction as a form of universal purification.

- In the end, whether the character was born to her evil nature or earned it though experience is largely irrelevant. The point is this: As your story begins, that image of herself now defines her identity and chosen way of life, and she considers the inner narrative that she uses to justify her actions totally willful and self-generated.

MORAL ARGUMENT—MORALITY AS MOTIVE

- Yearning implicitly suggests a moral code, for a way of life includes some sense of how one wants to be treated and intends to treat others.

- One's morality reflects the implicit balance the individual has struck between pursuing her own interests and respecting those of others.

- Self-interest converges with immorality when it goes beyond merely focusing on one's own interest to completely dismissing the merit of anyone else's. Taken to its extreme, this objectifies other people, stripping them of the humanity they deserve.

- Not all wrongdoers always pursue their self-interest blatantly. Some of the most compelling villains have justified their actions on the grounds that their actions serve a larger, benevolent purpose.
- The justification the villain gives for his actions often takes the form of a moral argument.
- The fact that a villainous moral argument has a compelling counterargument doesn't eliminate the need to make the villain's justification for his actions not just viable but convincing. This not only makes him more credible; it makes his more frightening.
- This battle between moral arguments expands the contest between protagonist and opponent to one of moral visions, including not just the two adversaries but the worlds they hope to maintain, create, or protect.

DIABOLICAL DISTINCTIONS

Opaque vs. Transparent

- Not all characters possess explicit biographies that might explain their turn toward criminality. Shakespeare provided us with two such villains—Iago and Richard III. A third is Frank Underwood of the American TV series *House of Cards*.
- These characters speak directly to the audience, allowing audience members to "lean in" to the story and provide their own motivations for why the characters act so reprehensibly.
- This can be a powerful technique, especially with a character whose actions are not just surprising but horrifying, and can intensify the terror she evokes.
- However, even if the character's motivation is withheld from the reader or audience, failure to explore why he acts as he does can result in a vague, unconvincing, or confusing depiction.
- This emphasizes the need to understand the character's subjective experience of her actions. As long as she is conscious, her intent is an expression of the dark avenger she longs to be, the righteous nightmare she hopes to bring to life.

- The main reason to reveal the villain's backstory is to reveal how his victims are chosen to negate his own suffering and his profound feelings of victimization.
- In many cases, those victims will serve as symbolic surrogates for her original tormentors: *I'm not the victim, you are.* In other cases, the victim will represent the innocence the killer has lost forever: *I'll show you what the world is really like.*
- There is no hard-and-fast rule as to which approach, opaque or transparent, is better. It ultimately depends on what effect you want to create, both throughout the story and especially at the end. For more on that, proceed to the next section.

Evil Incarnate vs. Fatally Human

- Many readers and audiences expect to be terrified by the villain, want to root against him, and crave a truly gratifying, cathartic climax where he receives what he deserves. This is far easier to do with a villain that embodies pure evil.
- To create the evil incarnate villain, you need to amplify her cruelty, her treachery, and her willingness to inflict unspeakable harm, and show her inflicting that harm on the most empathetic victims in your story.
- In terms of Yearning, such a villain must possess a single-minded longing to destroy what others find valuable. It is not enough for him to get what he wants; others must lose what they want, and that loss must be devastating.
- Humanizing the villain, however, also has benefits, though the emotional tone of the hero's victory will be significantly different.
- Humanizing the villain helps to blur the distinction between him and the hero, creating a moral no-man's-land between them.
- Often in stories of this type the hero will have to recognize in herself the negative qualities that give the villain his power and muster them within herself without succumbing to his immorality.
- Otherwise, she will to have to find different but equally forceful elements of her own personality to counteract the traits that make the

villain so formidable. This usually means that the hero, by employing virtues such as honesty, integrity, courage, compassion, etc. will rally others to her cause.

- Another unique facet of humanizing the villain is the ability to raise questions such as: Does he possess insight into his evil? Is he therefore possibly capable of change?
- The problem with a villain that can change is that it can diminish the Unity of Opposites between hero and villain, and thus lower the dramatic tension by offering the prospect of compromise rather than outright victory or defeat.
- However, just because a villain has insight or the capacity to change does not mean she does not embrace her position with her whole strength and will. You can justify that unwavering position through moral argument or personal history.

Devil vs. Monster

- The satanic villain typically possesses cunning, cruelty, and a certain magnificence, with a whiff of Old World decadence, considerable financial means, and a perverse sensuality.
- The true hallmark of the satanic villain, however, lies in his insight. He is utterly self-aware, and even in his hungers he exhibits an almost surgical cognizance. That self-awareness is anchored in a profound sense of his own superiority. He longs not so much to destroy as to dominate: "Better to reign in Hell than serve in heaven."
- In contrast, the bestial villain's criminal impulses lie largely beyond his control. This villain not only lacks the satanic villain's insight, he is largely the victim of unchecked impulse. That lack of insight, however, also creates this villain's greatest strength, for his commitment to his purpose, by being impervious to conscious control, is near absolute.
- Satanic and brutish villains are frequently paired together as a brains-and-brawn or general-and-soldier team. This duality between the leader and his henchmen provides a straightforward

means for the writer to employ the entire spectrum of villainy in developing the forces of evil within the story.

Psychopath (Pathological Individualism) vs. Sociopath (Defiant Individualism)

- The psychopath seeks his own interest, even at its most sadistic, with a callousness and remorselessness sometimes referred to as pathological individualism. His actions and motivations are solely self-directed, and he concerns himself with no one's welfare but his own.
- In contrast, there are those who identify with a certain social, ethnic, cultural, or political group who evidence some of the same sadism, callousness, and remorselessness who nonetheless confine their hurtful behavior to those outside the group. Members of criminal gangs, organized crime, and terrorist cells fall into this category, and their motivations are distinctly different from the lone-wolf psychopath. The term "defiant individualism" is sometimes used to define such individuals; so is "sociopath."
- The defiant individualist views the world at large as hostile to his interests, but also sees membership in a group as the best means to maximize his own personal efforts at success.
- In depicting such individuals in a story, neglect of this us-versus-them dynamic risks creating at best an inaccurate portrayal. In contrast to the utterly self-involved psychopath, the sociopath combines a sense of general injustice with group allegiance in justifying whatever harm he inflicts on others.

The Villain in Secret Search of Punishment

- Sometimes the villain secretly wishes to be caught and punished.
- The dramatic problem created by such a character is obvious: Why not just surrender? Usually, an explicit and implicit Yearning are in conflict, and the character has through most of the story an intense investment in the explicit Yearning, which in this case is to continue her criminal activities.

- Contrarily, the character can feel so overwhelmed by self-contempt that only a prolonged journey of self-destruction can purify his soul so that he might change.
- Recovery and rehabilitation narratives often follow a similar logic. The individual's escalating wrongful acts, whether related to addiction or criminal behavior, act as a kind of crucible to burn away her weakness, her cowardice, her self-contempt.
- This sort of character has charted a course he believes is leading toward gratification. But that belief is based on cynicism, which may not be groundless; he may consider his bad acts a legitimate form of rebellion.
- But there is also an element of self-hatred, a sense of weakness and futility, often colored by a caustic defiance against the world. At some level, she believes that only by burning it all to the ground—including and especially herself—can a genuinely new day commence. In this way her motivations resemble those of the Dystopian or Apocalyptic Villain, but the scope of her need for destruction is much narrower.

10

Divided Desire

←—————————————————————————→

> Let me but remark that the Evil One, with his single passion of
> satanic pride for the only motive, is yet, on a larger, more modern
> view, allowed to be not quite so black as he used to be painted.
> With what greater latitude, then, should we appraise the exact
> shade of mere mortal man, with his many passions and his mis-
> erable ingenuity in error, always dazzled by the base glitter of
> mixed motives, everlastingly betrayed by a short-sighted wisdom.
> —Joseph Conrad, *Under Western Eyes*

In the final episode of the award-winning TV series *Breaking Bad,* Walter White finds himself trapped in a snowbound car while police hunt
for him just outside. Hoping to escape arrest, he prays to whatever God
he thinks might listen: "Just let me get home. … Just let me get home."

With these words, mild-mannered Walt—aka the meth lord Heisenberg—reaches back in thematic time, echoing the same sentiment the
Greek hero Odysseus embraced in his famous ten-year journey from
the ruins of Troy to his palace in Ithaca.

But Walt and Odysseus share much more than a desire to get back
home. In the psychological complexity and moral tension they exhibit, they stand among a variety of avatars with names like Lazarillo
de Tormes, Moll Flanders, Adolph Verloc, Humbert Humbert, Augie
March, John Yossarian, Randle Patrick McMurphy.

There's no one set of pat traits that categorically encompasses all of
these characters, though the epithet *anti-hero* routinely gets slapped
beside their names.

But *anti-hero* defines them by negation, emphasizing what they're
typically not—altruistic, honest, idealistic, courageous—which does
nothing to explain their appeal. Their attractiveness to readers and

viewers is not just enduring but, judging from recent trends in television, inexhaustible. For a mere handful of examples, consider Tony Soprano (*The Sopranos*), Dexter Morgan (*Dexter*), Patty Hewes (*Damages*), Don Draper (*Mad Men*), Nancy Botwin (*Weeds*), "Red" Reddington (*Blacklist*)—and, of course, Walter "Heisenberg" White.

What *anti-hero* does get at, though somewhat indirectly, is the fundamental antagonism at the core of this character's existence, the wily rebellion, the refusal to bow. And that helps explain the timing of when these characters have often emerged, for they typically blossom in times of reaction to cherished ideals that, for one reason or another, seem to have grown outdated, if not rancid.

Some sources point to the disfigured, vulgar, dimwitted Greek soldier Thersites as the true progenitor of the anti-hero. But he plays such a minor role in the *Iliad* that he seems more a suggestion than a model. Appearing in just one scene, he dares speak "truth to power," condemning Agamemnon as cowardly and motivated solely by greed (something all the other warriors are thinking but refuse to say out loud).

In contrast, the warrior Odysseus, who rebukes Thersites and beats him until he weeps from shame, possesses enough heft and complexity to present something truly unique, even revolutionary.

This is especially clear when he's compared to the other great warriors in the Achaean camp: Achilles and Ajax.

The *Iliad* is a transitional narrative, dramatizing the eclipse of an era championing heroic values to one prizing rhetorical ones. Achilles and Ajax, despite their limitations—volatility of temper and vanity in the first case, a certain beef-wittedness (Shakespeare's term) in the other—both represent the courage and ambition for glory typical of the great hero. And both die before the walls of Troy: Achilles in battle, Ajax by his own hand. Their deaths signal an end to the heroic age.

From that point on, Odysseus commands the stage, and he is not just a great warrior. He is also the consummate deceiver, a descendent of both the Olympian trickster Hermes and the thief Autolycus. Known as much for his cunning as his courage, he performs a great many feats of valor but also feigns lunacy in an attempt to avoid combat, corrupts

Achilles's son Neoptolemus by coaching him to lie, deceives Clytemnestra about the death of her daughter, Iphigenia, and famously enjoys the sexual hospitality of Circe and Calypso while dallying on his return to his devotedly faithful wife, Penelope.

It's this essentially dual nature—a warrior's warrior on the one hand, a shamelessly amoral opportunist on the other—that keys our fascination. We're never sure exactly which Odysseus will appear at any given moment, and this creates a kind of character-driven suspense unrivaled in ancient Western literature. The doubt of Moses, the ignorance of Oedipus, the licentiousness of David don't even come close—underscoring the distinction between a heroic flaw and a psyche at war with itself.

As it turned out, there would be no hero like Odysseus in Western literature for centuries. His disappearance is largely due to the fact the Romans despised him—he violated their sense of duty, their belief in the preeminence of honor.

This is one reason the Romans traced the founding of Rome to the hero Aeneas, preferring the defeated Trojans to the victorious Greeks, whom they considered immoral and corrupt. Virgil in particular seldom referred to Ulysses, the Roman name for Odysseus, without the adjectives *cruel* or *deceitful.*

Glimpses of Odysseus could still be found in the satires and comedies of Menander, Plautus, and Terence, as well as bawdy Milesian tales such as *The Golden Ass* by Apuleius and Petronius's *Satyricon.* But these representations were largely satiric and lacked the epic stature of the warrior Odysseus.

The chivalric romance of the late Middle Ages and early Renaissance was largely an aristocratic form, and as the Golden Age of Hapsburg Spain began to curdle into corruption and decline, the fantastic adventures of the intrepid knight errant were losing a bit of their sheen.

An entirely new form of novel emerged on the Iberian Peninsula, based in part on the Arabic genre of *maqamat* and Slavic folktales, such as those featuring Till Eulenspiegel, imported from Germany under Charles V. The first novel of this kind appeared in 1554 and was titled *The Life of Lazarillo de Tormes and of his Fortunes and Adversities.*

Due to its scandalous subject matter and blasphemous disregard for the Church, it was banned almost everywhere, and the identity of its author remains in debate. And yet it proved not just wildly popular but profoundly influential.

Instead of steadfast knights, these novels featured lovable, wandering rogues and thieves, known as *picaros*, and the stories recounted their morally questionable but never explicitly wicked exploits.

Principally, the stories concerned the plight of the poor, forced to live by their wits in a patently corrupt and hypocritical society. There was often an element of redemptive conversion near the end, despite the blatant attacks on priests and other clerical officials.

In short, we have a return to something like the dual nature of Odysseus, with both virtue and vice residing in the hero's heart, enjoying a tricky equilibrium.

The appeal of the picaresque novel spread across Europe and took solid root in England, where its popularity survived into the nineteenth century in novels featuring rakish heroes such as Tom Jones, Moll Flanders, Barry Lyndon, and Martin Chuzzlewit.

None of these protagonists were irredeemably evil or, in the end, completely reformed, though the good in their natures tended to overshadow the bad. Rather, all possessed a duality of character forged by the misfortunes of poverty and birth in a society premised on the crowing of virtue amid the worship of privilege and greed.

As the popularity of the English picaresque novel was cresting in the late eighteenth and early nineteenth centuries, another type of hero was taking shape. Like the *picaro* and the wanderer, he was a social outsider, but it was temperament rather than class that defined his iconoclasm.

A kind of orphan child of Romanticism, he possessed a brooding intelligence that defied the coal-stoked ambition and pompous vulgarity of the Industrial Revolution.

With Hamlet as forebear and Lord Byron as mastermind, this hero gave us the Gothic novel and found himself incarnated in characters as diverse as the Brontë sisters' Heathcliff and Rochester, Victor Hugo's Quasimodo, Alexandre Dumas's Count of Monte Cristo, and the original vampire, Lord Ruthven.

Byron, describing the pirate hero of his verse tale *The Corsair*, provided a kind of template:

He knew himself a villain—but he deem'd
The rest no better than the thing he seem'd;
And scorn'd the best as hypocrites

Or, as Lady Caroline Lamb said of Byron himself, this new breed of icon was "mad, bad, and dangerous to know."

Again, the theme of defining a new, more authentic morality in a society rotten with falsity found voice in a hero neither evil nor virtuous, but revealing instead an uneasy marriage of both.

Europe was hardly alone in this reconsideration of what it meant to be heroic. The American West, especially in the hands of sensationalist newspapermen and hagiographic dime novelists, presented a multitude of characters, some working on the side of the law, others conspicuous outlaws, many others occupying a curious middle ground, that were ultimately epitomized in what became known as the "Good Bad Man."

This new breed of hero was born in the shadow of the Civil War, which exhibited a form of organized butchery never before seen in warfare. He was forged as well in encounters with Native Americans, whose warrior values and imperviousness to suffering seemed "savage" to Christian settlers. Finally, he was set loose in the vast and virtually lawless frontier which provided safe haven for every variety of desperado, hooligan, renegade, and hellhound imaginable. Given this background, he often found it necessary to be as evil as the day required, given who he had to deal with. It wasn't enough to be upstanding, courageous, and strong. Without a certain devilish cunning, mercenary greed, and willing embrace of violence, this outlaw-lawman couldn't hope to tame the territories in his charge.

None, however, more captures the imagination or better personifies the unique American embodiment of the anti-hero than John Henry "Doc" Holliday.

Although Wyatt Earp defended him to his dying days as one of the most loyal and courageous men he ever knew, Doc Holliday had few other friends. The wives of both Wyatt and Virgil Earp detested him, and Bat Masterson described him in largely unflattering terms, saying he had "a mean disposition and an ungovernable temper, and under the influence of alcohol was a most dangerous man." Doc's reputation was so profoundly negative in Tombstone, it was used against the Earps in the trial following the gunfight at the O.K. Corral. But none of the negativity could quite dispel the lingering fascination with an intelligent, well-spoken, highly literate Southerner trained as a dentist who became not just a successful gambler but one of the most feared men in the West.

As the foregoing suggests, this maturation in the tradition of the anti-hero paralleled a similar development in the depiction of the hero, who evolved from the incorruptible vessel of virtue found in the chivalric romance to a more nuanced, complicated, flawed human being.

In truth, this hero had been with us since the time of Greek tragedy, though Aristotle, in his *Poetics*, emphasized that the hero should err not through some fault of character but a mistake in judgment. Even so, his term for this error, *hamartia*, gradually came to be understood as the hero's tragic flaw.

And as the English novel of self-improvement gained popularity in the early nineteenth century, heroes became capable of positive change. They were not prisoners of their flaws but, through insight, were capable of overcoming these limitations. In fact, the very definition of hero changed to incorporate this notion of inherent flaw, willful insight, and deliberate self-transformation.

But the skepticism that has traditionally given rise to the anti-hero remained unconvinced that such positive change was always possible— or desirable.

Even as Freud's development of psychoanalysis hinted at the potential for curative insight, his concept of the Unconscious so often resembled a monstrous darkness that it often seemed the best that even the sanest mind could hope for was an uneasy truce with its demons. And creativity in particular seemed to require a willingness to risk imbalance.

The vision of the divided hero, a person equally capable of infamy or greatness, with a moral compass never pointing squarely toward true north, continued to haunt the Western tradition, especially amid the feverish partisanship and ideological rigidity that characterized the twentieth century, with its seemingly constant warfare and its mastery of propaganda.

The concept of nobility and the heroes who embody it took a serious hit in the trenches of the World War I, and the carpet-bombed cities of World War II. The Holocaust and Hiroshima redefined our understanding of Hell and the kind of soul that might inhabit it.

Slaughter and butchery are not ennobling, especially when systematized. A sense of the random, the meaningless, infected the Western psyche. The abyss wasn't just waiting. The abyss was us.

As World War II drew to a close, and for a decade afterward, we saw a flood of B movies and paperbacks characterized as noir, with morally compromised heroes straining to grab that alluring, illusive brass ring.

The pushback was both fierce and fun—Joseph McCarthy, Joe Friday, Doris Day, Technicolor, CinemaScope—and so the anti-hero remained a kind of cultural shadow. But he reemerged with a vengeance in the sixties as the Vietnam conflict wound down, putting the lie to the jingoistic sloganeering of the Cold War, appearing in such neo-noir classics as *Cool Hand Luke, Bonnie and Clyde, Mean Streets, Midnight Cowboy, Catch-22, The Killing of a Chinese Bookie, Dog Day Afternoon, Taxi Driver, The Godfather, Chinatown.*

But the forces of idealism, conformity, and normalcy struck back again, rising up against the dark tide. We got box office blockbusters like *Jaws* and *Star Wars.* We got Ronald Reagan's "Morning in America."

It didn't take long for this largely contrived optimism to grow stale. The nineties arrived, and as novelist Dennis Lehane has remarked, trying to describe the reasons behind but another resurgence of noir—which he considers working-class tragedy—it was clear the so-called prosperity of the Clinton economy and the dot-com boom was a massive house of cards.

There seemed to be a lot of money flying around, but it was landing less and less in middle-class neighborhoods, never mind the working class, let alone the poor. And writers, as always, responded to the Great Lie with characters who saw through the hypocrisy and refused to play nice.

It's tempting to believe that the proliferation of anti-heroes on cable TV since the appearance of *The Sopranos* in 1999 is a continuation of the neo-noir resurgence of the preceding decade. The housing collapse revealed the Bush economy to be an even worse pump-and-dump scheme than the tech stock disaster that plagued the previous regime.

Call it the "New American Anxiety," the recognition that something's gone horribly wrong and won't get better, especially as long as politics continues its degeneration into what Henry Adams blithely described as the systematic organization of hatreds.

The anti-hero seems perfectly suited to the time. Dread smothers all hope while the chattering class indulges in a sanctimonious orgy of blame. The Socratic ideal of the just man, who takes satisfaction solely from his own virtue, seems not only ancient but quaint.

But there's another, far more practical reason for the anti-hero's newfound popularity. In an era of long-format storylines, where a show's narrative arc doesn't stop at the end of this week's episode—it continues not just to the end of the season but on to the next and the season after that—the psychological depth and moral complexity of the anti-hero provide a greater range of dramatic action than a hero constrained by virtue.

Just as with Odysseus, we're never quite sure which half of the divided self will appear in any given scene, and that helps sustain suspense. Tony Soprano's careening between loyalty and cynical narcissism, the clash of Don Draper's capacity for genuine kindness despite an obsession with his fabricated image, Patty Hewes's scorched-earth careerism balanced against a scathing, ruthless honesty, especially about herself— each exemplifies how a soul at war with itself creates a dramatic engine with limitless possibilities.

Which returns us finally to good old Walter White. In the pilot episode of *Breaking Bad*, Walt learns he has terminal cancer and wants to provide financial security for his family, something he realizes is impossible given the new economic reality and his meager salary as a high school chemistry teacher. But this awakens in him something deeper, a need in the truest sense of the word: *to live.*

That war between familial love and a dying man's resurgent self-interest created the defiant Frankenstein we came to know as Heisenberg, with his need to avenge himself against all those who sold him short or stole his promise. He wanted a vengeful, pristine excellence, not mere success.

In the final episode, Walt reveals this exact same divide, though deepened and deftly articulated through five brilliant seasons. Challenged by his wife, who refuses to hear one more time that his criminality came from nothing more than a desire to care for the family, he stands exposed, and finally admits the dark ambition that also drove him: "I was good at it."

Like the tragic hero, the anti-hero stands before a vast, impersonal force—not God or fate but hypocrisy, or the end of an era. Unlike the tragic hero, he avails himself the weapon of amorality, plumbing the darker aspects of his nature. This provides an excellent means to dramatize the seemingly endless struggle between the proud, resourceful individual and the corrupt society that gladly would crush him. And though his turn toward the darkness may help him survive, it also taints whatever victory he manages to come by.

It's a great dramatic trope, with little risk of seeming irrelevant, especially given America's current trajectory. We may see the anti-hero recede into the shadows for a while, as he has before, but it's unlikely he'll vanish anytime soon.

Then again, it may be that the wholesale hypocrisy, corruption, and sanctimonious rage of the current era may tilt dramatic impulses in a new direction toward credible virtue. Such was the view expressed by the actor Brendan Gleeson after his appearance in John Michael McDonagh's *Calvary*, a film centered on Father James, a priest trying his best to help the people under his care in a small Irish town:

> [A]t this point, with the distrust that's there and the disillusionment with leadership that is so acute, we need some kind of a focus on taking the irony out and taking the anti-hero element away. Are there people to aspire to? Can people be strong enough to withstand all of this disillusionment? Maybe the time is right for people to emerge from the easy cynicism and try to get back to a place where we can actually believe

in people and trust people to have proper motivations. I think it's doubly important, now that we see so many people failing. When the norm is an anti-hero, there's a serious loss when you cannot portray a decent person on screen without it becoming slightly sentimental or feeling like it's unrealistic. This [character, Father James] is a seriously flawed man with a lot of failings in his life that he continues to struggle with. He's not a cool, clean hero. He's a very, very ravaged man, who's fighting as hard as he can. I think he's more inspirational, in that way.[1]

EXERCISES

- If you have a character in your story you believe would make a strong candidate for an anti-hero, describe the qualities that make her heroic. (Hint: Look to her Yearning and to those attributes you discovered while exploring her Persistent Virtues.) Then do the same for the qualities that make her immoral. (Hint: similarly, look to her Resistance, especially Flaws, and her Pathological Maneuvers.) Assess the relative weight, i.e., influence upon the character, of these two opposing inclinations. Are they in balance, with neither having a distinct upper hand? If not, what could you change to make it that way? Try to imagine a situation where she has to choose between acting kindly or cruelly, for example, or patiently or angrily, peaceably or violently. What determines which option she takes? How do you know? Analyze the moment in detail—what was it about the situation, the others who were there, what had happened just previously, that impelled the character to act one way rather than the other. Now envision working your way through your entire story with just that sort of delicate equilibrium—can you see yourself continuing indefinitely? Or do you instead see a need to create some kind of reckoning? (Remember that those two options are not mutually exclusive.)

---

1 "Brendan Gleeson Talks *Calvary*, Collaborating with John Michael McDonagh, Reteaming for *The Lame Shall Enter First, Heart of the Sea*, and More," Christina Radish, *The Collider*, August 12, 2014.

Epilogue

Character Work as the Examined Life

> The most fundamental aggression to ourselves, the most fundamental harm we can do to ourselves, is to remain ignorant by not having the courage and the respect to look at ourselves honestly and gently.
>
> —Pema Chödrön, *When Things Fall Apart*

I would be surprised if all the foregoing discussion of how characters long for a better way of living and a more authentic self, and the dozens if not hundreds of ways they get in their own way, did not cause you from time to time to stop for a moment and experience a certain frisson of self-recognition. The approach outlined in this book is very much based in what might be considered psychological realism, and its merits largely reside in its ability to mirror how individuals in real life go about their days. One such individual, of course, would be you.

If you have not already done so, you might want to ask yourself many of the same questions we have posed to our characters in the preceding pages, if for no other reason than to gain a more intimate, personal, intuitive understanding of the material.

Specifically, with as much honesty as you can muster, answer these questions:

- How does your life feel incomplete? What seems missing?
- How does what is missing from your life affect your attitude: Are you confused, morose, restless, anxious, all the more motivated? Take a moment. Settle into your body and be honest with yourself before answering—and remember that no answer is absolute.
- Was there ever a time in your life when you experienced either a feeling or an image that spoke to you as a kind of calling, a crystallization of who you wanted to be and how you hoped to live? If so, when did that happen? How did it change you, if at all? Have you continued to honor that sense of calling ever since? If not, why not?

- If you have never experienced such a moment of clarity, what has defined your sense of purpose or direction in life? How have you known when you were "on track" and when you weren't? Have others contributed to your sense of purpose—i.e., have you had mentors or allies or loved ones who have helped shape your goals or enhanced confidence that you can achieve them? Who are these people? How did they enter your life? Are they still there?
- How would you define your dream of life: the kind of person you want to be, the way of life you want to live? How firmly do you believe in that dream, i.e., do you expect to fulfill the promise of your life? How close do you feel to being who you want to be and living as you should?
- If your dream of life remains unfulfilled, ask yourself why.
- What happens when you sense that you are not living up to your own expectations? How do you think and feel and react?
- What Weaknesses—e.g., laziness, cowardice, lack of confidence, cynicism, despair—are holding you back?
- What Wounds or personal losses have undermined your confidence that pursuing your dreams is worthwhile? How responsible do you feel for those Wounds—i.e., what feelings of shame or guilt do they elicit?
- What Limitations—youth, old age, inexperience, lack of intelligence, poor health, poverty—are constraining your ability to pursue what you want? How might you overcome them?
- What forces of exterior Opposition or Obligation to others inhibit your ability to pursue your dream with your whole heart and soul? How might you change that situation?
- How have the foregoing influences generated behavior that not only holds you back but also hurts others?
- How have these various forces of Resistance become habits of behavior—i.e., what are your Pathological Maneuvers, the habitual responses you have to stress, conflict, frustration, criticism, serious setbacks? Do you retreat into your isolation, preoccupy yourself with distractions or keeping busy, deny your feelings, lash out at others, drink or indulge in some other obsessive or addictive behavior? What do you tell yourself to mitigate the pain of failure (e.g.,

"I didn't really want it that much. ... There will be other opportunities. ... I was never going to get it anyway. ... The whole thing is rigged. ... It's not what you know, it's who you know. ...")?

- Can you look back into your past and identify certain moments of helplessness—specifically moments of fear, guilt, shame, betrayal, or sorrow—that helped form those forces of Resistance within you and the Pathological Maneuvers that resulted? How did you get from there to here?

- Similarly, what moments of courage, forgiveness, pride, trust, and love have shaped your confidence in your ability to pursue what you want from your life? How have those moments helped shape what you consider your virtues?

- How would you rate your confidence in the merit of pursuing the promise of life? How optimistic do you feel that you will achieve what you are trying to accomplish at this stage in your life? How happy do you feel, and how confident are you that this happiness will last—or even grow? Do you believe, to use the Aristotelian term, that you are "flourishing?"

- How strongly does the need to protect yourself from the pain of life affect your decision making? One way to answer this question is to ask what goals, relationships, or improved connection with others you have gainfully pursued on the one hand, and which others have you abandoned, avoided, or neglected out of fear, guilt, shame, mistrust, or sadness?

- Where do you sit right now in the balance between pursuing the promise of life and protecting yourself from the pain of life? Which impulse has the upper hand? If protecting yourself is the dominant force, what would need to happen to change that?

- When have you pursued something only to discover that getting it left you dissatisfied? Why was that? What should you have pursued instead? Why didn't you?

- Have you ever pursued a goal and failed? How profoundly did the objective speak to your sense of who you are and what you want from your life? How did that failure affect your confidence, your sense of worth? What did you do immediately afterward?

- Have you ever felt a deep longing for someone or something, so deep it seemed to define your dream of life—the perfect love, the perfect opportunity—only to have it yanked away, destroyed, or otherwise kept from you? How did you adjust? Does the pain still linger? How does that affect your daily life?
- Have you ever felt a profound longing for someone or something only to discover upon having that longing gratified that it wasn't at all what you imagined? How did you respond? How did it affect your confidence in your own judgment? Did you recover?
- When have you had to choose between two or more options knowing that meant you would lose the other(s) forever? How has the loss of those other possibilities affected you since? Has the choice you made justified giving up the other alternative(s)?
- Have you ever been forced to choose between two or more devastating options? Again, analyze how it affected you, how you responded, what you did afterward, how your life changed.

In answering these questions and any others that arise as you're going about this work, it's extremely helpful to answer not in terms of information but in scenes, and to do so as vividly as possible so that the memory has its full emotional impact on you. That memory and effect will form the imaginative template for your understanding of these circumstances in your own life and create the foundation for building from there to the inner life of your characters.

This use of personal experience as a starting point to imagine the experiences of your characters is known in acting as "personalization." Its critics argue that this brings all characters down to the size of the person trying to depict them, but that argument neglects the role of imagination in completing the job. Becoming self-aware is necessary but not sufficient to the task of storytelling. It provides a crucial foundation, but then one must ask "What if" and enter imaginatively into the life of the character.

The foregoing self-examination most likely generated a sense of humility, not just because you examined in detailed and specific ways how you are not living up to your own expectations of who you should be and how you should live. I would be surprised if you did not also feel a certain elusiveness to your own identity, as though the sense of self that previously felt so serviceable now seems to possess serious cracks and fault lines, and the ground below feels as though it may give way any moment.

As the Albert Camus quote used at the beginning of Part II of this book states, we can explore various aspects of our character, but aspects do not form a solid self. This elusiveness of identity is one of the principle characteristics of our sense of Lack, just as the sense of a gravitational pull toward one pole of certainty or another is how we experience Yearning. In some of us that pull is pronounced and the destination seems reasonably apparent. In others there is just a vague notion that we are not where we need to be and that movement is required, though in which direction is unclear. In others, there is a profound desire to stay put and wait.

Even in those instances where confidence and clarity abound, life is simply so unpredictable, and circumstances change so relentlessly, that any concrete notion that we have discovered the final truth about ourselves or our lives is not merely an illusion, it's a lie. Honesty requires us to accept the inescapable ambiguity of our condition. We are always in a state of becoming what we might be. The only person with a rightful claim that he is who he is and will never change resides in a grave.

As for us, so our characters. The sneaky, subtle truth about truly compelling characters is that they possess the capacity, at any moment in the story, to surprise us. All of the work you will do exploring Lack, Yearning, Resistance, Desire, Pathological Maneuvers, and Persistent Virtues will create not a perfectly formed and immutable entity but a collection of possibilities. Ignore the work, or give it short shrift, and you will end up with a tangle of uncertainties. The backstory work, therefore, though fundamental, is just the beginning. The creative part, the immersion in the string of present moments that will form your story, follows. But once you have an intuitive sense of the vibrant, ineffable presences that represent your characters, you're ready to write. Listen to them. Let them guide you toward not just what is possible but what you never could have imagined without them.

INDEX